APPLICATIONS OF POSITIVE PSYCHOLOGY

Arpita Kackar
Assistant Professor in the Department of Psychology,
Jai Narayan Vyas University, Jodhpur

SCIENTIFIC® PUBLISHERS
New Delhi • Jodhpur

SCIENTIFIC PUBLISHERS
New Delhi • Jodhpur

Published by:

Jodhpur
5 A, New Pali Road, P.O. Box 91
Jodhpur - 342 001, Rajasthan (India)
E-mail: info@scientificpub.com
Website: www.scientificpubonline.com

New Delhi
4806/24, Ansari Road, Daryaganj,
New Delhi - 110 002 (India)

Applications of Positive Psychology
Arpita Kackar

ISBN: 978-93-6346-392-9 (HB)
eISBN:978-93-6346-740-8

Printed in India

PREFACE

Positive Psychology is a recent field of study and research having spanned a trajectory of not more than 20 years. Peterson (2006) has marked that positive psychology has a long history and a short span. He means that the positive side of human nature has been of long-standing interest to both philosophers and psychologists, but it is only recently that the positive side of human behavior has attracted serious and more widespread empirical study. At present, positive psychology is an evolving mosaic of research and theory from many different areas of psychology, tied together by a common focus on positive aspects of human behavior. By shifting the focus from pathology and dysfunction to strengths, virtues, and factors that contribute to a fulfilling life, it offers a holistic approach to human development. My book endeavors to bridge the gap between theoretical research and practical application, thereby offering useful insights and tools of positive psychology and tried to present them to students.

The primary goal of this book is to synthesize the rich body of research in positive psychology into an engaging and understandable format. I have summarized major empirical findings and theories within the field, presenting them in a way that is accessible to students regardless of their prior knowledge or experience. By doing so, I aim to provide a comprehensive introduction to positive psychology that is both informative and inspiring.

Another key objective of this book is to explore the core areas where positive psychology can be applied. It's principles are relevant across various domains of life, including health and well-being, relationships, education, work, the domain of disability, parenting, multicultural perspective, and community well-being. Each chapter examines the aforementioned areas, demonstrating how positive psychology can be integrated into everyday life to enhance well-being and bring positive change. Through practical examples, I have tried to illustrate the versatility and practical benefits of positive psychology interventions.

Understanding that not all readers may have a background in research methodology, I have focused on presenting the applications of positive psychology in a straightforward and practical manner. My aim is to provide practical tools and strategies that readers can use to improve their own lives and the lives of those around them without getting burdened by academic complexities.

This book is structured to guide readers through the foundational concepts of positive psychology before exploring its applications across different domains. The introductory chapter provides an overview of the history, principles, key concepts and theories of positive psychology, setting the stage for a deeper understanding of the field. Subsequent chapters are dedicated to specific applications, integrating empirical findings, along with related theories of each field with practical strategies to offer a holistic view of how positive psychology can enhance various aspects of life.

I extend my heartfelt gratitude to many individuals and institutions who have contributed to the creation of this book. I am deeply thankful to the researchers and practitioners whose pioneering work has laid the foundation for positive psychology. I also appreciate the valuable feedback from our colleagues and reviewers, and the unflinching enthusiasm and curiosity of my students, which has been a constant impetus to make an efficacious compendium on positive psychology.

I truly hope is that my book will prove a potent treasure trove for both the students as well as educators. providing a thorough understanding of positive psychology and practical tools for enhancing well-being. By applying the principles outlined in this book, readers can develop environments that promote flourishing and fulfilment. I invite you to embark on this journey of discovery and growth, exploring how positive psychology can make a profound difference in your life and the lives of others.

I wish you an engaging reading !!

ACKNOWLEDGMENT

To acknowledge is to avail the opportune moment to genuinely thank all those who have facilitated one's cherished enterprise and pursuits. As such I take the opportunity to extend my heartfelt gratitude and thankfulness toward all the individuals who have been highly instrumental in bringing my book to its long-cherished fruition.

First and foremost, I extend my deepest gratitude to the universe for the wealth of experiences and opportunities that have shaped my understanding and passion for psychology. The synchronicities and moments of inspiration that have guided me on this path are truly remarkable, and I am profoundly thankful for the unseen forces that have supported this endeavor.

I would like to express my sincere appreciation to all my **Teachers** who have imparted wisdom and knowledge throughout my academic and professional journey. Their dedication to education and their commitment to develop a love for learning have been instrumental in shaping my approach to psychology. Their teachings have not only informed this book but have also profoundly influenced my personal and professional growth.

A special thanks is to my dear friend and colleague, **Dr. Hemlata Joshi** whose insightful suggestions sparked the very idea of this book. Her belief in the importance of sharing the applications of positive psychology with a wider audience inspired me to embark on this project. Her intellectual companionship and constructive feedback have been invaluable throughout the writing process. Thank you, Hemlata, for your vision and encouragement.

I extend my deep and profuse thankfulness to my rock of support- my family members, particularly my mother Mrs. Veena Kackar and my sisters Ashita and Apurva for their love and encouragement that facilitated this intellectual journey of mine and speeded the apt culmination of my book. Concurrently, I feel thankful toward my friends who have always been there on this intellectual journey of mine.

A special debt of thanks is owned by my dear students whose enthusiasm, encouragement, and perennial curiosity provided the impetus to me to explore deeper and produce the compendium of knowledge on positive psychology to the best of my ability and efforts. This book is, in many ways, a response to their belief in me as someone who can significantly contribute to the field of psychology, and thus a reflection of our shared journey in the pursuit of knowledge and well-being.

While acknowledging the many contributions to this book, I also accept full responsibility for any flaws or shortcomings within its content. Writing is a continuous process of learning and refinement, and I am open to the lessons that come from both success and imperfection.

I want to express my heartfelt thanks to everyone who has been a part of this journey. Your contributions, whether big or small, have collectively made this book possible. It is with deep gratitude that I offer these acknowledgments, knowing that this book is a testament to the support, inspiration, and love of many.

Thank you all for being part of this journey.

CONTENTS

CHAPTER 1

INTRODUCTION TO POSITIVE PSYCHOLOGY

Introduction

Positive psychology is a relatively new field within modern psychology that emerged two decades ago, with a specific focus on understanding the nature of happiness and well-being and identifying the conditions that promote these states across different cultures and societies. Unlike traditional psychology, which often emphasizes the treatment of mental illness and dysfunction, positive psychology seeks to explore and enhance the positive aspects of human experience, such as happiness, well-being, and fulfillment. This field was pioneered by Martin Seligman in the late 1990s, who envisioned a science that studied what makes life worth living. Positive psychology investigates concepts such as positive emotions, strengths, virtues, and the factors that contribute to a meaningful life.

By examining how individuals can cultivate positive traits and emotions, build strong relationships, and find purpose, positive psychology provides a comprehensive framework for enhancing well-being. Its applications extend to various domains, including education, workplace environments, therapy, and personal development, offering strategies to improve mental health and overall life satisfaction. Through its research and practical interventions, positive psychology aims to unlock human potential and promote a balanced, flourishing existence.

Definition of Positive Psychology

Let us break down the word Positive Psychology to understand it better.

Positive: Displaying optimism and confidence and moving towards improvement or progress. It refers to a constructive and affirmative quality or attribute.

Psychology: The study of the mind and behavioral characteristics typical of an individual or group about a particular field of knowledge or activity

According to Gable & Haidt, 2005; Sheldon &King, 2001: "Positive Psychology is the scientific study of human flourishing and an applied approach to optimal functioning. It has also been defined as the study of the strengths and virtues that enable individuals, communities, and organizations to thrive."

According to the Positive Psychology Center 2016: "Positive Psychology is grounded in the belief that people want to lead meaningful and fulfilling lives, to cultivate what is best within them, and to enhance their experiences of love, work, and play."

According to Robert Biswas-Diener 2003: "Positive Psychology is the study of factors that make life more fulfilling, meaningful and enjoyable."

According to Peterson 2008: "Positive psychology is the scientific study of what makes life most worth living."

According to Martin Seligman and Mihaly Csikszentmihalyi (2000): Positive psychology is "the scientific study of positive human functioning and flourishing on multiple levels that include the biological, personal, relational, institutional, cultural, and global dimensions of life."

According to Sheldon 2009: It is a conceptual movement in both the research and applied arms of the psychological community which seeks to rectify the negative biases of traditional psychology so that a full accounting of human nature and behavior can emerge."

According to Hugo Alberts: Positive psychology is "the scientific and applied approach to uncovering people's strengths and promoting their positive functioning."

Thus, we can say that Positive psychology is the scientific study of human flourishing and optimal functioning, emphasizing strengths, virtues, and factors that contribute to a fulfilling, meaningful, and enjoyable life. It focuses on positive human functioning at multiple levels, including biological, personal, relational, institutional, cultural, and global dimensions. This field aims to enhance individuals' and communities' experiences of love, work, and play by fostering positive attitudes, optimism, and confidence.

History of Positive Psychology

1. **Founding of Positive Psychology:** The concept of eudaimonia, described in Aristotle's Nicomachean Ethics, emphasized human flourishing, virtue, and happiness. This ancient foundation focused on cultivating virtues to attain well-being. The formal establishment of

positive psychology as a distinct field is credited to Martin Seligman in 1998, during his tenure as President of the American Psychological Association. Seligman was motivated by the belief that mainstream psychology had become overly focused on disease, disorders, and disabilities. He sought to redirect the field's methodological, scientific, and organizational strengths towards facilitating well-being, resilience, and recovery rather than solely addressing illness and disease.

2. **Humanistic and Psychodynamic Influences:** Positive psychology did not emerge in a vacuum; it was influenced by earlier humanistic and psychodynamic approaches. Humanistic psychologists such as Abraham Maslow, Carl Rogers, and Erich Fromm had already laid the groundwork with their theories on human happiness and flourishing. These approaches emphasized the holistic study of individuals, advocating for a focus on positive human potential and well-being.
3. **Pioneering Research Models:**
   a) **Ed Diener's Tripartite Model (1984):** Diener proposed a model of subjective well-being that included three components:
      - Frequent positive affect
      - Infrequent negative affect
      - Cognitive evaluations such as life satisfaction

      This model highlighted the importance of both affective and cognitive dimensions in understanding well-being.

   b) **Carol Ryff's Six-Factor Model (1989):** Ryff identified six key factors of psychological well-being:
      I. Self-acceptance
      II. Personal growth
      III. Purpose in life
      IV. Environmental mastery
      V. Autonomy
      VI. Positive relations with others

      Her model emphasized the multifaceted nature of well-being.

   c) **Corey Keyes'-Flourishing Concept:** Corey Keyes, in collaboration with Carol Ryff, expanded the concept of well-being by emphasizing "flourishing," which integrates hedonic (emotional), psychological, and social well-being. His tripartite model encompasses emotional well-being (positive feelings and life satisfaction), psychological well-being (self-acceptance, personal growth, purpose), and social well-being (positive relations, social integration). This model has received cross-cultural empirical support, underscoring its robustness and universal applicability. It highlights the comprehensive nature of well-being, advocating for a balanced approach to achieving a fulfilling and meaningful life.

4. **Development and Growth:**
   - **1999:** The first Positive Psychology Summit was held, marking a significant step in the field's development.
   - **2002:** The First International Conference on Positive Psychology took place, further solidifying the field's academic and practical relevance.
   - **2005:** The University of Pennsylvania launched the first Master's Program in Applied Positive Psychology (MAPP), reflecting the growing interest and institutional support for the field.
   - **2006:** A course on positive psychology at Harvard University became one of the most popular offerings, indicating widespread student interest.
   - **2009:** The First World Congress on Positive Psychology was held in Philadelphia, showcasing the field's global reach and collaborative potential.
5. **Establishment as a Scientific Discipline:** Martin Seligman and Mihaly Csikszentmihalyi played pivotal roles in establishing positive psychology as a scientific discipline. In their seminal 2000 paper, they outlined the explicit goal of investigating human potential to counter the dominance of psychopathology and to build a science of human flourishing. This marked a significant shift towards a more balanced and comprehensive approach to psychology, one that emphasizes both the treatment of mental illness and the promotion of well-being.
6. **Contemporary Perspectives and Debates:** Positive Psychology has evolved through two major phases, known as Positive Psychology 1.0 (PP1) and Positive Psychology 2.0 (PP2), each with its own distinct focus and approach. PP1, championed by Martin Seligman, emphasized the study of positive emotions, traits, and institutions. It aimed to balance the traditional psychological focus on mental illness by promoting well-being through happiness, resilience, and positive character strengths. This phase was characterized by its optimistic outlook and the development of interventions to enhance positive aspects of human life.

In contrast, PP2, advanced by Paul T. Wong, integrates existential and humanistic perspectives, emphasizing the role of adversity, pain, and suffering in achieving true well-being. Wong's approach, known as Existential Positive Psychology, argues that overcoming challenges and finding meaning in suffering is essential to a fulfilling life. This perspective incorporates the concept of "tragic optimism," where individuals find hope and purpose despite hardships, thus providing a more holistic and balanced understanding of well-being that includes both positive experiences and the transformative potential of negative ones. Together, PP1 and PP2 offer a comprehensive framework for understanding human flourishing, blending the enhancement of positive experiences with the deep insights gained through facing life's inevitable difficulties.

Important Figures in Positive Psychology

1. **William James:** William James, a philosopher, physician, and psychologist, holds the distinction of being the first educator to introduce a psychology course in the United States. His curiosity was aroused by the question of why certain individuals could prosper and overcome challenges while others struggled with mental health issues. James contended that investigating subjective experiences was crucial for understanding optimal human functioning. By integrating realistic and functionalist viewpoints, he sought to establish connections between the mind and body, exploring the tangible aspects of inner experiences. Many regard James as America's inaugural positive psychologist, attributing this title to his holistic approach to human functioning and his exploration of the complete spectrum of subjective experiences, extending beyond the realm of psychopathology.
2. **Abraham Maslow:** While humanistic psychology's 'third force' contributed significantly to establishing the foundational concepts of positive psychology, Abraham Maslow exerted the greatest influence. Maslow is credited with coining the term "positive psychology" in his book "Motivation and Personality" (Maslow, 1954). He criticized psychology's focus on disorder and dysfunction, asserting that it failed to grasp human potential accurately. Maslow asserted that previous approaches, like psychoanalysis and behaviorism, were informative about human flaws and mental health issues, but overlooked the exploration of human virtues and aspirations.

3. **Martin Seligman:** Martin Seligman, an esteemed American psychologist, educator, researcher, and author, assumed the presidency of the American Psychological Association in 1996, with a notable focus on positive psychology. He asserted that mental well-being surpasses the mere absence of illness, pioneering a new era of inquiry into the sources of human happiness and fulfillment. Seligman's early exploration of learned helplessness and pessimism laid the groundwork for his subsequent collaboration with Christopher Peterson, aimed at offering a positive alternative to psychopathology classification. Their research, drawing from diverse cultures across history, culminated in the groundbreaking work "Character Strengths and Virtues," which delineated six fundamental categories of virtues.
4. **Mihaly Csikszentmihalyi:** Mihaly Csikszentmihalyi, born in Hungary in 1934, endured the upheavals of the Second World War, with his family facing significant challenges due to the political changes in Hungary. His exposure to psychology began when he attended a lecture by Carl Jung in Switzerland, where Jung discussed the psychological impact of post-war trauma on European individuals. This encounter ignited Csikszentmihalyi's interest in psychology, prompting him to pursue further studies in the United States. He earned his PhD from the University of Chicago in 1965 and subsequently joined the faculty as a professor in 1969. His deep passion for painting and creativity inspired his exploration of the concept of the "flow state," which he believed epitomized the optimal human experience. Csikszentmihalyi dedicated his career to scientifically investigating the various pathways to achieving flow. His research has attracted considerable public attention and has found extensive application in the examination of creativity, productivity, and happiness, both at the individual and organizational levels.
5. **Christopher Peterson:** Christopher Peterson was a distinguished Professor of Psychology at the University of Michigan and served as chair of the Department of Clinical Psychology. He made significant contributions to positive psychology, particularly through his work on character strengths and virtues. Alongside Martin Seligman, he co-authored the seminal book "Character Strengths and Virtues" in 2004, which has been influential in the field. Peterson's research delved deeply into the study of optimism, hope, and well-being, highlighting the importance of these attributes in fostering a fulfilling life. He was renowned for his emphasis on identifying and nurturing individual strengths and virtues, and his work continues to

inspire both academic research and practical applications in promoting mental health and resilience. Peterson's legacy in positive psychology remains impactful, shaping the way we understand and cultivate human potential and well-being.

6. **Donald Clifton:** Donald Clifton pursued a path similar to Martin Seligman by developing strengths-based psychology (Clifton & Harter, 2019). He researched successful individuals to uncover how they attained optimal workplace performance. His findings have helped employees identify fulfilling careers that can utilize their strengths. In 2002, the American Psychological Association recognized Clifton as the father of strengths-based psychology with a Presidential Commendation (Galluo, 2002).
7. **Albert Bandura:** Albert Bandura's self-efficacy theory, an integral component of his broader social-cognitive theory, focuses on an individual's belief in their ability to achieve goals by performing required tasks (Bandura, 1994). This concept has significantly enriched positive psychology by emphasizing the role of personal belief systems in driving motivation and behavior. High self-efficacy is linked to greater resilience, persistence, and success in facing challenges. It encourages individuals to set ambitious goals and persist in the face of setbacks, developing a proactive and confident approach to life. Bandura's work on self-efficacy underscores the importance of fostering these beliefs to enhance overall well-being and achievement, aligning closely with the aims of positive psychology to cultivate human potential and flourish.
8. **Deci and Ryan:** Edward L. Deci and Richard M. Ryan developed Self-Determination Theory (SDT) during the 1980s (Deci & Ryan, 1985). Deci was a professor in the Department of Clinical and Social Sciences at the University of Rochester, New York. Ryan was a clinical psychologist and professor at the Institute for Positive Psychology and Education at the Australian Catholic University in Sydney, Australia. Their pioneering work on self-determination revised Abraham Maslow's hierarchy of needs, identifying three key components that drive human motivation: autonomy, competence, and relatedness (Deci & Ryan, 2008). This theory has significant implications for the field of positive psychology.
9. **Ed Diener:** Ed Diener, known as "Dr. Happiness," is a prominent researcher who introduced the term subjective well-being as a scientifically measurable aspect of human happiness. His research revealed a significant genetic component to happiness and has stimulated numerous studies on

the internal and external conditions necessary for developing well-being (Diener, 2009). Diener has also explored the relationship between income and well-being, as well as the impact of cultural influences.

10. **Barbara Fredrickson:** Barbara Fredrickson is a prominent psychologist in positive psychology, best known for her broaden-and-build theory. This theory suggests that positive emotions expand people's cognitive and behavioral capacities, leading to the development of lasting personal resources such as resilience, social connections, and knowledge. Her research has significantly advanced our understanding of how positive emotions contribute to overall well-being and mental health. Her work has been instrumental in highlighting the transformative power of positive emotions in everyday life.
11. **C.R. Snyder:** C.R. Snyder was a pioneering psychologist known for his development of Hope Theory, which emphasizes the role of goal-directed thinking in developing well-being. His research demonstrated how having clear goals, pathways to achieve them, and the motivation to pursue them significantly contributes to positive psychological health. Snyder's work has been influential in understanding how hope can be cultivated to improve mental health and resilience. His contributions have provided valuable insights into the mechanisms that drive human motivation and success.
12. **Daniel Glibert:** Daniel Gilbert is a prominent psychologist known for his work on affective forecasting, which examines how people predict their future emotional states. He revealed that people often misjudge the intensity and duration of their future emotions, leading to incorrect decisions about what will make them happy. His book, "Stumbling on Happiness," explores these concepts and has brought significant attention to the study of happiness and human judgment. Gilbert's research emphasizes the complexities of predicting happiness and has influenced the field of positive psychology by highlighting cognitive biases in emotional forecasting.
13. **Carol Dweck:** Carol Dweck is renowned for her groundbreaking work on mindset theory, which distinguishes between fixed and growth mindsets. She demonstrated that individuals with a growth mindset, who believe that abilities and intelligence can be developed through effort and learning, tend to achieve higher levels of success and resilience. Her influential book, "Mindset: The New Psychology of Success," has had a profound impact on education, business, and personal development. Dweck's research

has significantly contributed to positive psychology by highlighting the importance of beliefs and attitudes in personal growth and achievement.

Aims of Positive Psychology-1 (Martin Seligman)

According to Seligman and Csikszentmihalyi (2000), the agenda of Positive Psychology includes the following aims:

- To articulate a vision of the good life that is evidence-based, understandable, and attractive.
- To demonstrate actions that can lead to well-being, positive individuals, and flourishing communities.
- To document what kinds of families result in children who flourish, what work settings support the greatest satisfaction among workers, what policies result in the

The Positive Psychology Manifesto emphasizes the study of optimal human functioning across multiple levels—biological, experiential, personal, relational, institutional, cultural, and global. It focuses on understanding the dynamics of these processes, how humans create meaning from adversity, and how the good life can emerge from these interactions. Positive Psychology aims to discover and promote factors that enable individuals and communities to thrive, shifting attention from disease to psychological health. Christopher Peterson described it as the scientific study of what goes right in life. To advance these goals, Martin Seligman established the Positive Psychology Center at the University of Pennsylvania, highlighting strengths that lead to fulfilling lives. According to Angela Duckworth, Paul Rozin, and Martin Seligman, the three central concerns of Positive Psychology are:

1. Understanding positive experiences or positive emotions, which involves studying contentment with the past, pleasure in the present, and hope for the future.
2. Understanding positive individual traits involves studying strengths and virtues such as the capacity to love, altruism, creativity, curiosity, integrity, moderation, self-control, spirituality, and humor.
3. Understanding positive institutions involves studying strong families, communities, and corporations, along with the virtues that nourish them, such as justice, responsibility, civility, work ethic, leadership, teamwork, purpose, and tolerance.

Aims of Positive Psychology-2.0 (Paul T. Wong)

Dr. Paul T. Wong, Founding President of the Meaning-Centered Counseling Institute, Inc. (MCCI) and creator of 'meaning-centered counseling and therapy' (MCCT), emphasizes the importance of suffering in human flourishing and growth. He refers to his approach as "Existential Positive Psychology (2.0) of Flourishing Through Suffering," also known as the second wave of Positive Psychology (PP2). Wong asserts that Positive Psychology is intrinsically existential because it addresses fundamental questions about human existence, such as what constitutes the good life, what makes life worth living, and how happiness can be achieved. He argues that these questions cannot be fully explored without acknowledging existential anxieties, and thus, a mature Positive Psychology must return to its existential-humanistic roots to rediscover the richness of lived experiences and the many pathways to meaning in life (Wong, 2016).

While Seligman's Positive Psychology 1.0 (PP1) focuses primarily on positive emotions, Wong criticizes this approach for neglecting the significance of negative emotions. Existential-humanistic psychologists, like Viktor Frankl, believe that both pleasure and pain contribute to well-being. Frankl, who survived the Holocaust, developed 'logotherapy,' which emphasizes finding meaning in suffering. He argued that the absence of meaning leads to depression, anxiety, and a pursuit of hedonistic pleasures or neurotic obsessions (Frankl, 1992). Wong, therefore, integrates suffering and meaning as essential aspects of Positive Psychology.

Wong describes Existential Positive Psychology (EPP) as a natural combination of Positive Psychology and existential psychology, addressing fundamental questions about self-identity, happiness, and the human condition (Wong, 2016). These questions include: "Who am I? What defines me?"; "How can I be happy? Why am I dissatisfied with life?"; "What is the good life? Is this all there is to life?"; "What should I do with my life? What is my calling?"; "How do I make the right choices?"; "Where do I belong? Why do I feel alone?" and "What is the point of striving when life is short?" (Wong, 2016).

Research has identified eight sources of a meaningful life:

- Happiness and fulfillment,
- Achieving something worthwhile,
- Intimacy (marriage and family),
- Good relationships with friends and people,
- Self-acceptance,

- Self-transcendence or altruism,
- Religion,
- Fairness or justice

Scope of Positive Psychology

Subject matter of positive psychology can be classified into three domains (Seligman, 2002):

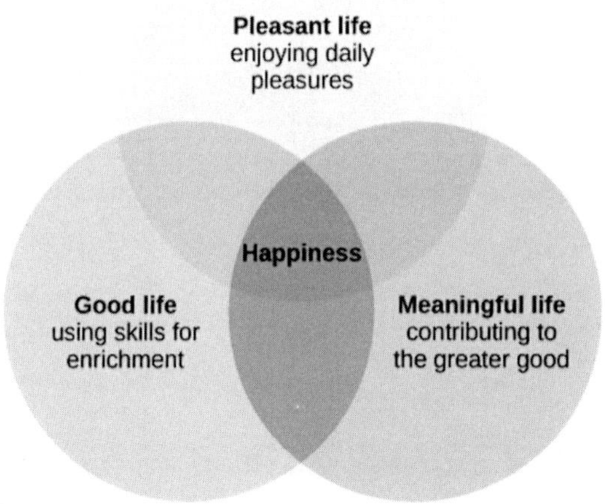

- **The first domain**, the pleasant life, focuses on developing positive emotions about the past, present, and future. It involves enhancing feelings of happiness, gratitude, and contentment while minimizing experiences of negative emotions like sadness and regret. This domain encourages practices such as savoring joyful moments, expressing gratitude, and maintaining an optimistic outlook to boost overall well-being. By fostering a positive emotional state, individuals can experience a greater sense of life satisfaction and joy.
- **The second domain**, the engaged life, emphasizes developing positive individual traits and fully immersing oneself in activities that are both enjoyable and challenging. This involves finding activities that create a state of flow, where one becomes deeply absorbed and loses track of time. Engaging in such activities helps individuals harness their strengths, build skills, and experience a sense of accomplishment and fulfillment. This domain is crucial for personal growth and the development of a strong sense of self-efficacy.

- **The third domain**, the meaningful life, revolves around positive institutions and having a sense of purpose and meaning in one's life. It involves connecting to something greater than oneself, such as contributing to community, nurturing relationships, or committing to personal values and causes. This domain encourages individuals to seek out and cultivate roles and activities that provide a sense of significance and purpose, leading to a deeper sense of fulfillment. By finding meaning, individuals can face life's challenges with resilience and a stronger sense of direction.

Pillars of Positive Psychology

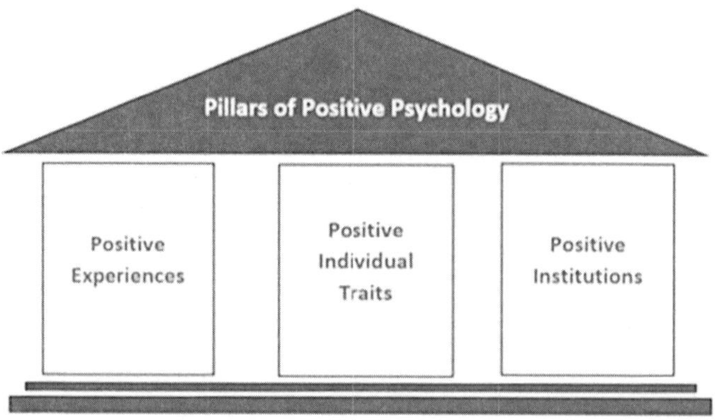

The three pillars of positive psychology—positive experiences, positive individual traits, and positive institutions—form the foundational framework for understanding and promoting well-being.

1. **Positive Experiences:** This pillar focuses on the various emotions and experiences that contribute to a sense of well-being. It includes feelings of joy, gratitude, love, contentment, and other positive emotions. Positive experiences are essential for enhancing happiness and life satisfaction. They involve in moments of pleasure, fulfillment, and engagement with life, such as enjoying a beautiful sunset, spending time with loved ones, or achieving personal goals.
2. **Positive Individual Traits:** This pillar emphasizes the unique strengths and virtues that individuals possess, which enable them to flourish and lead fulfilling lives. These traits include qualities such as resilience, optimism, creativity, courage, kindness, and perseverance. Positive individual traits play a crucial role in personal growth, success, and overall psychological well-being. They contribute to resilience in the face of adversity, the search of meaningful goals, and the development of healthy relationships.

3. **Positive Institutions:** This pillar focuses on the social and cultural contexts that support and nurture individual well-being. Positive institutions include elements of community, such as supportive families, strong friendships, effective leadership, and inclusive organizations. They provide environments where individuals can flourish and thrive, developing a sense of belonging, purpose, and connectedness. Positive institutions promote collective well-being by creating opportunities for collaboration, cooperation, and growth, ultimately contributing to the greater good of the society.

Together, these three pillars form a comprehensive framework for understanding the factors that contribute to human flourishing and well-being. By cultivating positive experiences, nurturing individual strengths, and fostering supportive institutions, positive psychology seeks to enhance the quality of life for individuals, communities, and the society as a whole.

Theories of Positive Psychology

1. **PERMA Model:**

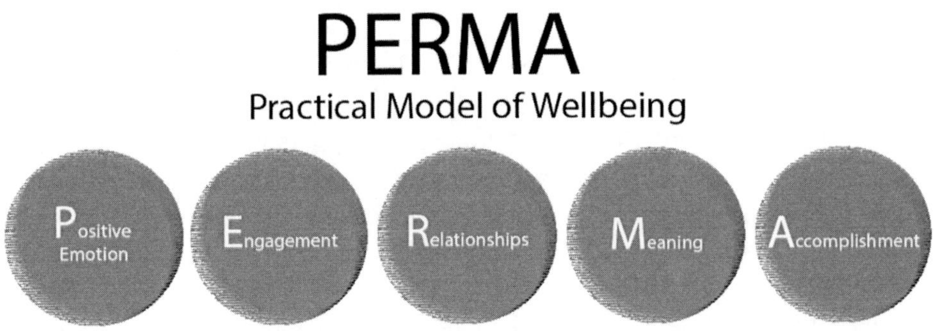

The PERMA model is a cornerstone of positive psychology, developed by Martin Seligman to provide a comprehensive framework for understanding and enhancing well-being. The model identifies five key elements that contribute to human flourishing:

a) **Positive Emotions (P):** Positive emotions involve experiencing feelings of joy, gratitude, satisfaction, and contentment. While the search of positive emotions alone may not fully sustain well-being, they are essential components. Experiencing the positive emotions allow individuals to enjoy life's moments and can contribute to a more fulfilling existence.

b) **Engagement (E):** Engagement refers to being deeply involved in activities that interest and challenge us, often leading to a state known as "flow." When we are engaged, we lose track of time and become absorbed in the task at hand. This sense of engagement is crucial for well-being as it provides a sense of purpose and satisfaction from being fully immersed in activities we enjoy and excel.

c) **Relationships (R):** Relationships are fundamental to the human well-being. As a social beings, humans prosper on connections with others. Deep and meaningful relationships provide support, love, and a sense of belonging. Positive relationships enhance our well-being by offering emotional support, developing a sense of community, and allowing us to share experiences with others.

d) **Meaning (M):** Meaning involves having a sense of purpose and understanding that there is something greater than oneself. This can be achieved through dedication to causes, participation in communities, or finding personal significance in life's activities. Having a sense of meaning is irreplaceable and contributes significantly to the overall well-being, as it helps individuals feel that their lives are valuable and worthwhile.

e) **Accomplishment (A):** Accomplishment or achievement is the search and attainment of goals, which provides a sense of success and fulfillment. Striving for and reaching personal milestones boosts self-esteem and gives a sense of progress and competency. Without a drive for accomplishment, individuals might miss out on an essential aspect of well-being that comes from achieving goals and bettering themselves.

The PERMA model is evidence-based and provides a robust structure for both understanding and improving well-being. By focusing on these five elements, individuals can create a more balanced and fulfilling lives. Each element can be pursued for its own sake, and together they form a holistic approach to enhancing well-being. This framework not only helps individuals manage life's challenges more effectively but also promotes a meaningful life with reducing psychological distress.

2. **Broaden-and-Build Theory:** The Broaden-and-Build Theory, developed by Barbara Fredrickson in 1998, explores the role of positive emotions in human psychology. This theory contrasts with traditional models focused on negative emotions and their specific action tendencies.

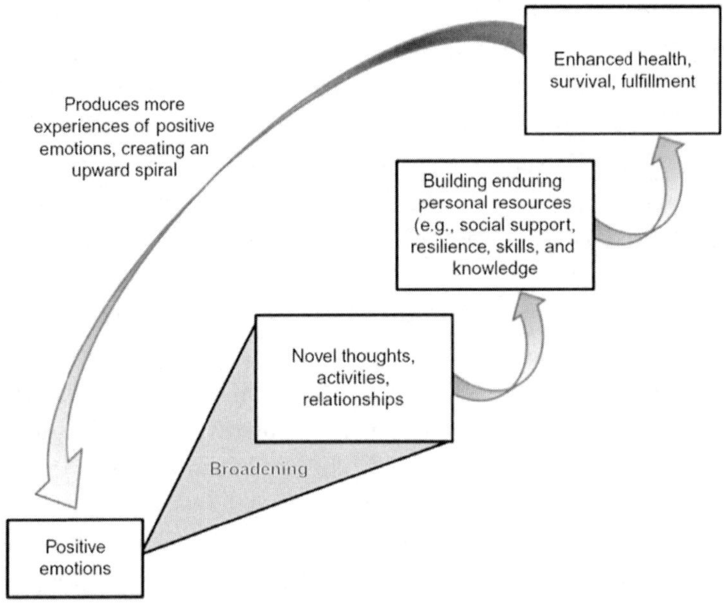

a) **Broaden Thought:** Positive emotions, such as joy, interest, and love, expand our range of thoughts and actions. These emotions encourage exploratory behaviors, creativity, and the pursuit of new ideas and experiences. For example, joy can lead to playful behavior, interest can lead to curiosity and learning, and love can also promote social bonding and support.

b) **Build Personal Resources:** The broadened mindset induced by positive emotions helps in building enduring personal resources. These resources include physical (e.g., health and stamina), social (e.g., friendships and social networks), intellectual (e.g., knowledge and skills), and psychological (e.g., resilience and optimism). These resources can be drawn upon later, during times of need or adversity.

c) **Undoing Negative Emotions:** Positive emotions can counteract the effects of negative emotions. They facilitate quicker cardiovascular recovery from stress and anxiety. This "undoing" effect helps maintain overall emotional balance and resilience.

d) **Increasing Psychological Resilience:** Regularly experiencing with positive emotions develops psychological resilience. Resilient individuals use positive emotions to cope with and recover from life's challenges. Positive emotions contribute to a positive cycle, promoting further resilience and well-being.

e) **Promoting Physical Health:** Positive emotions are linked to better physical health outcomes. They reduce the risk of chronic diseases and improve overall health. Individuals experiencing more positive emotions report fewer health issues and better quality of life.

f) **Creating Upward Spirals:** Positive emotions trigger upward spirals, increasing the likelihood of experiencing further positive emotions. This compounding effect enhances long-term well-being and life satisfaction. Positive moments lead to further positive experiences, creating a reinforcing cycle of positivity.

The Broaden-and-Build Theory emphasizes the importance of positive emotions in expanding our cognitive and behavioral repertoires, building valuable personal resources, and promoting overall health and resilience. By developing positive emotions, individuals can enhance their ability to cope with challenges and lead more fulfilling lives.

3. **Flow Theory:** Flow Theory, introduced by Mihaly Csikszentmihalyi, explores a mental state of deep absorption and enjoyment during activities. This state, known as "Flow," is characterized by intense focus, loss of self-consciousness, and a sense of timelessness. Csikszentmihalyi's pioneering research has significantly influenced the fields of positive psychology, creativity, and performance. Csikszentmihalyi's interest in Flow began in the 1960s while studying the creative process with Jacob Getzels. Observing artists who were deeply engrossed in their work, Csikszentmihalyi noted their single-minded focus and persistence despite discomfort. This led him to explore flow in various fields; Flow is a state where individuals are completely absorbed and involved in their activities, experiencing enjoyment and fulfillment. It occurs when the challenge of the task matches one's skills, leading to effortless and enjoyable performance. This state is marked by intense focus and intrinsic motivation. Characteristics of Flow are as follows:

a) **Challenge-Skill Balance:** Engaging in tasks that are well-matched to one's skill level, neither too easy nor too difficult.

b) **Action-Awareness Merging:** A deep sense of involvement where actions become spontaneous and automatic.

c) **Clear Goals:** Having specific objectives that provide direction and purpose.

d) **Unambiguous Feedback:** Receiving immediate and clear feedback on performance, allowing for adjustments and improvements.

e) **Concentration on the Task at Hand:** Intense focus and concentration, excluding distractions.

f) **A Sense of Control:** Feeling in command of the situation and capable of meeting the challenges.

g) **Loss of Self-Consciousness:** Becoming so absorbed that self-awareness diminishes.

h) **Transformation of Time:** Altered perception of time, often feeling that it passes quickly.

i) **Autotelic Experience:** Finding the activity intrinsically rewarding and enjoyable for its own sake.

Flow is central to positive psychology, which examines factors that contribute to human flourishing and well-being. Researchers like Deci and Ryan have studied Flow in the context of intrinsic motivation, while Seligman has highlighted its role in living a meaningful life. Flow helps individuals use their strengths and virtues, reducing time spent on mundane or overly challenging tasks. To achieve flow, individuals should choose activities that challenge their skills appropriately, set clear goals and seek immediate feedback, minimizing distractions and engaging in activities that are intrinsically rewarding. Flow Theory highlights the profound impact of being deeply engaged and absorbed in activities. By understanding and developing Flow, individuals can improve their performance, creativity, and emotional well-being. Csikszentmihalyi's work encourages us to seek out opportunities for Flow, making life more meaningful and enjoyable.

4. **Self Determination Theory:** Self-Determination Theory (SDT), developed by Edward L. Deci and Richard M. Ryan, explores the interplay between intrinsic and extrinsic motivation and how these forms of motivation impacts personality, human behavior, and optimal functioning. Originating from their research in the 1970s and 1980s and formalized in their 1985 book, SDT has evolved to emphasize the subtle roles of different motivational types and their influence on well-being and performance. There are different types of motivation.

   a) **Intrinsic Motivation:** This arises from internal drives and personal satisfaction. It is driven by core values, interests, and a personal sense of morality. For example, engaging in a hobby purely for enjoyment is intrinsically motivated.

   b) **Extrinsic Motivation:** This stems from external sources and results in external rewards such as grades, salaries, or social approval. For instance, working for a paycheck or studying to receive good grades is forms of extrinsic motivation.

c) **Autonomous vs. Controlled Motivation:** Autonomous Motivation includes intrinsic and extrinsic motivation that align with one's values and sense of self. When people feel their actions are self-endorsed and follow their core values, they experience autonomy and self-direction. Controlled Motivation involves acting under pressure from external sources or internal pressures like guilt or the desire for approval. This includes external regulation (acting to obtain rewards or avoid punishments) and introjected regulation (acting to avoid internal pressures like guilt or to boost self-esteem).

The Motivation Continuum: SDT proposes a continuum ranging from non-self-determined to self-determined motivation:

- **Amotivation:** Lack of intention to act, resulting from not valuing an activity or feeling incompetent.
- **External Regulation:** Behavior driven by external rewards and punishments.
- **Introjected Regulation:** Behavior driven by internal pressures like shame or ego enhancement.
- **Identified Regulation:** Behavior driven by personal goals and values.
- **Integrated Regulation:** Behavior aligned with one's sense of self and fully internalized values, though still externally motivated.
- **Intrinsic Regulation:** Behavior driven by inherent interest and enjoyment.

Basic Psychological Needs: SDT identifies three basic psychological needs essential for optimal functioning and well-being:

- **Autonomy:** The need to feel in control of one's own behavior and goals.
- **Competence:** The need to gain mastery and effective interaction with the environment.
- **Relatedness:** The need to feel connected and involved with others.

Self-Determination Theory (SDT) is central to positive psychology as it emphasizes the role of intrinsic motivation in achieving personal fulfillment and well-being. By satisfying the basic psychological needs of autonomy, competence, and relatedness, individuals can develop greater life satisfaction and resilience. SDT highlights how developing these needs can lead to optimal functioning and increased psychological growth. In positive psychology, SDT provides a framework for understanding how self-motivated actions contribute to a meaningful and engaged life.

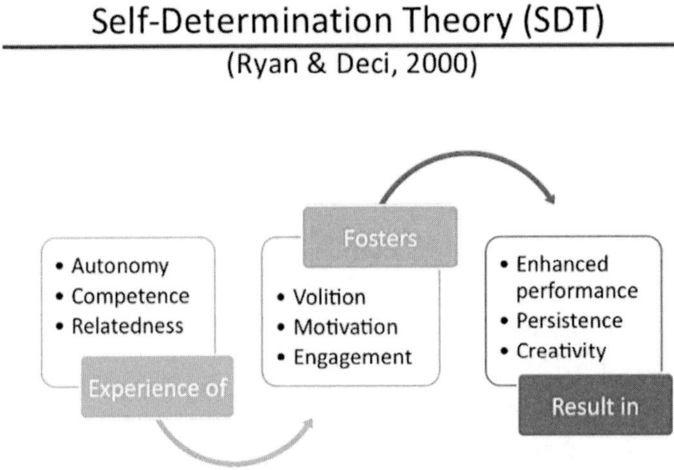

5. **Character Strengths Theory:** The notion of character strengths was first introduced by psychologists Martin Seligman and Christopher Peterson. Seligman and Neal Mayerson, another psychologist, created the Values in Action (VIA) Institute on Character, which uses the VIA Inventory of Strengths developed by Peterson to identify people's positive character strengths.

Classification of Character Strengths

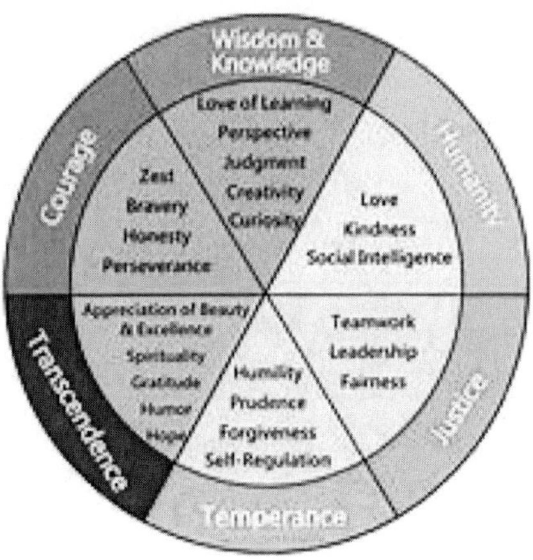

The 24 character strengths are divided into six classes of virtues:

- Wisdom
- Courage
- Humanity
- Justice
- Temperance
- Transcendence

The six virtues and the positive character strengths that are grouped with each of them are as follows:

1. **Wisdom:** Those who score high in wisdom tend to have character strengths that lead them to acquire knowledge and use it in creative and useful ways. The core wisdom character strengths are:
   - **Creativity:** Thinking of new ways to do things.
   - **Curiosity:** Taking an interest in a wide variety of topics.
   - **Open-mindedness:** Examining things from all sides.
   - **Love of learning:** Mastering new topics, skills, and bodies of research.
   - **Perspective:** Being able to provide wise counsel to others; looking at the world in a way that makes sense.
2. **Courage:** People who score high in courage have emotional character strengths that allow them to accomplish goals despite any opposition they face–whether internal or external. The character strengths associated with courage are:
   - **Honesty:** Speaking the truth; genuine.
   - **Bravery:** Embracing challenges, difficulties, or pain; not shrinking from threat.
   - **Persistence:** Finishing things once they are started.
   - **Zest:** Approaching all things in life with energy and excitement.
3. **Humanity:** Those who score high in humanity have a range of interpersonal character strengths that involve caring for others. These core character strengths are:
   - **Kindness:** Doing favors and good deeds.
   - **Love:** Valuing close relations with others.
   - **Social Intelligence:** Being aware of other people's motives and feelings.

4. **Justice:** People who are strong in justice tend to possess civic strengths that underscore the importance of a healthy community. The character strengths in the justice group are:
   - **Fairness:** Treating all people the same.
   - **Leadership:** Organizing group activities and making sure they happen.
   - **Teamwork:** Working well with others as a group or a team.
5. **Temperance:** Those who score high in temperance tend to have strengths that protect against the excesses in life. These strengths are:
   - **Forgiveness:** Forgiving others who have wronged them.
   - **Modesty:** Letting one's successes and accomplishments stand on their own.
   - **Prudence:** Avoiding doing things they might regret; making good choices.
   - **Self-regulation:** Being disciplined; controlling one's appetites and emotions.
6. **Transcendence:** People who are strong in transcendence tend to forge connections with God, the universe, or religions that provide meaning, purpose, and understanding. The core positive character strengths associated with transcendence are:
   - **Appreciation of beauty:** Noticing and appreciating beauty and excellence in everything.
   - **Gratitude:** Being thankful for the good things; taking time to express thanks.
   - **Hope:** Expecting the best; working to make it happen; believing good things are possible.
   - **Humor:** Making other people smile or laugh; enjoying jokes.
   - **Religiousness:** Having a solid belief about a higher purpose and meaning of life.

Thus, we can say that Character Strengths and Virtues Theory developed by Martin Seligman and Christopher Peterson is a cornerstone of positive psychology, focusing on identifying and cultivating core virtues and strengths in individuals. This theory suggests that emphasizing character strengths leads to greater well-being and resilience. Seligman's work emphasizes the importance of acknowledging and nurturing positive traits such as courage, wisdom, and kindness. By promoting the cultivation of these strengths, Seligman's theory offers a proactive approach to increasing individuals' overall life satisfaction and fulfillment. In positive psychology, this framework encourages a shift toward utilizing human potential and developing personal growth.

7. **Hope Theory:** Snyder's Hope Theory is a psychological framework developed by Charles Richard Snyder, which focuses on the cognitive and affective processes that enable individuals to pursue and achieve their goals. Hope, in this context, is defined as the perceived capability to devise pathways to desired goals and the motivation to use those pathways. The three key components of Hope Theory are as follows:
    a) **Goals:** Central to hope theory, goals are the targets that drive human behavior. They need to be specific, valuable, and attainable to create a sense of direction and purpose.
    b) **Pathways Thinking:** This cognitive component refers to the individual's ability to generate multiple routes or strategies to achieve their goals. It involves planning and identifying various ways to overcome obstacles and reach the desired destination.
    c) **Agency Thinking:** This affective component involves the motivation and determination to pursue the identified pathways. It reflects the individual's confidence and commitment to follow through on their plans and adapt to challenges.
    d) **The Cyclical Relationship:** The cyclical relationship between pathways thinking and agency thinking is central to Snyder's Hope Theory. When individuals can envision multiple ways to achieve their goals, they feel more capable of navigating obstacles, which enhances their cognitive flexibility and problem-solving skills. This ability to generate various strategies, known as pathways thinking, is crucial for maintaining momentum toward goal achievement. Simultaneously, agency thinking, which involves a strong belief in one's ability to execute these plans and stay motivated, plays a vital role. Positive emotions and self-confidence are essential in this process, as they reinforce the intention to pursue the chosen pathways. Thus, pathways thinking and agency thinking work together in a dynamic cycle, where each component strengthens and supports the other, fostering a resilient and proactive approach to goal attainment.
    e) **Overcoming Barriers:** Hope theory suggests that barriers, though inevitable, can be reframed as challenges rather than insurmountable obstacles. This perspective transforms setbacks into opportunities for growth and adaptation. Strengthened pathways, thinking empower

individuals to devise new strategies and alternative routes when confronted with difficulties, developing strength and flexibility. Additionally, maintaining a positive emotional state is crucial for sustaining motivation and resilience. Positive emotions enhance both pathways and agency thinking, making it easier to generate and pursue different strategies to achieve goals. This dual focus on cognitive flexibility and emotional positivity ensures that individuals remain motivated and capable of overcoming obstacles on their path to success.

Snyder's Hope Theory offers a comprehensive understanding of how hope operates as a motivational force. By emphasizing goal setting, strategic planning, and sustained motivation, it provides a framework for enhancing personal growth, achievement, and well-being. In positive psychology, hope is seen as a critical component for achieving well-being and resilience. Pathways thinking involve generating multiple strategies to reach desired outcomes, enhancing problem-solving abilities. Agency thinking, the belief in one's capacity to execute these strategies, reinforces motivation and perseverance. Together, these elements cultivate a proactive and optimistic mindset, enabling individuals to face challenges effectively and maintain a positive emotional state.

Summary

Positive psychology represents a transformative shift in the field of psychology, emphasizing the study and promotion of strengths and virtues that enable individuals and communities to thrive. Historically, psychology focused predominantly on mental illness and dysfunction, aiming to alleviate suffering and restore normalcy. However, positive psychology seeks to balance this approach by exploring factors that contribute to a fulfilling and meaningful life, offering a more holistic perspective on human well-being. Central to positive psychology are several key theories and models that elucidate the components and mechanisms of well-being. Martin Seligman's PERMA model is foundational, identifying five pillars essential to human flourishing: positive emotion, engagement, relationships, meaning, and accomplishment. These elements collectively contribute to an individual's overall sense of well-being and life satisfaction.

In addition to the PERMA model, other theories provide deeper insights into the motivational aspects of well-being. Hope Theory, for instance, highlights the role of goal-directed thinking and the belief in one's capacity to achieve those goals, developing resilience and optimism. Self-Determination Theory (SDT) further expands on motivation by identifying three basic psychological needs—autonomy, competence, and relatedness—that are crucial for fostering intrinsic motivation and psychological growth.

Positive psychology's scope extends beyond individual well-being to include relational and community well-being. It emphasizes the cultivation of strengths, such as resilience, gratitude, and empathy, which can enhance personal and collective resilience. By fostering positive relationships and nurturing intrinsic motivation, positive psychology provides a comprehensive approach to human potential, aiming to create not only more resilient individuals but also healthier and more vibrant communities.

The field of positive psychology continues to evolve, its principles and practices hold significant promise for enhancing well-being on multiple levels. By integrating these insights into various domains of life, from education and work to healthcare and community development, positive psychology seeks to foster environments where individuals and communities can thrive and flourish.

CHAPTER 2

APPLICATION OF POSITIVE PSYCHOLOGY IN HEALTH, STRESS MANAGEMENT, AND POST-TRAUMATIC GROWTH

The integration of positive psychology into healthcare represents a paradigm shift, expanding the focus from mere disease management to holistic well-being. Positive psychology, emphasizing on strengths, virtues, and optimal functioning, offers a transformative way to view health and healing. At its core, positive psychology seeks to find out the factors that contribute to a fulfilling life, not just the absence of illness. In healthcare, this approach has big effects, going beyond just physical sickness to include mental, emotional, social, and spiritual well-being. By using positive emotions, personal strengths, and resilience, healthcare providers can help people not just deal with problems but also do well even when things are tough. This chapter explores the harmony between positive psychology and healthcare. The chapter talks about how positive psychology and healthcare work well together. It shows how using positive psychology ideas can make people healthier and happier.

Stress is an inevitable part of life, affecting our thoughts, emotions, and behaviors. While short-term stress can be beneficial, enhancing our resilience and motivation, chronic stress can have detrimental effects on our physical and mental health, as well as our relationships. This chapter investigates into the nature of stress, examining its impacts and the dangers of burnout. Practical techniques based on positive psychology principles designed to reduce the harmful effects of stress, helping us to reframe our perceptions of pressure and regain a sense of control over our lives will be studied.

Post-traumatic growth (PTG) refers to the positive psychological changes that can occur after an individual processes and copes with trauma, leading to personal development beyond their previous levels of functioning. This chapter explores the significant impact of positive psychology on PTG, highlighting how the principles of positive psychology facilitate this transformative process. By emphasizing the potential for growth and resilience in the face of adversity, it provides a framework for understanding how individuals can flourish despite experiencing trauma. This perspective helps reframe traumatic events as opportunities for profound personal growth, fostering a deeper sense of meaning and purpose in life.

Introduction

In psychology, there has traditionally been more attention given to studying negative aspects rather than positive ones. However, in recent years, there has been increasing acknowledgment and investigation into positive mental health. This change is noticeable in the scientific literature, where the majority of studies have historically concentrated on topics like stress, anxiety, and depression, while comparatively fewer have explored concepts related to health and well-being.

Health has been a subject of significant study and interest within psychology due to its profound influence on psychological behavior. Psychological well-being is intricately linked to physical health, with various aspects such as stress, mood, and cognition being affected by one's health status. Moreover, mental health conditions can impact physical health outcomes and vice versa. Over time, the concept of health has undergone various definitions, each serving different purposes. Initially, health was viewed from a biomedical perspective, focusing on the body's ability to function and defining health as absence of disease. It was seen as a state of normal bodily function that could be disrupted by illness. In 1948, the World Health Organization (WHO) introduced a groundbreaking definition that broadened the understanding of health. This definition connected health not only to the absence of disease but also to overall well-being, encompassing physical, mental, and social dimensions. It emphasized the importance of factors beyond mere bodily function, such as mental and social well-being.

"Health is a state of complete physical, mental, and social well-being and not merely the absence of disease or infirmity" (WHO, 1948).

The World Health Organization's definition of health encourages us to consider health in positive terms, not just as absence of disease. Positive health can be characterized not only as a long and disease-free life but also in terms of:

a) Less frequent and briefer ailments
b) Greater recovery capacity
c) Rapid wound healing

d) Increased physiological capacity
e) Chronic but non debilitating diseases

Different types of health include:

- **Physical Health:** This relates to the condition of the body and its ability to function optimally. It involves aspects such as fitness, nutrition, and disease prevention.
- **Mental Health:** Mental health involves emotional and psychological well-being. It includes factors like mood, cognition, and coping skills, and affects how individuals think, feel, and behave.
- **Social Health:** Social health refers to the quality of relationships and social interactions. It involves aspects such as communication, support networks, and sense of belonging within communities.

Each type of health is interconnected and contributes to overall well-being, highlighting the importance of addressing all dimensions for holistic health.

Positive Health

The concept of positive health represents a transformation in how we perceive well-being, emphasizing the importance of considering factors beyond the absence of disease. It includes not only physical health but also psychological and social dimensions, reflecting an overall state of vitality and growth. Positive health can be characterized not only as a long and disease-free life but also in terms of:

a) Less frequent and briefer ailments
b) Greater recovery capacity
c) Rapid wound healing
d) Increased physiological capacity
e) Chronic but non debilitating diseases

In epidemiology, various population-level concepts like DALYs (disability adjusted life years), HALYs (health-adjusted life years), and QALYs (quality-adjusted life years) combine measures of sickness and death into single measures. Similarly, HLEs (happiness-adjusted life expectancies) measure a nation's quality of life by multiplying average life expectancy with average happiness levels. Positive health intersects with related approaches like disease prevention and wellness, emphasizing the importance of considering good health rather than solely the absence of illness.

While extensive research exists on negative psychological factors and their health risks, less explored are the protective roles of positive psychological factors. Positive and negative feelings are somewhat connected but affect different parts of the brain. Now, scientists are studying how things that promote good health, like positive emotions, work together with things that can harm health, like stress, to understand how they both influence our health.

Well-done research indicates that certain positive aspects of health predict good health in different ways. Some of these positive factors from positive psychology include:

- Feeling positive emotions
- Being satisfied with life
- Having optimism about the future
- Practicing forgiveness
- Being able to control oneself
- Having energy and enthusiasm
- Finding meaning and purpose in life
- Helping others and volunteering
- Having strong social relationships
- Having a sense of spirituality or religiosity

There are two reasons why people bother about their health and well-being:

a) People desire well-being above and beyond the relief of their sufferings.

b) Positive emotions, engagement, purpose, positive relationships, positive accomplishments act as a buffer against mental disorders.

Link between Healthy Lifestyles and Positive Psychology

Achieving positive health includes a holistic approach that integrates physical health habits with positive mindsets and activities. Positive psychology interventions, combined with traditional healthy habits like a plant-based diet and regular exercise, play an important role in developing healthy behavior changes. These interventions not only lead to positive emotions but also offer direct physiological benefits, such as enhancing the parasympathetic nervous system. The reciprocal relationship between healthy lifestyles and positive emotions reinforces the adoption of healthy behaviors, creating a powerful cycle of well-being. Health practitioners can facilitate this process by initiating discussions with patients about incorporating positive activities into their lifestyle, thereby enhancing vitality and overall health. Furthermore, the adoption of a healthy lifestyle by health practitioners themselves can contribute to personal well-being and alleviate burnout.

Theories of Health

1. **Broaden-and-Build Theory:** Proposed by Barbara Fredrickson, the theory claims that positive emotions, like happiness and interest, broaden an individual's awareness, leading to exploratory thoughts and actions. Over time, this broadened behavior builds valuable skills and psychological resources, enhancing overall well-being. Unlike negative emotions, which prompt narrow, survival-oriented behaviors, positive emotions develop a cycle of increased well-being, resilience, and success. Barbara Fredrickson's research supports this theory, showing that positive emotions enhance creativity, inventiveness, and long-term psychological resilience. Additionally, practices like meditation and religious participation have been found to generate positive emotions, promoting psychological well-being and physical health.

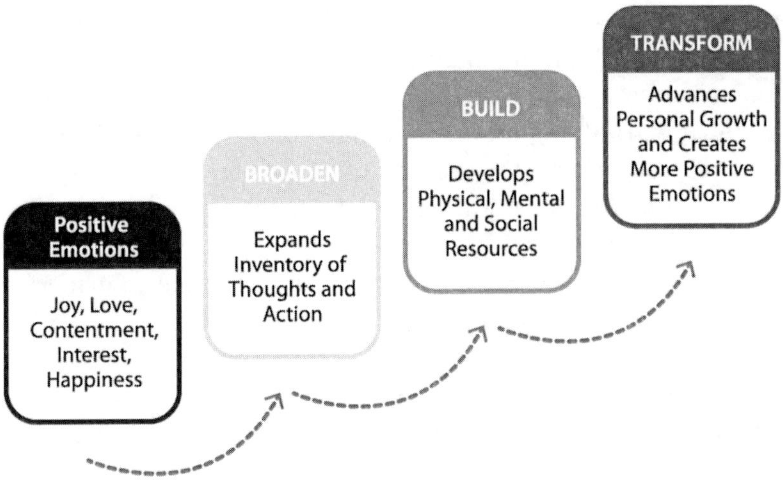

2. **PERMA Model:** Developed by Martin Seligman, the PERMA model provides a comprehensive framework for enhancing health and well-being. By focusing on five key elements - Positive emotions, Engagement, Relationships, Meaning, and Accomplishment - the PERMA model offers a holistic approach to promoting physical and mental health. Positive emotions, such as joy and contentment, not only contribute to subjective well-being but also have tangible effects on physical health, including reduced stress levels and improved immune function. Engagement in activities that foster a state of flow promotes mental health by enhancing

focus, creativity, and resilience. Healthy relationships are fundamental to well-being, as social support and connectedness have been linked to better physical health outcomes and decreased risk of mental health disorders. Finding meaning in life provides individuals with a sense of purpose and direction, which can protect against stress and contribute to overall life satisfaction. Finally, the pursuit of accomplishment and achievement develops a sense of competence and mastery, leading to increased self-esteem and motivation. By incorporating these elements into daily life, individuals can cultivate a thriving existence characterized by optimal health and well-being.

3. **Socioemotional Selectivity Theory: (SST).** Proposed by Laura Carstensen, sheds light on how individuals prioritize their goals and invest their resources, particularly in old age. This theory suggests that as individuals perceive their time horizons to be shrinking, they become more selective in their efforts, prioritizing emotionally meaningful goals and activities. This selective focus on positive emotional experiences and relationships is believed to contribute to enhanced psychological well-being and reduced emotional risks as individuals grow older. From a health perspective, SST implies that older adults may benefit from a greater emphasis on social and emotional targets in their lives. By prioritizing emotionally gratifying interactions and meaningful relationships, older adults may experience lower levels of stress, improved mood and better overall mental health. Additionally, the theory suggests that the efforts of present-oriented and pleasure-related goals may lead to increased happiness and life satisfaction among older individuals. Furthermore, the positivity effect observed in older adults, where they tend to focus more on positive stimuli and memories, may contribute to their overall sense of well-being. This bias toward positivity in perception and recall could help buffer against negative experiences and enhance resilience in the face of challenges, ultimately promoting better emotional and mental health outcomes in older age. Overall, SST highlights the importance of social and emotional factors in promoting health and well-being as individual's age.
4. **Self-Determination Theory (SDT):** Developed by Edward Deci and Richard Ryan, SDT holds significant importance in the context of health by emphasizing the intrinsic motivations and psychological needs that drive human behavior. By acknowledging the universal needs for autonomy, competence, and relatedness, SDT provides insights into developing psychological well-being and promoting positive health outcomes. When

individuals feel a sense of autonomy, competence, and connection in their lives, they are more likely to engage in health-promoting behaviors such as regular exercise, balanced nutrition, and seeking medical care when needed. Moreover, SDT highlights the importance of intrinsic motivation in sustaining long-term behavioral changes, as opposed to relying solely on external rewards or punishments. SDT also emphasizes the role of social support and interpersonal relationships in promoting health and well-being. By promoting environments that support autonomy and relatedness, such as through empathetic communication and collaborative decision-making in healthcare settings, SDT can enhance patient satisfaction, adhering to treatment plans and overall health outcomes. Overall, SDT provides a valuable framework for understanding the psychological factors that influence health behaviors and outcomes, emphasizing the importance of intrinsic motivation, autonomy, competence, and social connection in promoting holistic well-being.

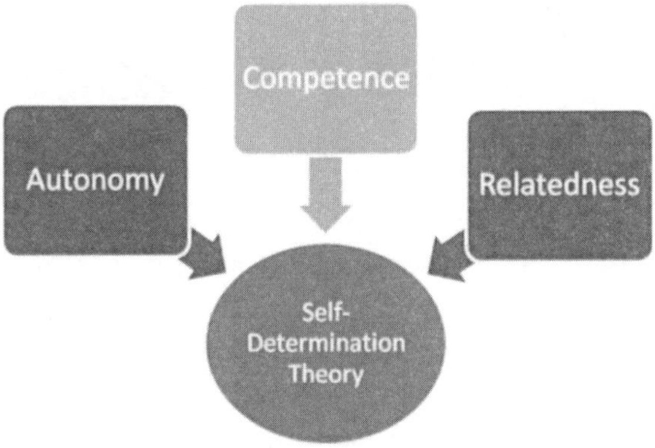

5. **Flourishing Theory:** Developed by Corey Keyes, Flourishing theory offers a comprehensive framework for understanding mental health and well-being. At its core, flourishing theory say that mental health extends beyond the absence of mental illness to incorporate the presence of positive emotions, high levels of psychological functioning, and strong social connections. It emphasizes the importance of individuals not just surviving, but growing in various domains of life. Keyes conceptualizes flourishing as the pinnacle of mental health, where individuals experience positive emotions such as happiness, interest in life, and satisfaction, alongside optimal psychological and social functioning. This state is characterized by a sense of vitality, purpose and engagement with life's challenges and opportunities. The theory provides a profound understanding of mental

health along a continuum, with flourishing representing the highest level, moderate mental health falling in between, and languishing indicating a state of poor mental health. Keyes' research has shown that flourishing individuals not only have lower rates of mental illness but also enjoy greater resilience, higher levels of life satisfaction, and better overall quality of life.

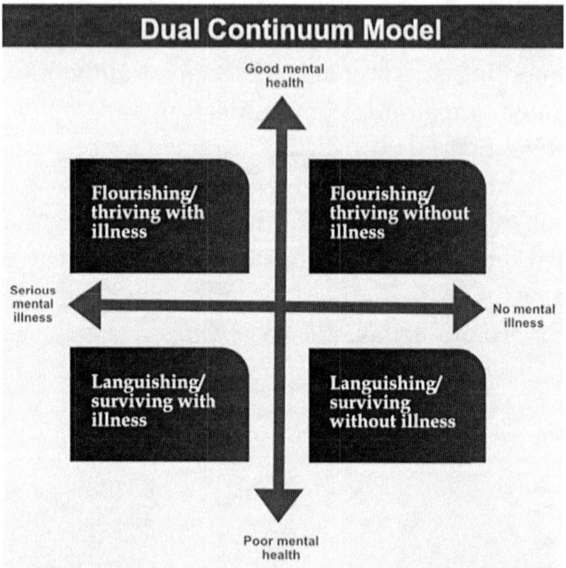

6. **Learned Optimism:** Seligman's approach to learned optimism has significant implications in the area of health. By training individuals to reframe their responses to adversity, it equips them with powerful tools to manage stress and enhance their overall well-being. One significant impact of learned optimism on health is its potential to prevent and relieve depression. By teaching individuals to challenge negative beliefs and interpretations of adverse events, this approach can disrupt the patterns of rumination and self-blame that often characterizes depression. Instead of feeling overwhelmed and helpless in the face of challenges, individuals learn to cultivate a more adaptive mindset, characterized by resilience and hopefulness. Moreover, learned optimism can have a chain reaction on various aspects of physical health. Chronic stress and negative emotions are known contributors to a range of health problems, including cardiovascular disease, weakened immune function, and chronic pain. By promoting positive thinking and constructive coping strategies, learned optimism may help to lessen the physiological effects of stress, thereby reducing the risk of these health conditions. Additionally, the vitalization component

of Seligman's method encourages individuals to actively celebrate their successes in disputing negative beliefs. This positive reinforcement can reinforce optimistic thinking patterns, further enhancing mental and emotional well-being. Overall, by fostering a more optimistic outlook on life, Seligman's method of learned optimism offers a promising pathway to improved health outcomes, both mentally and physically.

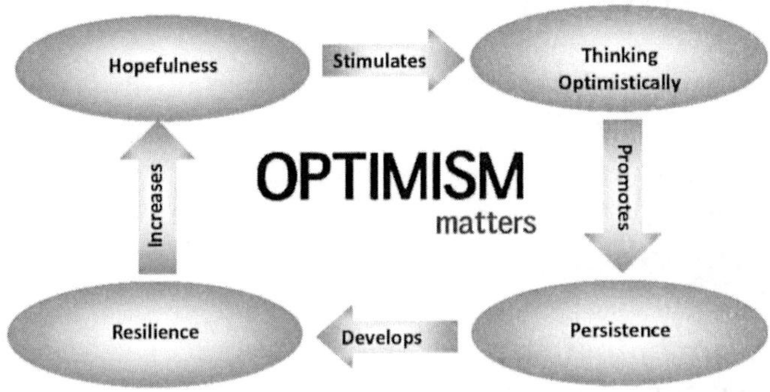

7. **Resilience Theory:** The resiliency treatment model emphasizes the dynamic nature of adjustment to chronic stress, providing a framework for developing coping skills essential for maintaining well-being. By integrating elements such as the Relaxation Response (RR), stress awareness and management, and adaptive strategies, the model addresses both the physiological and psychological aspects of resilience. Through the Stress Management and Resiliency Training/Relaxation Response Resiliency Program (SMART-3RP), individuals can cultivate resilience by actively practicing these core skills. Stress management techniques derived from cognitive behavior therapy aid in reducing psychological symptoms like anxiety and depression, while adaptive strategies rooted in positive psychology foster positive psychological states and social connectedness. This holistic approach acknowledges the bidirectional relationship between these processes and resilience, highlighting their collective influence on overall health and well-being.

Positive Psychology Intervention Techniques for Health

Positive psychology interventions (PPIs) aim to promote both mental and physical well-being. Here are some techniques used in these interventions:

1. **The PERMA model:** Developed by psychologist Martin Seligman, identifies five essential elements for well-being: Positive emotions, Engagement, Relationships, Meaning, and Accomplishment. Each

dimension plays a crucial role in enhancing both physical and mental health.

a) **Positive Emotions:** Positive emotions like happiness, gratitude, and joy contribute to improved mental and physical health by reducing stress, boosting the immune system, and promoting overall well-being. Cultivating positive emotions through activities such as mindfulness, meditation, or spending time with loved ones can lead to better health outcomes.

b) **Engagement:** Engagement refers to being fully absorbed and involved in activities that challenge and interest us. Engaging in activities that provide a sense of flow and accomplishment promotes mental health by reducing feelings of boredom and increasing feelings of fulfillment. Physically, engagement can lead to improved cardiovascular health and overall fitness.

c) **Relationships:** Strong social connections are essential for both mental and physical health. Building and maintaining meaningful relationships provide emotional support, reduce feelings of loneliness, and contribute to a sense of belonging and purpose. Social support has been linked to lower rates of depression, improved immune function, and increased longevity.

d) **Meaning:** Finding meaning and purpose in life is essential for well-being. Having a sense of meaning gives individuals a reason to live, motivates them to overcome challenges, and provides a sense of direction. Meaningful activities contribute to mental health by promoting a sense of fulfillment and satisfaction, while also developing resilience in the face of adversity.

e) **Accomplishment:** Accomplishment refers to setting and achieving goals that are meaningful and challenging. Accomplishing goals provides a sense of competence, confidence, and self-esteem, which are important for mental health. Additionally, achieving goals related to physical health, such as exercising regularly or maintaining a healthy diet, contributes to overall well-being by promoting physical fitness and reducing the risk of chronic diseases.

2. **Counting Blessings:** Counting blessings is a powerful gratitude practice that significantly contributes to holistic health by fostering a positive mindset and enhancing emotional well-being. When individuals take time to reflect on and acknowledge the positive aspects of their lives, such as meaningful relationships, personal achievements, or joyful moments,

they cultivate an attitude of gratitude. This intentional focus on the good things experienced can shift attention away from stressors and negative thoughts, promoting a more balanced and optimistic outlook. Research has shown that practicing gratitude through counting blessings can lead to improved mental health by reducing symptoms of depression and anxiety, while also increasing overall life satisfaction. Furthermore, this practice encourages mindfulness and presence as individuals become more aware of the positive elements in their daily lives. Physically, gratitude can lower blood pressure, improve sleep quality, and boost the immune system, contributing to better physical health. Socially, expressing gratitude can strengthen relationships, develop a sense of community, and increase social support, which are all vital components of holistic well-being. In essence, counting blessings is a simple yet effective tool for enhancing holistic health, encompassing emotional, physical, and social dimensions of well-being, and ultimately leading to a more fulfilling and balanced life.

3. **Utilizing Signature Strengths:** Utilizing signature strengths involves identifying and using one's core qualities and attributes that are most authentic and fulfilling. These strengths, such as kindness, perseverance, or creativity, play a significant role in shaping an individual's thoughts, behaviors, and interactions. By intentionally applying these strengths in daily activities and challenges, individuals can experience a sense of accomplishment, fulfillment, and improved well-being, contributing positively to both mental and physical health.
4. **Kindness Activities:** Kindness activities involve performing acts of kindness toward others without expecting anything in return. These activities can range from small gestures like holding the door open for someone to larger acts like volunteering or donating to charity. Engaging in kindness activities has been shown to boost positive emotions, reduce stress levels, and enhance overall well-being. Moreover, practicing kindness can develop a sense of connection with others and promote a healthier, more compassionate society.
5. **Cultivating Optimism:** Cultivating optimism involves developing a positive outlook on life by focusing on hopeful and positive thoughts about the future, even in challenging situations. This technique encourages individuals to interpret events in a more favorable light, emphasizing possibilities for positive outcomes. By developing optimism, individuals may experience reduced stress levels, improved coping abilities, and

better overall mental and physical well-being, as they approach life with a constructive and hopeful mindset.

6. **Mindfulness Meditation:** It is a practice that involves focusing one's attention on the present moment without judgment. It typically involves techniques such as focused breathing, body scans, or mindful movement. By cultivating awareness of sensations, thoughts, and emotions as they arise, mindfulness can promote stress reduction, emotional regulation, and increased self-awareness, contributing to improved mental well-being. Additionally, research suggests that regular mindfulness practice may lead to physical benefits such as reduced blood pressure, improved immune function, and better sleep quality, supporting overall physical health.
7. **Self-Affirmation:** Self-affirmation involves reflecting on and affirming one's core values, strengths, and positive attributes. This practice can increase self-esteem, resilience, and a sense of identity, which in turn can protect against stress and adversity. By reinforcing a positive self-image, self-affirmation may reduce anxiety and depression, improve coping abilities, and enhance overall mental well-being. Additionally, self-affirmation has been linked to healthier behaviors and outcomes, such as increased physical activity, better adherence to medical treatments, and lower levels of physiological stress markers, contributing to improved physical health.
8. **Healthy Lifestyle Habits:** Healthy lifestyle habits encompass behaviors such as regular exercise, balanced nutrition, adequate sleep, stress management, and avoiding harmful substances like tobacco and excessive alcohol. These habits promote good physical health by improving cardiovascular function, strengthening the immune system, maintaining a healthy weight, and reducing the risk of chronic diseases. Additionally, healthy lifestyle habits can positively impact mental health by reducing stress, improving mood, enhancing cognitive function, and fostering a sense of well-being and resilience. Overall, adopting a healthy lifestyle contributes to better physical and mental health outcomes.

Summary

The growing field of positive psychology offers a compelling framework for understanding and promoting total well-being and positive health. While the application of positive psychology to health is promising, much work remains to be done to fully understand its impact on physical health outcomes. Research has shown that positive psychological assets, such as positive emotions, life satisfaction, optimism, positive relationships, and life purpose, are prospectively associated with good health. Furthermore, interventions aimed at increasing these assets have demonstrated promising results, although long-term effects require sustained lifestyle changes.

However, it is essential to approach the potential of positive psychology interventions with cautious optimism. As researchers and practitioners continue to explore the links between positive psychological assets and health, it is important to maintain a skeptical yet open-minded attitude. Attention to underlying mechanisms and rigorous empirical investigation will be critical in advancing our understanding of how positive psychology interventions can promote good health. Moreover, while freedom from disease and longevity are important goals, quality of life should not be overlooked. Research consistently demonstrates that cultivating positive psychological and social assets, such as experiencing frequent positive emotions, having a sense of life purpose, and fostering social connections, is associated with greater overall well-being and happiness across the lifespan.

Concept of Stress

Stress, a common human experience, is a response to challenges and difficult circumstances that can either enhance or impair an individual's performance and well-being. Stress is similar to electricity; it provides energy and increases arousal, thereby affecting performance. However, excessive stress can lead to negative consequences, just as a high electric current can damage appliances. Conversely, insufficient stress may result in low motivation and inefficiency. Therefore, not all stress is inherently detrimental. "Eustress" refers to a beneficial level of stress that helps individuals achieve peak performance and manage crises effectively. However, eustress can transform into "distress," which causes physical and psychological harm.

Stress originates from the Latin words "strictus" (tight or narrow) and "stringere" (to tighten), reflecting the physical sensations often associated with stress, such as muscle tension and restricted breathing. Stressors, which are events that trigger the stress response, can range from environmental factors like noise and crowding to personal issues such as bad relationships or daily commuting. The body's reaction to these stressors is known as "strain."

Hans Selye, a pioneer in stress research, defined stress as the body's nonspecific response to any demand. However, this definition is disputed, as different stressors may elicit varying responses, and individuals may react differently to the same stressor. Stress is not merely an internal or environmental factor but a dynamic process involving individuals interacting with their social and cultural environments. This process includes appraising stressful encounters and coping with them.

Richard Lazarus' cognitive theory of stress emphasizes the role of appraisal in the stress response. Primary appraisal involves evaluating an environment as positive, neutral, or negative, while secondary appraisal assesses one's ability to cope with the stressor. These appraisals determine our cognitive, behavioral, emotional, and physiological responses. Factors influencing appraisal include past experiences and perceived control over the situation. For instance, a sense of self-confidence can reduce the perception of a threat.

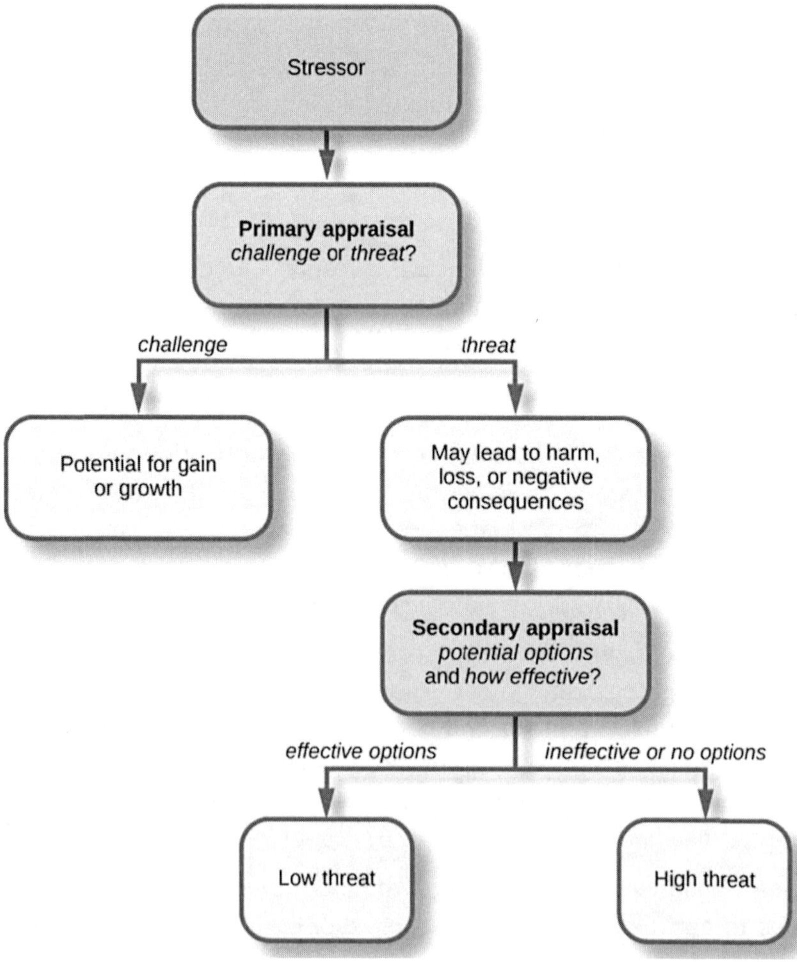

Stress reactions vary in intensity, duration, complexity, and predictability. More intense, prolonged, complex, and unexpected stresses typically have more negative effects. Individual differences, such as physical health, mental health, and temperament, also influence stress experiences. Cultural contexts shape the meaning of events and expected responses, while personal resources like money, social skills, and support networks impact stress appraisal.

Signs and Symptoms of Stress

1. **Psychological Signs:**
   - **Difficulty Concentrating:** Finding it hard to focus on tasks or maintain attention.
   - **Worrying:** Excessive concern about various aspects of life.
   - **Anxiety:** Experiencing feelings of nervousness, restlessness, or tension.
   - **Trouble Remembering:** Having issues with memory recall or experiencing forgetfulness.
2. **Emotional Signs:**
   - **Anger:** Feeling unusually irritable or having frequent outbursts of anger.
   - **Moodiness:** Experiencing frequent mood swings or feeling emotionally unstable.
   - **Frustration:** Feeling easily frustrated or overwhelmed by minor issues.
3. **Physical Signs:**
   - **High Blood Pressure:** Elevated blood pressure levels, which can be a sign of chronic stress.
   - **Changes in Weight:** Noticeable weight gain or loss due to changes in eating habits or metabolism.
   - **Frequent Colds or Infections:** Reduced immune function leading to increased susceptibility to illnesses.
   - **Changes in Menstrual Cycle and Libido:** Irregular menstrual cycles or changes in sexual desire.
4. **Behavioral Signs:**
   - **Poor Self-Care:** Neglecting personal hygiene, diet, exercise, or sleep.
   - **Lack of Enjoyment:** Not engaging in or finding time for activities once enjoyed.

- **Substance Reliance:** Increasing use of drugs, alcohol, or other substances to cope with stress.

Types of Stress

There are three major types of stress.

1. **Physical and Environmental Stress:** Physical stressors are external factors that exert pressure on the body, such as intense physical exertion or exposure to extreme temperatures. Environmental stressors include elements in the surroundings like noise pollution or air quality that impact well-being and may cause tension or discomfort.
    - **Physical Stress:** Demands that change the body's state, such as overexertion, lack of sleep, or injury.
    - **Environmental Stress:** Aspects of surroundings that is unavoidable, like air pollution, noise, or extreme weather conditions.
    - **Catastrophic Events:** Sudden and severe environmental stresses like earthquakes, floods, or fires.
2. **Psychological Stress:** Psychological stress originates from the mind and is unique to each individual, representing internal sources of stress. It includes a range of emotions such as worrying, anxiety, or depression, which not only indicate stress but also contribute to its perpetuation.
    - **Frustration:** Results from obstacles that hinder the achievement of desired goals, often stemming from social discrimination interpersonal conflicts, or setbacks in academics or careers.
    - **Conflicts:** Arise from incompatible needs or motives, forcing individuals to choose between different paths or values. Examples include decisions regarding career options or balancing personal and professional aspirations.
    - **Internal Pressures:** Stem from self-imposed expectations and beliefs, leading to unrealistic standards and eventual disappointment. This may manifest as striving for perfection in all endeavors or setting unattainable goals.
    - **Social Pressures:** Result from external demands imposed by others, leading to stress in interpersonal relationships. Examples: Excessive demands from colleagues, conflicts with family or friends.
3. **Social Stress:** Social stress arises from interactions with others and various social events, representing externally induced sources of stress. Examples of social stress are:

- **Family Emergencies:** Situations such as illnesses or financial crises within the family can lead to considerable stress.
- **Strained Relationships:** Conflicts and tensions within relationships, whether with family members, friends, or romantic partners, can be significant sources of stress.
- **Conflicts with Neighbors:** Disputes or disagreements with neighbors over issues such as noise, property boundaries, or other matters can cause stress.
- **Individual Variability:** Social stresses vary widely among individuals based on personality traits and preference. Example: Introverts vs. Extroverts may experience social stress differently; while attending social gatherings like parties may be stressful for introverts who prefer solitude, extroverts may find being alone or in quieter settings to be stressful.

Sources of Stress

A wide range of events and conditions can generate stress. Among the most important of these are major stressful life events, such as death of a loved one or personal injury, the annoying frequent hassles of everyday life and traumatic events that affect our lives.

- **Life Events:** Changes, big and small, sudden and gradual affect our life from the moment we are born. We learn to cope with small, everyday changes but major life events can be stressful, because they disturb our routine and cause turmoil. If several of these life events that are planned (e.g. moving into a new house) or unpredicted (e.g. break-up of a long-term relationship) occur within a short period of time, we find it difficult to cope with them and will be more prone to the symptoms of stress.
- **Hassles:** These are the personal stresses we face as individuals due to the happenings in our daily life, such as noisy surroundings, commuting, quarrelsome neighbors, electricity and water shortage, traffic snarls, and so on. Attending to various emergencies are daily hassles experienced by a housewife. There are some jobs in which daily hassles are very frequent. These daily hassles may sometimes have devastating consequences for the individual who is often the one coping alone with them as others may not even be aware of them as outsiders. The more stress people report as a result of daily hassles, the poorer is their psychological well-being.

- **Traumatic Events:** These include being involved in a variety of extreme events such as a fire, train or road accident, robbery, earthquake, tsunami, etc. The effects of these events may occur after some lapse of time and sometimes persist as symptoms of anxiety, flashbacks, dreams and intrusive thoughts, etc. Severe trauma can also strain relationships.

Effect of Stress on Psychological Functioning and Health

Physiological Effects:

1. **Cardiovascular Disorders:** Prolonged stress can lead to the development of cardiovascular issues such as heart disease, heart attacks, and stroke. This occurs due to increased heart rate, elevated blood pressure, and the release of stress hormones like cortisol and adrenaline, which can damage blood vessels over time.
2. **Immune System Changes:** Chronic stress suppresses the immune system, making individuals more susceptible to infections and illnesses. This is because stress hormones can inhibit the function of immune cells, reducing their ability to combat pathogens.
3. **Gastrointestinal Problems:** Stress is closely linked to gastrointestinal disorders such as ulcers, irritable bowel syndrome (IBS), and acid reflux. The digestive system is sensitive to stress, leading to symptoms like stomach pain, nausea, diarrhea, or constipation.
4. **Respiratory Issues:** Stress can exacerbate respiratory conditions such as asthma and allergies. During times of stress, individuals may experience heightened inflammation in the airways, triggering asthma attacks or allergic reactions.
5. **Musculoskeletal Tension:** Stress often manifests physically, causing muscle tension, stiffness, and pain. Prolonged stress can contribute to conditions like tension, headaches, and migraines.

Cognitive Effects

1. **Impaired Concentration and Memory:** Stress can impair cognitive function, leading to difficulties with concentration, memory retrieval, and decision-making. High levels of stress hormones can interfere with neural pathways involved in learning and memory.
2. **Reduced Mental Flexibility:** Chronic stress can decrease cognitive flexibility, making it challenging to adapt to new situations of

problem-solving effectively. Individuals may become rigid in their thinking patterns, leading to increased feelings of frustration and overwhelm.

3. **Impaired Judgment:** Stress can cloud judgment and impair logical reasoning, leading individuals to make impulsive or irrational decisions. This can have consequences in various areas of life, including work, relationships, and personal health.

Emotional Effects

1. **Mood Changes:** Stress often contributes to mood disturbances such as irritability, anxiety, and depression. Fluctuations in stress hormones can disrupt neurotransmitter levels in the brain, affecting mood regulation and emotional stability.
2. **Feelings of Helplessness and Hopelessness:** Prolonged stress can evoke feelings of helplessness and hopelessness, making individuals feel overwhelmed by their circumstances and unable to cope. This can lead to a sense of despair and resignation.
3. **Increased Risk of Burnout:** Chronic stress is a significant risk factor for burnout, characterized by physical, emotional, and mental exhaustion. Burnout often occurs in high-pressure environments where individuals feel chronically overwhelmed and depleted.

Health Effects

1. **Increased Risk of Chronic Illness:** Stress has been implicated in the development and aggravation of various chronic illnesses, including cardiovascular disease, diabetes, autoimmune disorders, and certain cancers. Prolonged stress weakens the body's ability to maintain homeostasis, contributing to the onset and progression of these conditions.
2. **Compromised Quality of Life:** Persistent stress can significantly diminish overall quality of life, impairing physical health, mental well-being, and social functioning. Individuals may experience reduced productivity, strained relationships, and a diminished sense of fulfillment and satisfaction.
3. **Shortened Lifespan:** Chronic stress has been associated with a shortened lifespan, primarily due to its detrimental effects on physical health and increased risk of mortality from stress-related illnesses. Managing stress effectively is crucial for promoting longevity and well-being.

General Adaptation Syndrome

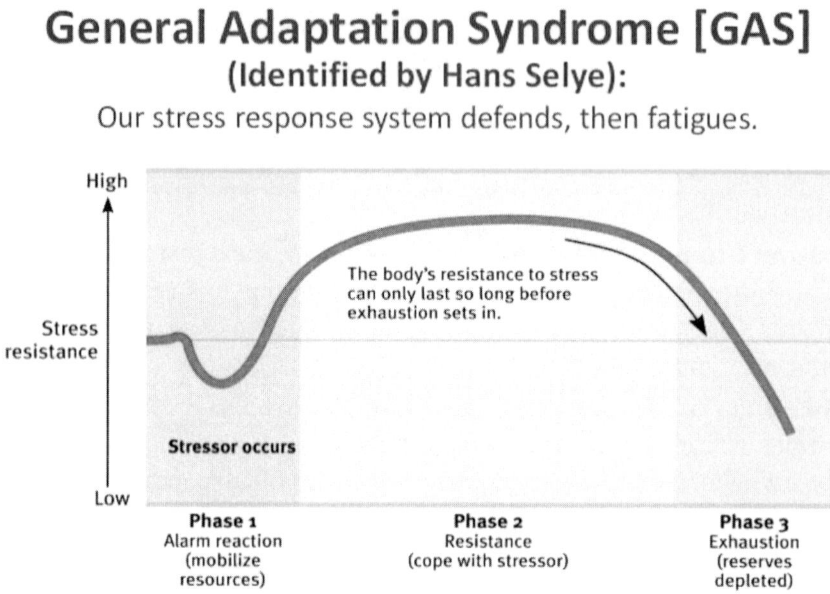

The General Adaptation Syndrome (GAS) model, developed by Hans Selye, outlines the body's physiological response to prolonged stress. This model identifies three distinct stages: alarm reaction, resistance, and exhaustion. Each stage represents a different level of response and adaptation by the body to ongoing stressors.

1. **Alarm Reaction Stage:** The initial stage begins with a noxious stimulus or stressor, activating the adrenal-pituitary-cortex system. This triggers the release of stress hormones like adrenaline and cortisol, preparing the body for "fight or flight." Physiological changes include increased heart rate, heightened senses, and a burst of energy.
2. **Resistance Stage:** If stress continues beyond the initial alarm stage, the body transitions into the resistance stage. During this phase, the parasympathetic nervous system attempts to restore equilibrium by conserving energy and resources. Although the body remains on high alert, it tries to adapt to the ongoing stressor through various coping mechanisms, which may include direct confrontation or other adaptive behaviors to decrease the stressor's impact. The body continues to secrete stress hormones, although at a more controlled rate, to sustain its defenses over an extended period, effectively managing its resources to cope with the prolonged stress.

3. **Exhaustion Stage:** Prolonged exposure to the stressor without adequate recovery leads to the exhaustion stage. During this phase, the body's resources, which were heavily taxed during the alarm and resistance stages, become depleted. The physiological systems involved in responding to stress, such as the immune system and adrenal glands, become less effective. As a result, the body's ability to resist becomes compromised, making it more susceptible to stress-related illnesses and diseases such as high blood pressure, heart disease, and other chronic conditions.

Criticisms of the GAS Model

- **Limited Role of Psychological Factors:** Selye's model has been criticized for not adequately considering psychological factors. Psychological appraisal—how individuals perceive and evaluate stressors—plays a crucial role in determining the impact of stress.
- **Individual Differences:** People respond to stress differently based on their perceptions, personalities, and biological make-ups. Factors such as resilience, coping strategies, and previous experiences significantly influence how one deals with stress.
- **Complexity of Stress Response:** Modern research emphasizes that the stress response is more complex than the physiological processes described in the GAS model. Emotional and cognitive factors are integral to understanding how stress affects individuals.

Positive Psychology Strategies/Techniques for Management of Stress

Positive psychology techniques encompass physical, cognitive, behavioral, and effective strategies that effectively aid in stress reduction. These techniques use the power of positive thinking, physical activity, and emotional regulation to develop resilience and well-being. Let us understand each aspect and how it helps in reduction of stress.

A) Physical Aspect

1. **Physical Exercise:** It is a powerful tool for reducing stress, offering numerous benefits for both physical and mental health. Physical exercise refers to any bodily activity that enhances or maintains physical fitness and overall health. It involves engaging in structured and repetitive

movements that target various muscle groups, cardiovascular system, and flexibility. Examples include jogging, weightlifting, swimming, and yoga.

a) **Physical Benefits:** Regular physical activity, such as aerobics, jogging, swimming, and cycling, significantly improves cardiovascular health by enhancing heart efficiency and lowering the resting heart rate, which indicates more efficient heart function and reduces physiological strain on the body. Additionally, physical activity helps regulate stress hormones by lowering cortisol levels, the body's primary stress hormone. Exercise also triggers the release of endorphins, often referred to as "feel-good" hormones. These endorphins act as natural painkillers and mood elevators, providing a sense of well-being and relaxation, thereby promoting both physical and mental health.

b) **Mental and Emotional Benefits:** Engaging in physical activities such as playing tennis, walking, or swimming provides a valuable mental diversion from daily stressors, allowing individuals to focus on the activity at hand rather than ruminating on stress-inducing thoughts. Regular exercise also enhances mood by reducing symptoms of anxiety and depression through the release of neurotransmitters like serotonin and dopamine, which are crucial for mood regulation. Additionally, regular physical activity can improve sleep patterns, which is essential for stress management as good sleep allows the body and mind to recover and regenerate, thereby enhancing overall resilience to stress.

c) **Social and Psychological Benefits:** Participating in group sports or fitness classes provides valuable social interaction, helping to build social connections that enhance emotional support networks and reduce feelings of isolation and stress. Additionally, setting and achieving fitness goals, whether it's running a certain distance or mastering a new sport, can significantly boost self-esteem and self-efficacy. This sense of accomplishment fosters a positive self-image and a greater sense of control over one's life, contributing to overall mental and emotional well-being.

2. **Relaxation Techniques:** Relaxation techniques like Jacobson Progressive Muscle Relaxation (JPMR) are effective for stress reduction because they utilize the body's physiological responses to induce a state of calmness and reduce the effects of stress. JPMR is a technique that effectively utilizes the reciprocal inhibition of the nervous system to relieve stress. By actively engaging the Parasympathetic Nervous System (PNS) through

relaxation techniques, JPMR reduces the dominance of the Sympathetic Nervous System (SNS), responsible for the "fight or flight" response. This shift promotes relaxation and recovery, countering the physiological effects of stress. Additionally, JPMR involves a cycle of tension and relaxation in various muscle groups, enhancing awareness of physical sensations associated with tension and relaxation. By systematically relaxing specific muscles, overall muscle tension diminishes, contributing to a sense of overall calm and further reducing stress levels.

The steps of JPMR offer numerous benefits. Beginning with deep breathing, individuals enhance oxygen intake and activate the PNS, resulting in immediate relaxation. Sequential muscle contraction and relaxation engage individuals in mindfulness, diverting attention from stressors and aiding in the recognition and release of muscle tension. This process develops a profound sense of physical and mental relaxation, promoting overall well-being and stress reduction.

- **Psychological and Emotional Benefits:**
  a) **Mindfulness and Present Focus:** JPMR requires individuals to focus on the present moment and their bodily sensations. This mindfulness practice helps reduce rumination on past events or anxiety about the future, both of which are common in stress. Concentrating on the process of muscle relaxation provides a mental distraction from stress-inducing thoughts and worries.
  b) **Reduction of Anxiety and Stress:** Regular practice of JPMR has been shown to reduce symptoms of anxiety. The relaxation response counteracts the physical and mental effects of anxiety, promoting a sense of calm and control. By systematically reducing muscle tension and promoting relaxation, JPMR helps lower overall stress levels. This makes it easier for individuals to cope with daily stressors and improves their overall resilience to stress.

3. **Meditation:** Meditation is a practice that involves focusing the mind on a particular object, thought, or activity to achieve mental clarity, relaxation, and inner peace. It encompasses various techniques such as mindfulness, deep breathing, or guided visualization, aimed at cultivating awareness and reducing stress. Through regular practice, meditation promotes emotional balance, enhances concentration, and fosters overall well-being. Following are the different types of meditation techniques.
   a) **Mindfulness Meditation:** Mindfulness meditation involves focusing on the present moment with a non-judgmental attitude. It

encourages awareness of one's thoughts, emotions, and sensations as they occur. Practitioners sit comfortably, focus on their breath, and gently bring their attention back to their breathing whenever their mind wanders. This practice shifts the mind from automatic pilot mode to a state of conscious awareness. By focusing on the present, mindfulness reduces the tendency to ruminate on past events or worry about the future, which are common sources of stress. Mindfulness develops a non-reactive awareness of emotions, allowing individuals to respond to stressors more calmly. Regular practice improves concentration and cognitive function, helping individuals handle stressful situations more effectively.

b) **Mantra Meditation:** Mantra meditation involves the repetition of a sound, word, or phrase (mantra) to achieve a state of focused attention and deeper consciousness. Practitioners repeat a mantra, such as "Om," either aloud or silently. The repetition helps quiet the mind and focus attention. The rhythmic repetition of a mantra creates a calming effect, reducing the physiological markers of stress, such as heart rate and blood pressure. Chanting a mantra provides a mental anchor, distracting the mind from stress-inducing thoughts. For some, mantra meditation offers a spiritual dimension that provides comfort and a sense of peace.

c) **Transcendental Meditation:** Transcendental meditation involves the use of a specific mantra assigned to each practitioner, aiming to transcend ordinary thought processes and reach a state of pure consciousness. Practitioners silently repeat a specific mantra for about 15–20 minutes, typically twice a day. The technique is designed to be easy and natural, allowing the mind to settle into a state of restful alertness. Transcendental meditation induces a state of deep relaxation that helps reduce chronic stress. The practice helps individuals transcend surface-level thoughts and access a deeper state of awareness, promoting inner peace. Studies have shown that this form of meditation can lower cortisol levels, the body's primary stress hormone.

- **General Benefits of Meditation for Stress Reduction**
  a) **Activation of the Parasympathetic Nervous System:** Meditation activates the body's "rest and digest" response, counteracting the "fight or flight" response triggered by stress.

b) **Improved Sleep:** Regular meditation practice enhances sleep quality by promoting relaxation and reducing insomnia, a common consequence of chronic stress.

c) **Enhanced Emotional Resilience:** Meditation cultivates emotional resilience, making individuals more adept at handling stress and less likely to be overwhelmed by it.

d) **Reduced Physical Symptoms of Stress:** Meditation help to alleviate physical symptoms associated with stress, such as headaches, muscle tension, and gastrointestinal issues.

e) **Improved Overall Well-being:** By developing a sense of calm, clarity, and self-awareness, meditation contributes to improved mental and physical well-being, helping individuals lead more balanced and less stressful lives.

4. **Biofeedback:** Biofeedback is a powerful technique for stress reduction, using real-time data on physiological processes to help individuals gain conscious control over their body's stress responses. Biofeedback involves using electronic devices to monitor and display physiological activities such as heart rate, breathing, blood pressure, muscle tension, and brainwave patterns. This information is then presented to the individual, usually through visual or auditory signals, allowing them to become aware of their involuntary bodily processes.

- **Benefits of Biofeedback:**

a) **Increased Self-Awareness:** By making normally unconscious physiological processes perceptible, biofeedback helps individuals become more aware of their body's reactions to stress. People can identify specific physiological changes that occur when they are stressed, such as increased heart rate or muscle tension.

b) **Enhanced Self-Regulation:** With the help of biofeedback, individuals can learn to control their physiological responses through conscious effort. For example, they can learn to slow their heart rate or reduce muscle tension by practicing relaxation techniques. Techniques such as deep breathing, progressive muscle relaxation, or mindfulness can be applied more effectively when individuals can see their immediate impact on physiological measures.

c) **Reduction of Physical Symptoms:** Biofeedback can help individuals lower their blood pressure by teaching them how to relax their muscles and breathe more deeply. By learning to consciously relax muscles, individuals can reduce the physical tension often associated with stress, thereby alleviating related symptoms like headaches and back pain.

d) **Stress and Anxiety Management:** Regular practice with biofeedback can help reduce the secretion of cortisol, the body's primary stress hormone, thereby reducing overall stress levels. Enhanced control over physiological responses contributes to better emotional regulation, helping individuals respond to stressors more calmly and effectively.

e) **Behavioral Changes:** Seeing real-time improvements in physiological metrics can motivate individuals to continue practicing stress-reduction techniques, reinforcing positive behaviors. Over time, the conscious control over physiological responses can become more automatic, leading to lasting behavioral changes that support stress management.

B) Cognitive Aspect

1. **Cognitive Restructuring:** It is the key component of Cognitive Behavioral Therapy (CBT) developed by Aaron Beck, is a powerful technique for stress reduction. It involves identifying and changing irrational or maladaptive thought patterns that contribute to emotional distress and maladaptive behaviors. Cognitive restructuring is based on the idea that our thoughts, beliefs, and perceptions about events significantly influence our emotional and behavioral responses. By changing these cognitive patterns, we can alter our reactions to stressors, thereby reducing stress. The ABC (Antecedent, Belief, and Consequence) model illustrates how our beliefs about an event influence our emotional and behavioral outcomes.
   - **Antecedent (A):** The event or situation that triggers a response.
   - **Belief (B):** The interpretation or thought about the event.
   - **Consequence (C):** The emotional and behavioral response to the belief about the event.
   - **Steps in Cognitive Restructuring:**

     a) **Identify Irrational Thoughts:** Recognize and acknowledge negative or irrational thoughts triggered by stressful events.

     b) **Challenge Irrational Thoughts:** Evaluate the evidence for and against these thoughts, questioning their validity and accuracy.

c) **Develop Alternative Thoughts:** Generate more balanced, rational, and positive thoughts to replace irrational ones.

d) **Practice and Reinforce:** Continuously practice and reinforce the new, rational thoughts until they become more automatic and replace the old, irrational patterns.

- **Benefits of Cognitive Restructuring for Stress Reduction:**

a) **Enhanced Emotional Regulation:** By changing negative thought patterns, individuals can regulate their emotions more effectively. This reduces feelings of anxiety, sadness, and frustration associated with stress.

b) **Improved Coping Mechanisms:** Cognitive restructuring helps individuals develop healthier ways of interpreting and responding to stressful events, leading to more adaptive coping strategies.

c) **Reduction in Catastrophic Thinking:** It helps in diminishing catastrophic thinking (expecting the worst possible outcome), which often exacerbates stress. Replacing such thoughts with more realistic appraisals reduces overall stress levels.

d) **Positive Behavioral Changes:** As thoughts become more rational and positive, behaviors also change. This leads to proactive problem-solving, better decision-making, and constructive actions that mitigate stress.

e) **Improved Self-Esteem and Confidence:** Replacing self-defeating thoughts with positive affirmations boosts self-esteem and confidence, reducing the stress associated with feelings of inadequacy and incompetence.

2. **Positive Attitude:** Positive attitude refers to adopting an optimistic mindset where one believes that good things will happen and is confident in their ability to overcome challenges. It involves focusing on the positive aspects of situations, events, and people, rather than dwelling on the negative side. Characteristics of positive attitude include optimism, hope, divergent thinking, and resilience.

- **Benefits of Positive Attitude:**

a) **Confidence and Problem-Solving:** Positive attitude makes individuals more confident in their abilities and encourages proactive problem-solving approaches when faced with challenges. This proactive mindset helps in effectively managing stressors.

b) **Reduction of Stress:** Adopting a positive attitude reduces stress by reframing negative thoughts and emotions into more constructive and optimistic ones. This shift in mindset allows individuals to approach stressful situations with resilience and adaptability.

c) **Inner Strength:** Cultivating a positive attitude strengthens inner resilience and mental fortitude, enabling individuals to cope better with stressors and bounce back from setbacks.

d) **Cognitive Restructuring:** Positive attitude involves cognitive restructuring, where individuals deliberately engage in positive thinking and focus on the best possible outcomes in challenging situations. This practice helps in managing stress by shifting the focus from negative to positive aspects.

3. **Expressing Gratitude:** Expressing gratitude involves actively showing appreciation and thankfulness for the positive aspects of life, including the kindness of others, the beauty of nature, and the blessings we receive. It can take various forms, such as verbal expressions of thanks, writing gratitude letters, keeping a gratitude journal, or engaging in gratitude visits where one personally expresses gratitude to others.

- **Benefits of Expressing Gratitude for stress reduction:**

a) **Shifts Focus:** Expressing gratitude redirects attention from negative aspects of life to positive ones, fostering a more optimistic and appreciative outlook. This shift in focus reduces rumination on stressors and promotes feelings of contentment and satisfaction.

b) **Promotes Positive Emotions:** Gratitude elicits positive emotions such as happiness, joy, and appreciation, which counteract negative emotions associated with stress. The release of neurotransmitters like dopamine and serotonin enhances mood and overall well-being.

c) **Enhances Resilience:** Practicing gratitude enhances resilience by cultivating a mindset of abundance and positivity. It encourages individuals to find value and meaning in challenging situations, facilitating adaptive coping strategies and the ability to bounce back from setbacks.

d) **Widens Perspective:** Expressing gratitude broadens one's perspective by acknowledging the interconnectedness of life and recognizing the contributions of others. This expanded view helps in reframing difficulties as opportunities for growth and learning.

e) **Promotes Self-Awareness:** Expressing gratitude encourages self-awareness by prompting individuals to reflect on their own strengths, accomplishments, and the positive aspects of their identity. This self-affirmation fosters self-esteem and self-confidence, reducing stress related to self-doubt and insecurity.

4. **Coping Strategies:** Coping strategies are the conscious efforts individuals make to manage and reduce the negative effects of stressful situations. These strategies can be adaptive or maladaptive, problem-focused or emotion-focused, and acceptance-oriented. There are three types of coping strategies:

a) **Problem-Focused Coping:** It addresses the stressor directly by taking action to remove or mitigate its cause. Example- Seeking information or assistance to resolve the problem causing stress, such as seeking help from a supervisor or developing a plan of action. The benefit of using problem focused coping strategies is that it provides a sense of control and empowerment, reduces the impact of the stressor by addressing its root cause.

b) **Emotion-Focused Coping:** Focuses on managing the emotional response to the stressor rather than directly addressing the stressor itself. Example: Seeking social support, engaging in relaxation techniques, or distracting oneself from the stressor. This strategy helps to regulate emotional distress, promotes relaxation, and provides temporary relief from the stressor.

c) **Acceptance-Oriented Coping:** It involves accepting the stressful situation as it is, recognizing that some things are beyond one's control. Example: Coming to terms with a loss or setback and finding meaning or acceptance in the experience. The benefit of using this strategy is that it facilitates psychological adaptation, reduces feelings of helplessness, and promotes resilience in the face of adversity.

- **Benefits of Using Coping Strategies in Stress Reduction:**

a) **Enhanced Problem-Solving Skills:** Coping strategies, particularly problem-focused coping, help individuals develop effective problem-solving skills. By actively addressing stressors, individuals become more adept at finding solutions and managing challenges.

b) **Improved Emotional Regulation:** Coping strategies, such as emotion-focused coping and acceptance-oriented coping, help individuals regulate their emotions in response to stressors. This leads to greater emotional stability and resilience.

c) **Reduced Physiological Stress Responses:** Engaging in coping strategies can help reduce physiological stress responses, such as elevated heart rate, blood pressure, and cortisol levels. This contributes to overall physical health and well-being.

d) **Increased Sense of Control:** Coping strategies provide individuals with a sense of control over their circumstances, even in the face of adversity. This empowerment promotes feelings of self-efficacy and confidence in one's ability to cope with stress.

e) **Improved Quality of Life:** Ultimately, coping strategies contribute to a higher quality of life by reducing the negative impact of stress on physical, emotional, and psychological well-being. They help individuals adapt to adversity and thrive in the face of challenges.

C) Affective Aspect

1. **Emotional Intelligence:** Emotional Intelligence (EI) refers to the ability to recognize, understand, and manage one's own emotions as well as the emotions of others. It involves being aware of how emotions influence thoughts and behaviors, and using this awareness to navigate social interactions, make decisions, and manage stress effectively. Daniel Goleman, who popularized the concept of EI, identified five components of emotional intelligence:

   a) **Self-awareness:** Ability to recognize and understand one's own emotions, including strengths, weaknesses, values, and motives. Self-aware individuals are attuned to their emotional reactions and can accurately assess their impact on themselves and others.

   b) **Empathy:** Capacity to understand and share the feelings, perspectives, and experiences of others. Empathetic individuals are sensitive to the emotions of others and can respond with compassion and understanding.

   c) **Self-regulation:** Ability to manage and regulate one's own emotions, impulses, and behaviors in various situations. Self-regulated individuals can control emotional reactions, adapt to changing circumstances, and maintain composure under pressure.

d) **Motivation:** Drive to pursue goals with energy, persistence, and enthusiasm, even in the face of challenges and setbacks. Motivated individuals are intrinsically driven to achieve personal and professional objectives, and they can channel their emotions in constructive ways to stay focused and resilient.

e) **Social skills:** Ability to effectively navigate social interactions, build and maintain relationships, communicate clearly, resolve conflicts, and collaborate with others. Individuals with strong social skills can establish rapport, influence others positively, and work cooperatively toward shared goals.

- **Benefits of Emotional Intelligence in Stress Reduction:**
    a) **Enhanced Self-awareness:** Recognizing and understanding one's own emotions helps individuals identify stress triggers, early warning signs of stress, and maladaptive coping patterns. This self-awareness enables proactive stress management and fosters emotional resilience.

    b) **Improved Coping Strategies:** Emotional intelligence equips individuals with a repertoire of adaptive coping strategies for managing stress effectively. By regulating emotions, problem-solving, and seeking support when needed, individuals can face stressful situations with greater ease.

    c) **Better Interpersonal Relationships:** Empathy and social skills enable individuals to connect with others on an emotional level, fostering supportive relationships and a sense of belonging. Strong social support networks serve as buffers against stress and provide avenues for seeking help and guidance.

    d) **Reduced Conflict and Misunderstandings:** Effective communication, conflict resolution, and negotiation skills minimize interpersonal conflicts and misunderstandings that can contribute to stress. Emotionally intelligent individuals can navigate disagreements constructively and maintain positive relationships.

    e) **Enhanced Decision-making:** Self-regulation and sound judgment enable individuals to make rational decisions under pressure, without being overwhelmed by emotions. Emotional intelligence facilitates thoughtful consideration of options, weighing consequences, and choosing the most appropriate course of action.

f) **Overall Well-being:** Emotional intelligence promotes psychological well-being by developing emotional balance, self-confidence, and a sense of purpose. Individuals with high emotional intelligence experience less anxiety, depression, and burnout, leading to a higher quality of life.

2. **Positive Visualization:** Positive visualization is a mental technique that involves using imagination to vividly visualize a desired future outcome or goal. It is a form of mental rehearsal where individuals create detailed mental images of achieving their goals, experiencing success, or overcoming challenges. Positive visualization can take two main forms:

   a) **Outcome Visualization:** It involves focusing on the desired end result or goal. Individuals imagine themselves achieving the outcome they desire, visualizing the end goal as if it has already been accomplished. Example: Visualizing oneself receiving a promotion, winning a competition, or completing a project successfully.

   b) **Process Visualization:** It focuses on the steps and actions required to reach the desired outcome. Individuals visualize themselves engaging in the process of achieving their goals, paying attention to the specific actions and behaviors involved. Example: Visualizing oneself studying diligently, practicing skills, or networking to advance career goals.

   - **Benefits of Positive Visualization for Stress Reduction:**

     a) **Stress Reduction:** Positive visualization promotes relaxation and reduces stress by shifting focus away from negative thoughts and worries. Imagining successful outcomes creates a sense of optimism and confidence, alleviating stress and anxiety.

     b) **Increased Resilience:** Engaging in positive visualization builds resilience by fostering a positive mindset and outlook. Visualizing oneself overcoming challenges and achieving goals reinforces belief in one's ability to overcome adversity, enhancing resilience in the face of stressors.

     c) **Enhanced Self-Confidence:** Visualization of success and achievement boosts self-confidence and self-efficacy. Imagining oneself accomplishing goals and overcoming obstacles instills a sense of belief in one's capabilities, reducing self-doubt and insecurity.

d) **Improved Focus and Concentration:** Visualization exercises require mental focus and concentration, which can enhance cognitive functioning and attention control. Visualizing specific tasks or actions helps individuals to maintain focus and clarity, reducing distractions and improving productivity.

e) **Motivation and Goal Attainment:** Positive visualization serves as a powerful motivator by providing a clear mental image of desired outcomes and goals. Visualizing success creates a sense of purpose and determination, increasing motivation to take action and work toward achieving goals.

f) **Optimism and Positive Outlook:** Engaging in positive visualization cultivates an optimistic outlook on life by highlighting possibilities and opportunities for growth and success. Visualizing positive outcomes fosters a hopeful attitude, reducing pessimism and negative thinking patterns.

g) **Mind-Body Connection:** Visualization techniques utilize the mind-body connection by activating neural pathways associated with positive emotions and relaxation responses. Imagining success and achievement triggers physiological changes that promote well-being and reduce stress.

D) Behavioral Aspect

1. **Engaging in Leisure Activities:** Engaging in leisure activities involves voluntarily participating in enjoyable and relaxing pursuits during one's free time. These activities are varied and can include hobbies, sports, and socializing, spending time in nature, artistic pursuits, gaming, and more. Research highlights leisure as a valuable coping resource with numerous benefits for both physical and mental health. Here are some examples of engaging in leisure activities and the benefits of using this technique for stress reduction: Examples of Leisure Activities are:

   a) **Hobbies:** Engaging in hobbies such as painting, gardening, crafting, cooking, or playing a musical instrument allows individuals to express creativity, relax, and focus on enjoyable activities.

   b) **Physical Activities:** Participating in sports, exercise, yoga, or outdoor activities like hiking, biking, or swimming promotes physical well-being, releases endorphins and reduces tension and stress.

c) **Socializing:** Spending time with friends, family, or participating in group activities and events fosters social connections, provides emotional support, and reduces feelings of loneliness and isolation.

d) **Nature Exploration:** Being in nature, whether it's hiking in the mountains, strolling in a park, or spending time at the beach, promotes relaxation, reduces stress hormones, and restores mental clarity and calmness.

e) **Mindfulness and Relaxation:** Engaging in mindfulness practices, meditation, deep breathing exercises, or relaxation techniques promotes relaxation, reduces muscle tension, and calms the mind.

- **Benefits of Using Leisure Activities for Stress Reduction:**

  a) **Stress Reduction:** Leisure activities provide a natural outlet for stress reduction by promoting relaxation, enjoyment, and positive emotions. Engaging in pleasurable activities distracts from stressors and helps individuals unwind and recharge.

  b) **Physical Health Benefits:** Many leisure activities, such as exercise and outdoor pursuits, offer physical health benefits, including improved cardiovascular health, reduced risk of chronic diseases, and enhanced overall well-being.

  c) **Mental Health Benefits:** Participating in leisure activities contributes to mental well-being by reducing symptoms of anxiety, depression, and burnout. Enjoyable activities boost mood, increase feelings of happiness, and provide a sense of accomplishment.

  d) **Enhanced Coping Skills:** Engaging in leisure activities builds coping skills by providing opportunities for problem-solving, creative expression, and social interaction. It helps individuals develop resilience and adaptive coping strategies to manage stressors more effectively.

  e) **Improved Relationships:** Social leisure activities strengthen social bonds and relationships, fostering a sense of belonging and support. Spending quality time with loved ones enhances emotional connections and provides a buffer against stress.

  f) **Work-Life Balance:** Incorporating leisure activities into daily life promotes work-life balance by providing opportunities for relaxation and personal fulfillment outside of work responsibilities. It helps prevent burnout and enhances overall life satisfaction.

2. **Connecting with People:** Connecting with people involves engaging in meaningful social interactions and building supportive relationships with family, friends, neighbors, and the community. It encompasses both physical presence and perceived social connection, where individuals feel emotionally supported and connected even when physically apart. The benefits of connecting with people for stress reduction:

- **Benefits of Connecting with People for Stress Reduction:**

  a) **Emotional Support:** Social connections provide emotional support, empathy, and understanding, which help individuals cope with stress and adversity. Having someone to confide in and share concerns with reduces feelings of loneliness and isolation.

  b) **Catharsis and Emotional Release:** Engaging in open and honest conversations with others allows individuals to express their feelings and emotions, leading to catharsis and emotional release. Sharing burdens with trusted individuals help to alleviate stress and tension.

  c) **Sense of Belonging:** Connecting with others develops a sense of belonging and inclusion, which is essential for psychological well-being. Feeling part of a supportive social network reinforces one's identity and purpose, reducing feelings of alienation and disconnection.

  d) **Increased Confidence and Trust:** Building strong social connections boosts self-esteem, confidence, and trust in oneself and others. Knowing that there are people who care and support you enhances resilience and reduces the impact of stressors.

  e) **Positive Distraction and Enjoyment:** Spending time with others in enjoyable activities and social gatherings provides a welcome distraction from stressors. Laughing, sharing stories, and engaging in shared interests promote relaxation and enjoyment, reducing stress levels.

  f) **Physical Health Benefits:** Strong social connections are associated with improved physical health outcomes, including lower blood pressure, reduced risk of chronic diseases, and enhanced immune function. Positive social interactions contribute to overall well-being and resilience.

  g) **Problem-Solving and Perspective:** Connecting with others allows for collaborative problem-solving and gaining different perspectives on challenges. Sharing experiences and seeking advice from trusted individuals' helps individuals gain insight, find solutions, and manage stress more effectively.

Summary

Stress is an inevitable aspect of life, manifesting in various forms and situations. While it often prompts instinctive reactions of avoidance or resistance, adopting a mindset of acceptance can offer a more constructive approach. By acknowledging and accepting our feelings of stress, we can relieve the additional strain caused by resistance or denial, allowing us to redirect our focus toward our goals and priorities. Positive psychology techniques are instrumental in managing and reducing stress levels, transforming how we interact with our stressors. These techniques encourage individuals to use the power of positive thinking and behaviors, thereby enhancing resilience and resourcefulness. Physical activities, such as regular exercise and mindfulness practices, help reduce bodily tension and promote a state of relaxation, mitigating the physiological impacts of stress. Cognitive strategies like positive reframing and gratitude journaling shift our focus from negative ruminations to more optimistic and hopeful perspectives, helping us to view stress as a challenge rather than a threat.

Behavioral approaches, such as setting realistic goals and establishing structured routines, provide a sense of control and accomplishment. This proactive stance empowers individuals to confront stressors directly, rather than resorting to unhealthy coping mechanisms or avoidance behaviors. Affective techniques, including the cultivation of positive emotions and nurturing social connections, further enhance emotional resilience and stability. These strategies develop a supportive network and a compassionate self-view, both crucial for long-term stress management.

By integrating positive psychology techniques into our daily lives, we can reframe our relationship with stress. This shift not only helps in immediate stress reduction but also turns stress into a catalyst for personal growth. It encourages us to learn from challenges, develops resilience, and strives for continuous improvement. Consequently, facing life's inevitable pressures with these tools leads to enhanced well-being and a more fulfilling existence. Applying positive psychology techniques offers a pathway to managing stress effectively, promoting a holistic approach to mental health and personal development.

Post-traumatic Growth

The concept of post-traumatic growth (PTG) is deeply rooted in human history and literature, suggesting that adversity can lead to positive outcomes. This idea has been explored by numerous philosophers and psychologists. Viktor Frankl, in his pioneering work "Man's Search for Meaning" (2006), introduced the notion of "tragic optimism," which suggests that individuals can transform suffering into personal achievement and growth. Frankl emphasized that facing unavoidable suffering offers an opportunity to rise above oneself and achieve a greater sense of meaning and purpose. Similarly, Abraham Maslow (1970) suggested that adversities could act as antecedents to self-actualization, further highlighting the potential for personal growth following traumatic experiences.

Despite these philosophical bases, systematic empirical investigation of PTG began much later. In the 1980s and 1990s, researchers started to focus on positive changes following traumatic events. Initial studies reported positive transformations in various populations, such as rape survivors, bereaved individuals, and combat veterans (e.g., Affleck et al., 1987; Hooks, 1989). The term "post-traumatic growth" was officially coined by Tedeschi and Calhoun (1995) to describe the positive psychological changes observed in individuals coping with highly stressful events. Their pioneering work laid the foundation for a new research paradigm, shifting the focus from negative outcomes, such as PTSD, to the potential for positive transformation following trauma. This phenomenon includes several dimensions of growth. Their research highlights five key areas:

- Recognizing and embracing new opportunities
- Developing stronger relationships
- Cultivating inner strength
- Gaining a deeper appreciation for life
- Evolving in terms of religious and spiritual beliefs

Trauma, an almost inevitable aspect of life, typically occurs outside our control. However, the process of PTG illustrates how even the harshest and most traumatic events can lead to personal growth and a reevaluation of what is vital and meaningful in life (Schubert et al., 2015). PTG is characterized by changes that help individuals develop beyond their previous levels of functioning, enabling them to make sense of their world and their lives in new ways.

The concept of PTG corresponds closely with the principles of positive psychology, which suggest that the interplay of positive and negative life experiences is essential for human flourishing. According to this perspective, trauma is seen as a crucial aspect of growth, emphasizing the importance of learning from adversity rather than avoiding it. As Professor Stephen Joseph notes, living a life devoid of sadness and misfortune is naïve; instead, individuals must learn to live with and learn from adversity (Joseph, 2013).

PTG involves the tendency for individuals to change after experiencing stressful or traumatic events, developing beyond their previous level of psychological functioning. Joseph (2013) describes PTG as a process of change, suggesting that it should not only be viewed as an outcome but also as an ongoing journey. This process is closely tied to self-determination theory, which emphasizes the importance of making sense to increase our fitness for survival in the world (Ryan & Deci, 2018). In simple terms, PTG includes "experiences of positive change that may occur as the result of the struggle with traumatic events and major life crises" (Munroe & Ferrari, 2022). It typically occurs under conditions of severe stress, is accompanied by transformative life changes, and requires individuals to challenge and reconstruct their basic assumptions about life, moving beyond previously held views on flourishing.

While post-traumatic stress disorder (PTSD) is a complex reaction to trauma involving multiple factors and significant difficulty in coping and rebuilding one's life (Joseph, 2013), PTG offers a hopeful perspective. Even individuals suffering from PTSD can experience post-traumatic growth, illustrating the potential for positive change and development following trauma (Kiyimba et al., 2022).

Difference between Post-traumatic Growth and Resilience

Post-traumatic Growth	**Resilience**
Occurs only after exposure to trauma	Can be present before trauma, also available as part of individual's personality.
An outcome of highly stressful situation.	May not occur after exposure to trauma. But if a person shows PTG, he/she develops resilience in the person.
PTG always involve resilience	Resilience may or may not lead to PTG
Involves transformation in the personality- changes in ones's thinking, attitude and behavior	May not involve any change unless the person is required to show resilient behavior

Models of Post-traumatic Growth

1. **Therapeutic Spiral Model:** The Therapeutic Spiral Model (TSM) is a three-stage process designed to treat trauma through experiential trauma therapy, focusing on stabilizing the self, working through past traumas, and integrating post-traumatic growth (Hudgins, 2019).
   - I. **Stage 1:** In the first stage, the emphasis is on identifying roles essential for facing the impact of trauma with spontaneity, creativity, and a fully activated autonomous healing center (Hudgins & Durost, 2022). These roles include self-observation and strengths. During this stage, clients learn to utilize their strengths, develop engagement, and employ psychological functions such as observation, restraint, and rehabilitation to promote healthy self-organization (Hudgins & Durost, 2022).
   - II. **Stage 2:** The second stage involves demonstrating and working through dissociated feelings, survival defenses, and repetitive memories until it is safe for these feelings to be consciously expressed in the present (Hudgins & Durost, 2022). The primary focus here is to address the aftereffects of past trauma and their ongoing impact.
   - III. **Stage 3:** In the third stage, transformation is emphasized, where the autonomous healing center activates the body for self-healing when the conditions are right (Hudgins & Durost, 2022). This stage engages with the client's moments of insight, helping them understand how to use these insights in the future, ultimately realizing their potential. In this final phase that most of the growth occurs. The entire self-organization changes when new experiences lead to positive changes in the body, mind, heart, spirit, and relationships with oneself, others, and the world (Hudgins & Durost, 2022).
2. **Tripartite Model:** The tripartite model proposed by Judith Herman (1992) offers a structured and phased approach for therapists working with clients to revisit traumatic memories (Kiyimba et al., 2022).
   - I. **Safety and Stabilization:** This initial phase focuses on symptom management, emphasizing the importance of educating clients about how trauma impacts the brain and body. Therapists teach strategies for regulating emotional reactions, aiming to normalize symptoms, enhance daily functioning, and reduce the risk of re-traumatization (Kiyimba et al., 2022).
   - II. **Remembering and Mourning:** In the second phase, clients engage with their trauma memories or narratives for safe processing. This

process involves supporting clients as they gain increased awareness and control over their traumatic recollections, gradually shifting these distressing experiences into the past tense (Kiyimba et al., 2022).

III. **Reconnection:** The final phase focuses on helping clients to reconnect with their social networks and reintegrate into society. This phase aims to reduce symptoms and enhance personal and relational well-being by integrating the knowledge, skills, and awareness gained throughout therapy (Kiyimba et al., 2022).

This phased approach is particularly beneficial for individuals who have experienced prolonged or repeated trauma, as it provides the necessary psychological stabilizing resources before advancing through the therapeutic process (Kiyimba et al., 2022).

3. **Functional Descriptive Model:** According to the Functional-Descriptive Model developed by Tedeschi and Calhoun (1995, 2004), traumatic life events can often lead to positive outcomes, a process known as post-traumatic growth.

   I. **Initial Trauma and Emotional Distress:** The process begins with the experience of a traumatic event that is sufficiently distressing to challenge and destroy the individual's core beliefs and goals, resulting in extreme emotional distress. These core beliefs, or assumptive beliefs include general notions about the world, such as its predictability, controllability, and benevolence, guiding people's behavior and interpretation of life events (Tedeschi & Calhoun, 1995).

   II. **Shattering of Assumptive Beliefs:** Traumatic events challenge the validity of these core beliefs, causing survivors to question their understanding of the world and their place within it. This disruption leads individuals to engage in automatic and unintentional ruminations about the trauma in an attempt to come to terms with it and alleviate emotional distress.

   III. **Coping and Reconstruction:** The cognitive processes activated by trauma are typically unwanted, prompting individuals to adopt various coping strategies, such as self-disclosure and seeking support from others. These strategies help to manage emotional distress and aid in reconstructing damaged assumptive beliefs and goals (schemas).

   IV. **Transition to Intentional Reflection:** As some emotional distress are reduced, intentional reflections about how the event has changed the individual takes place. If these reflections are constructive and focused on finding meaning and benefits, positive growth is said to have occurred (Tedeschi & Calhoun, 1995).

V. **Seismic Metaphor and Rebuilding:** Tedeschi and Calhoun use the metaphor of a "seismic" event to describe how traumatic experiences shatter prior goals, beliefs, and pre-trauma schemas. The intentional rumination phase allows individuals to thoughtfully consider how they want to rebuild their lives, incorporating the realities of their circumstances and their survival of the traumatic event.

VI. **Development of Adaptive Beliefs and Resilience:** Through this process, individuals may develop adaptive beliefs that enhance resilience, enabling them to handle future challenges more effectively. By integrating positive changes into their life narratives, individuals recognize meaningful growth and improvement in their lives.

VII. **Recognition of Positive Change:** Although some trauma survivors may wish to forget the traumatic event, many acknowledge that these experiences have led to positive changes in their lives.

This model highlights the potential for significant personal growth following traumatic events, emphasizing the transformative power of constructive rumination and adaptive coping strategies.

4. **Organismic Valuing Process:** Joseph's (2004) Person-Centered Theory proposed that post-traumatic growth occurs following highly stressful life events because individuals have an inherent tendency to comprehend and integrate their experiences meaningfully while striving toward optimal well-being. However, this theory was considered too narrow in scope. Therefore, Joseph and Linley (2005) reviewed the Person-Centered Theory to develop a more comprehensive framework known as the Organismic Valuing Process (OVP) Theory.

The theory asserts that people are intrinsically motivated to move toward growth following traumatic experiences. Within the organismic valuing process, three possible cognitive outcomes to the psychological resolution of trauma-related difficulties are suggested (Hollon & Garber, 1988):

I. **Assimilation:** Trauma experiences are assimilated, leading to a return to the pre-trauma baseline. However, this leaves the individual vulnerable to future re-traumatization. For instance, if a person assimilates the trauma with the belief that "bad things happen," they recover but do not grow psychologically, remaining susceptible to future stressors.

II. **Negative Accommodation:** Trauma experiences are accommodated in a negative direction, leading to psychopathology and distress. This outcome is illustrated by the development of a philosophy that "bad things will always happen and nobody can prevent them," resulting in greater feelings of hopelessness and a higher likelihood of post-traumatic stress or depression (Janoff-Bulman, 1989).

III. **Positive Accommodation:** Trauma experiences are accommodated in a positive direction, leading to growth. In this scenario, the individual modifies their prior worldviews positively, such as beliefing that "bad things happen and life is unpredictable, so it should be lived to the fullest." This positive accommodation fosters psychological growth following trauma.

These cognitive outcomes highlight that the alleviation of distress alone does not guarantee growth. While alleviation of distress may facilitate growth, it is through positive accommodation that individuals experience significant psychological development. In contrast, assimilation may increase vulnerability to future re-traumatization (Joseph & Linley, 2005).

The Dimensions of Post-traumatic Growth

After trauma, individuals often develop greater strength, reasoning, and capability to handle future challenges, although these positive changes are often unnoticed or not linked to the traumatic events. Researchers and clinicians, such as Tedeschi and Calhoun (1996, 2004), suggest that post-traumatic growth can occur in five dimensions. The dimensions are as follows:

- **Personal Strength:** After experiencing trauma, individuals often feel an increased sense of personal strength, confidence, self-awareness, openness, empathy, creativity, maturity, humility, and ability to handle future challenges (Tedeschi & Calhoun, 1995). Survivors may develop a more positive self-view with a greater sense of resilience and strength. Research indicates that trauma leads to a greater appreciation of life and a better understanding that some life events cannot be predicted or controlled (Tedeschi & Calhoun, 2004).
- **Changed Priorities:** Lindstrom, Cann, Calhoun, and Tedeschi (2013) suggest that traumatic events lead to cognitive reconstruction, increasing life appreciation and shifting priorities. This change can result in healthier lifestyles, more selective friendships, and new life goals. In life-threatening situations, survivors might see their survival as a "second chance," leading

to learning new skills or changing occupations (Sank, 1979). According to Joseph and Linley (2006), trauma can inspire a renewed appreciation for life's simple pleasures previously overlooked.

- **Improved Relationship:** As a result of trauma, individuals often become more emotionally connected within their social networks, experiencing greater intimacy with family, friends, neighbors, and even strangers (Tedeschi & Calhoun, 1996, 2004). Survivors seek to understand the event and cope with distress by turning to their relations and friends for support. This process tends to result in stronger, warmer, and more intimate interpersonal relationships (Sawyer, Ayers, & Field, 2010) and a renewed sense of compassion for others facing extreme stress (Tedeschi & Calhoun, 1996, 2004). Survivors often report increased relationships and greater altruism toward others after a traumatic experience.
- **Change in Philosophy:** Tedeschi and Calhoun (1996, 2004) suggest that trauma exposure often leads individuals to engage cognitively with fundamental existential questions about death and life's purpose, developing a deeper understanding of meaning and purpose. This cognitive engagement involves questioning pre-trauma beliefs and developing a greater appreciation for existential or spiritual issues, resulting in feelings of vulnerability and mortality. For instance, trauma survivors frequently ponder questions like "Why do such events happen?" and "What is the essence of life and existence?", which promote a deeper awareness and a more meaningful life philosophy (Joseph & Linley, 2006; Tedeschi & Calhoun, 2004).
- **Spiritual Development:** Exposure to traumatic events and extreme adversities can lead to improvements in religious beliefs and a sense of growth in spiritual life, potentially strengthening the individual's coping mechanisms as they discover new avenues for life (Lindstrom et al., 2013; Calhoun & Tedeschi, 2001). Research indicates that individuals often turn to religion to explain their traumatic experiences and answer the questions when concrete reasons are absent (Tedeschi & Calhoun, 2004). Consequently, trauma survivors may experience enhanced religious or spiritual beliefs, including increased frequency of prayers, gratitude to God, strengthened faith, and a new life philosophy. These changes can lead to the emergence of new potentials and opportunities that did not exist before the traumatic event (Tedeschi & Calhoun, 1996, 2004; Pargament, Desai & McConnell, 2006).

Summary

Post-traumatic growth (PTG) represents a transformative framework within positive psychology, emphasizing the potential for psychological and emotional development following traumatic events. Unlike traditional perspectives that often focus on the negative aftermath of trauma, diagnosing conditions such as PTSD, PTG offers an alternative view that acknowledges the possibility of growth beyond pre-trauma functioning. Positive psychology techniques play a crucial role in facilitating this growth, providing a pathway for individuals to develop a deeper sense of self, revised belief systems, and improved coping mechanisms.

Physical techniques, such as regular exercise and mindfulness practices are fundamental in reducing bodily tension and fostering relaxation. These activities not only help mitigate the physiological impacts of stress but also create a foundation for emotional and cognitive recovery. Cognitive strategies like positive reframing and gratitude journaling shift individuals' perspectives from negative ruminations to more optimistic and hopeful outlooks. By encouraging a focus on positive aspects and potential growth opportunities, these techniques help individuals reframe their trauma experiences in a more constructive light.

Behavioral approaches are also integral to PTG. Structured routines, goal setting, and engaging in meaningful activities provides individuals with a sense of control and accomplishment. These methods promote proactive coping and a forward-looking mindset, essential for navigating the aftermath of trauma. Affective techniques, such as cultivating positive emotions through social connections and practicing self-compassion, further enhance emotional resilience and stability. These strategies help individuals build supportive networks and foster a compassionate self-view, crucial for long-term recovery and growth.

Despite challenges in measurement and definition, PTG offers valuable insights for clinicians aiming to assist clients in utilizing trauma-induced wisdom. By integrating positive psychology techniques into therapeutic practices, therapists can develop resilience and facilitate growth, helping individuals to lead more meaningful and fulfilling lives post-trauma. Embracing PTG not only enriches clinical practice but also inspires further research, promoting a more holistic understanding of trauma and recovery.

CHAPTER 3

APPLICATION OF POSITIVE PSYCHOLOGY IN WORK

In today's rapidly evolving business landscape, effective management goes beyond traditional paradigms. The ultimate goal for any organization is not just profitability but also sustainable growth and excellence. This necessitates the adoption of new principles where positivity and sustainability are core values. Leaders and managers across all levels and types of organizations must adopt a balanced approach to human behavior, focusing not only on addressing weaknesses and challenges but also on nurturing strengths and human capacities. This realization has given rise to a blooming field known as Positive Psychology in the Workplace (PPW). PPW surrounds the application of knowledge, concepts, and principles of positive psychology within organizational settings. Despite its significance, PPW did not receive the recognition it deserved until recent years. However, prominent publications such as 'The Wall Street Journal' have shed light on the increasing attention given to positivity in the workplace. Central to PPW is the study of psychological states such as self-efficacy, optimism, hope, resilience, and flow, among others, which influence how individuals cope with organizational demands, consequently impacting organizational performance. Moreover, PPW examines positive emotions and seeks to identify factors that contribute to the meaningfulness of work. It also emphasizes the importance of positive leadership, which helps develop human capabilities and emotions supportive of a flourishing work environment. At its core, PPW is concerned with enhancing organizational outcomes such as employee engagement. According to Ulrich (1997), engaging employees not only involves their physical presence but also capturing their minds and souls. Employees must feel valued and respected for their contributions, which in turn motivates them, increases their commitment to work, and ultimately leads to greater job satisfaction. This holistic approach to employee well-being includes physical, personal, psychological, economic, social, and organizational aspects. It is called by the term 'gainful employment' (Snyder, Lopez, & Pedrotti, 2011).

The application of PPW goes beyond theories. It shows up in real way through practical strategies. These strategies include various facets, including developing a positive work culture, providing opportunities for personal and professional growth, recognizing and celebrating achievements, promoting work-life balance, and cultivating authentic relationships among employees. One of the key aspects of PPW is the cultivation of a strengths-based approach to employee development. Rather than solely focusing on remedying weaknesses, organizations utilize employees' inherent strengths to maximize their potential and performance. This involves implementing practices such as strengths assessments, coaching, and mentoring programs tailored to individual strengths and aspirations. Furthermore, positive leadership plays an important role in driving organizational success through inspiring and empowering employees. Positive leaders exhibit traits such as empathy, optimism, resilience, and authenticity, creating a favorable environment where employees feel valued, motivated, and empowered to contribute their best efforts

Benefits of being Happy at Work

1. **Enhanced Productivity:** One of the primary benefits of being happy at work is enhanced productivity. Happy employees tend to have higher energy levels and greater focus, enabling them to complete tasks more efficiently. This increased productivity stems from their positive mindset, which fuels motivation and a desire to excel. When employees are content, they are more likely to go the extra mile, contributing significantly to the organization's overall performance. This boost in productivity not only benefits the individual but also leads to improved organizational outcomes and success.
2. **Increased Creativity and Innovation:** Happiness in the workplace develops an environment where creativity and innovation can flourish. Content employees are more inclined to think outside the box, propose novel solutions, and pursue their tasks with passion and vigor. This creative energy contributes to a culture of continuous improvement, allowing the organization to adapt to changing market demands and stay competitive. By promoting happiness, companies can harness the innovative potential of their workforce, driving growth and advancement.
3. **Stronger Engagement and Involvement:** Happy employees are deeply engaged in their roles, feeling a strong sense of purpose and connection to their work. This engagement is a result of their positive

outlook and satisfaction, which drive them to be more involved and committed. Engaged employees are more likely to invest time and effort into their tasks, seek opportunities for development, and contribute positively to the organization's mission. This heightened involvement ensures that employees are not just present but are actively participating in and contributing to the organization's success.

4. **Improved Collaboration and Teamwork:** A positive work environment, strengthened by happy employees, enhances collaboration and teamwork. Content workers are more likely to cooperate with their colleagues, developing a spirit of mutual support and collective problem-solving. This collaborative environment improves communication, synergy, and the ability to tackle challenges together, leading to better organizational effectiveness. When employees are happy, they are more willing to share ideas, offer assistance, and work toward common goals, strengthening the overall team dynamic.
5. **Positive Work Environment and Culture:** Happiness at work contributes significantly to creating a positive work environment and culture. Happy employees have a positive attitude, which can uplift the morale of their peers and cultivate a supportive and optimistic atmosphere. This chain reaction of positivity enhances the overall work environment, making it more enjoyable and conducive to productivity. A positive workplace culture not only improves employee satisfaction but also attracts and retains talent, ensuring long-term organizational success.
6. **Enhanced Physical and Mental Well-being:** The link between happiness at work and improved physical and mental well-being is well-established. Fulfilled employees experience lower levels of stress, burnout, and mental health issues. This improved well-being results in lower absenteeism and higher employee retention rates, creating a healthier and more resilient workforce. By prioritizing employee happiness, organizations can reduce healthcare costs, decrease turnover, and maintain a more stable and productive workforce.
7. **Sense of Purpose and Achievement:** Happy employees derive a strong sense of purpose and fulfillment from their work. This sense of purpose is critical for motivation and job satisfaction. When employees feel that their work is meaningful and aligned with their values, they are more likely to be motivated, engaged, and committed. Additionally, achieving goals and performing well contributes to a sense of accomplishment, further reinforcing their happiness and job satisfaction.

8. **Respect and Appreciation for Diversity:** A happy and positive workplace respects and appreciates diversity, recognizing the value that different perspectives and backgrounds bring to the organization. This respect fosters an inclusive environment where all employees feel valued and supported. When employees are happy, they are more likely to embrace and celebrate diversity, contributing to a richer and more dynamic workplace culture.
9. **Companionship and Loyalty:** Happiness at work strengthens companionship and loyalty among employees. When individuals are content, they are more likely to form strong bonds with their coworkers and develop a sense of loyalty to the company. This companionship enhances teamwork and creates a supportive network within the organization. Loyal employees are more committed to the organization's goals and are more likely to stay with the company, reducing turnover and maintaining organizational stability.

By considering these points, it is clear that happiness at work offers multifaceted benefits that not only improve individual well-being but also drive organizational success and growth. Prioritizing employee happiness is, therefore a strategic advantage for any organization aiming for sustained prosperity. As indicated by Snyder et al. (2011), gainful employment is characterized by nine features which can also be described as the benefits gaining from it.

Figure 1: Aspects of Gainful Employment

The Scientific Field of Positive Work and Organizations

Before investigating the application of Positive Psychology in the Workplace, it's essential to examine the existing research studies. The study of positive psychology in work settings has evolved into a comprehensive field known as Positive Work and Organizations (PWO). This domain includes the integration of three key research streams within positive psychology in the workplace:

a) **Positive Organizational Psychology (POP):** Positive organizational psychology is a dynamic field that explores how to create and increase positivity at work. Its core mission revolves around investigating and enriching the variety of positive experiences and outcomes that can be observed within workplaces. This includes a deep exploration of the profound impacts of positive emotions, individual strengths, resilience, and the pursuit of meaningful work on the overall well-being and performance of employees. Central to its approach is the recognition that by emphasizing the positive facets of work and organizational life, has the power to cultivate environments where individuals not only thrive but also contribute optimally to organizational success. Through rigorous research and practical interventions, positive organizational psychology seeks to facilitate the development of flourishing individuals and the cultivation of flourishing and succeeding organizations. It aims to create a symbiotic relationship where the well-being and fulfillment of employees are intricately linked with organizational effectiveness and vitality.

b) **Positive Organizational Behavior (POB):** Positive organizational behavior is a complex field that looks at how people act and think at work, focusing on things that lead to good results. Basically, it's about using the strengths of both individuals and organizations to make workplaces better for everyone's performance and happiness. Positive organizational behavior is about recognizing and supporting employees' strengths. It means focusing on what people are good at instead of what they lack. This approach is more about being proactive, making sure employees feel engaged, have good relationships at work, and are happy with their jobs. By making positive experiences at work a priority and using employees' strengths, positive organizational behavior helps create workplaces where people feel empowered, work together, and support each other. This kind of environment inspires people to do their best and contribute to the organization's goals.

c) **Positive Organizational Scholarship (POS):** Positive organizational scholarship represents a comprehensive approach to both research and application, drawing from the foundational principles of positive psychology and adapting them to the unique dynamics of organizational environments. It serves as a medium for exploring the transformative effects of applying positive practices within workplaces, ranging from the cultivation of gratitude and kindness to the integration of mindfulness techniques. At its core, positive organizational scholarship seeks to unravel the intricate mechanisms through which these positive practices influence not only the well-being of individual employees but also the broader organizational landscape. Through rigorous inquiry and practical interventions, it aspires to instill a sense of purpose, connectivity, and resilience within organizational ecosystems, thereby developing environments where both individuals and the collective entity can reach their full potential. In essence, positive organizational scholarship embodies a vision of organizational excellence grounded in the pursuit of positivity, well-being, and sustainable success.

Characteristics of Positive Work Environment

Establishing a favorable workplace for positive experiences lays the cornerstone for organizational flourishing. By prioritizing employee well-being and satisfaction, organizations build a culture of engagement, productivity, and innovation. This foundational approach cultivates a collaborative environment where both individuals and the organization thrive harmoniously.

There are two ways through which we can understand a positive work environment:

1. Work Design
2. Work Culture

1. **Work Design:** Work design involves setting up tasks, activities, relationships, and responsibilities within one's professional domain. It's about organizing work in a way that affects how well you do, how happy you are, and how good the results are. When work is designed well, it helps everyone do their best and meets the organization's goals. Good work design usually has three main parts. (Parker, Van den Broeck, & Holman, 2017):
   a) Job autonomy, characterized by empowerment and self-leadership
   b) Social support
   c) Reasonable level of job demands relative to job resources

a) **Job Autonomy:** Providing employees with job autonomy involves granting them a sense of control and decision-making authority over their work. Autonomy allows employees to exercise their strengths, creativity, and problem-solving skills, leading to increased job satisfaction and motivation. Organizations can promote job autonomy by delegating responsibility, encouraging innovation, and promoting a supportive and trusting work environment. This is characterized by empowerment and self-leadership.

   I. **Empowerment:** Empowerment within a work culture serves as a fundamental component of job autonomy, embodying the philosophy of entrusting individuals with the authority, resources, and support necessary to take ownership of their work. It involves granting employees the autonomy to make decisions, exercise discretion, and influence outcomes related to their tasks and responsibilities. At its core, empowerment instills a sense of confidence, accountability, and fulfillment among employees, supporting a deeper connection to their work and organization. By providing individuals with the freedom to innovate, problem-solve, and express their creativity, organizations access a valuable pool of talent and potential. Empowered employees are more likely to demonstrate initiative, take calculated risks, and proactively seek solutions to challenges, increasing organizational performance and adaptability. Furthermore, empowerment creates a culture of trust, collaboration, and continuous improvement, where individuals feel valued, respected, and supported in their professional endeavors.

   II. **Self-Leadership:** Self-leadership is a diverse practice rooted in understanding one's identity and directing oneself intentionally toward desired experiences. Initially introduced by Charles C. Manz in organizational management literature, it involves guiding oneself toward both inherently motivating tasks and less engaging responsibilities. Recognizing its vital role in effective team leadership, scholars such as Marieta Du Plessis have expanded its scope to incorporate insights from positive psychology. Du Plessis emphasizes the integration of signature strengths, value-based inspiration, and goal-setting into the self-leadership journey. By practicing self-leadership, individuals not only enhance their productivity and effectiveness but also deeper a sense of fulfillment and authenticity in their personal and professional lives.

b) **Social Support:** Promoting employee well-being and resilience depends on building strong friendships and help from coworkers in companies. This can be achieved by cultivating amicable relationships among colleagues, stimulating teamwork and collaboration, and instituting mentorship initiatives. By facilitating opportunities for employees to interact and bond, not only improve their personal well-being, but organizational culture and teamwork also flourish. Encouraging friendships and interconnectedness increases a sense of belonging and support network, strengthening employees against stressors and challenges. Emphasizing collective goals and shared achievements further consolidates this supportive environment.

Psychologists have long recognized the intrinsic human need for social connection. Interpersonal relationships profoundly impact mental health, health behavior, physical well-being, and mortality risk (Umberson & Montez, 2010). Our physiological responses are finely attuned to positive social interactions. Gable and Gosnell (2011) proposed that people have special brain systems for understanding others, and having close friends and family help to build these systems, which can protect us from feeling too stressed. Their study revealed that social interactions trigger the release of oxytocin, a potent hormone associated with trust and altruism in the workplace. Dunbar and Dunbar (1998) suggested that workplace isolation activates brain regions similar to physical pain, emphasizing the significance of social bonds. Conversely, cooperative, trustworthy, and fair workplace relationships activate the brain's reward center, increasing employee trust, respect, and mutual inspiration (Geue, 2017). Positive workplace interactions directly impact physiological processes, strengthening cardiovascular, immune, and neuro endocrine systems and promoting overall health (Heaphy & Dutton, 2008). In essence, positive relationships among employees enhances the body's capacity for self-regulation, benefiting both professional and personal well-being.

Benefits of Social Interaction at Work:

1. **Employee Engagement:** Employee involvement is significantly influenced by social interactions, which are integral to well-being. Companies boasting heightened employee involvement demonstrate reduced operational expenses, enhanced

performance metrics, diminished turnover rates, decreased absenteeism, and fewer safety mishaps (Gallup, 2015).

2. **Shared Knowledge:** In collaborative team environments or when senior and junior workers collaborate, social interaction can facilitate the transfer of knowledge and productivity, especially in low-skilled tasks and occupations (Cornelissen, 2016). For instance, Mas and Moretti (2009) observed enhanced productivity when employees teamed up with more proficient and efficient colleagues.
3. **Employee Satisfaction:** Employees who find satisfaction in the general quality of their workplace relationships tend to develop stronger bonds with the organization. Managers who promote informal interactions, such as social gatherings outside of work hours, can cultivate more favorable relationships and notably enhance employee satisfaction (Sias, 2005).
4. **Reduced Health Risks:** Lack of social interaction within the workplace may lead to adverse outcomes regarding social support. Numerous research endeavors have pointed to the potential health consequences stemming from feelings of isolation due to inadequate social support. These consequences include heightened susceptibility to cardiovascular ailments, weakened immune responses, elevated risks of depression, and shortened lifespan (Holt-Lunstad et al., 2015; Cacioppo, Hawkley, Norman, & Berntson, 2011; Mushtaq, Shoib, Shah, & Mushtaq, 2014).
5. **Innovation:** Establishing strong connections with colleagues through frequent social interactions increases an environment which is favorable to innovative thinking. As outlined by Wang, Fang, Qureshi, and Janssen (2015), these strong interpersonal bonds cultivated through social interactions help innovators in seeking inspiration, sponsorship, and support within the organizational setting.
6. **Connection:** Workplace social interactions help everyone understand things in the same way. As noted by Sias, Krone, and Jablin (2002), peer relationships, also known as equivalent-status relationships predominate among employee interactions. These peer connections occur among colleagues without formal hierarchical authority and serve as vital sources of both informational and emotional support. Employees gain a sense

of connection and inclusion as they exchange workplace insights and information through regular social engagement, increasing a shared understanding of their work environment.

7. **Positive Feelings:** Studies show that when people talk and connect with others at work, they feel happier by the end of the day. (Nolan & Küpers, 2009).
8. **Trust:** Frequent positive social interactions promote the accumulation of shared experiences and the incremental formation of trusting relationships (Oh, Chung, & Labianca, 2004). With trust established among team members, there's a greater tendency for positive, collaborative conduct, thereby increasing employees' access to valuable resources.
9. **Altruism:** Workers who participate in favorable social exchanges also demonstrate increased altruism by offering assistance, guidance, counsel, and feedback to colleagues on diverse work-related issues (Hamilton, 2007).
10. **Improved Motivation:** Interpersonal interaction and favorable relationships play important role in influencing various attitudinal, well-being, and performance-related outcomes. Basford and Offermann (2012) discovered that employees across different hierarchical levels, whether low- or high-status positions, exhibited heightened motivation levels when they developed positive interpersonal connections with coworkers.

c) **Jobs Demands and Resources:** Maintaining a positive work environment depends on skillfully handling both job demands and available resources. It's really important for organizations to make sure that employees have everything they need to do their jobs well. This includes good training, the right tools, and lots of support. Striking a balance between these demands and resources serves to alleviate stress, strengthen job satisfaction, and elevate overall well-being and performance levels. When employees have the necessary support and tools at their disposal, they're better positioned to find their roles with confidence, leading to enhanced productivity and a more fulfilling work experience. Morgeson and Humphrey (2006) developed a Work Design Questionnaire (WDQ) to assess various aspects of job design.

Components of WDQ: It assesses five core components of work design:

a) **Skill Variety:** This dimension assesses the extent to which a job requires employees to use a variety of skills and abilities.

b) **Task Identity:** Task identity measures the degree to which a job involves completing a whole and identifiable piece of work, contributing to a sense of completeness.

c) **Task Significance:** Task significance examines the impact and importance of the job in affecting the lives or work of other people, emphasizing the social relevance of the work.

d) **Autonomy:** Autonomy refers to the degree of independence and freedom of employees in scheduling and performing their work.

e) **Feedback:** Feedback measures the extent to which employees receive clear information about the effectiveness of their performance.

2. **Work Culture:** Positive work culture refers to a workplace environment where employees feel valued, respected, and supported. It includes shared values, beliefs, and behaviors that promote collaboration and mutual respect. In such cultures, communication is open and transparent, building trust and friendship among coworkers. Recognition of employee contributions and achievements is common, leading to increased job satisfaction. Moreover, positive work cultures encourage creativity and innovation, as individuals feel enabled to share ideas and take risks. Overall, a positive work culture contributes to higher morale, improved performance, and a sense of belonging among employees. Some ways to build a positive work culture are as follows:

a) **Values and Beliefs:** A good work atmosphere comes from everyone sharing similar beliefs and values that match with positive thinking. It's vital for organizations to clearly outline and convey their fundamental values—like trust, respect, collaboration, and growth—to establish a solid cultural framework. These values serve as guiding principles, shaping decision-making, interactions, and behaviors across the organization. When ingrained within the company's ethos, these values encourage an environment where employees feel supported and empowered. By following these same rules together, companies create a friendly and supportive work environment where people do well and help the company to succeed.

b) **Social Connections:** Positive relationships among coworkers play an important role in nurturing a supportive and collaborative work culture. Open communication channels, actively encouraged by organizations, facilitate the exchange of ideas and information, developing a sense of unity and cooperation among team members. Encouraging teamwork means people work together to reach goals, which makes work better and helps everyone achieve more.

c) **Rituals and Practices:** Introducing rituals and practices that promote positive values and behaviors can shape the culture of an organization. For example, arranging regular team-building activities help employees bond and work together better. Programs that acknowledge individual achievements encourage appreciation and motivation, encouraging everyone to keep doing their best. Also, offering opportunities for personal and professional development gives employees a sense of purpose and investment, making them happier and more committed.

Theories of Positive Psychology in Work

1. **Growth Mindset:** The growth mindset theory, developed by positive psychologist Carol Dweck, has profound implications for organizational development and employee performance. At its core, the theory distinguishes between two types of mindsets: fixed and growth. A fixed mindset is characterized by the belief that one's abilities and qualities are static and unchangeable. In contrast, a growth mindset embraces the idea that abilities and qualities can be developed and enhanced through dedication, effort, and learning. The Core Principles of Growth Mindset are as follows:

   a) **Belief in Development:** The growth mindset suggests that talents and intelligence are not fixed traits but can be cultivated over time. Employees with a growth mindset see challenges as opportunities to improve rather than insurmountable obstacles. They are more likely to embrace new tasks and persist in the face of setbacks, viewing effort as a path to mastery.

   b) **Emphasis on Learning:** Continuous learning and improvement are central to the growth mindset. Employees are encouraged to acquire new skills, seek feedback, and view failures as learning experiences. This approach develops an environment where innovation and adaptation are part of the organizational culture.

   c) **Effort and Persistence:** Effort is seen as a crucial component of success in a growth mindset. Employees understand that sustained effort and resilience are necessary to achieve their goals. This perspective reduces the fear of failure and promotes a more resilient and proactive workforce.

d) **Adaptability:** A growth mindset encourages adaptability in the face of change. Employees are more willing to step out of their comfort zones, take on new responsibilities, and adjust to evolving circumstances. This adaptability is particularly valuable in dynamic industries where agility and innovation are critical.

Implementing a Growth Mindset in the Workplace

a) **Leadership and Role Modeling:** Leaders play an important role in developing a growth mindset. By modeling growth-oriented behaviors, such as embracing challenges, showing enthusiasm for learning and acknowledging their own development journeys, leaders can inspire employees to adopt similar attitudes.

b) **Feedback and Recognition:** Constructive feedback is vital for nurturing a growth mindset. Feedback should focus on effort, strategies, and progress rather than innate abilities. Recognizing and rewarding persistence and improvement encourages employees to continue developing their skills.

c) **Learning Opportunities:** Providing ample opportunities for professional development is essential. Organizations can offer training programs, workshops, mentorship, and access to learning resources. Encouraging employees to set learning goals and providing support for achieving them helps reinforce a growth mindset.

d) **Encouraging Collaboration:** A collaborative environment develops a growth mindset by allowing employees to share knowledge, learn from each other, and collectively solve problems. Teamwork and open communication help to create a culture where learning from one another is valued.

e) **Addressing Fixed Mindset Triggers:** It's important to identify and address triggers that may lead to a fixed mindset, such as excessive focus on outcomes, fear of failure, and comparison with others. By shifting the focus to the learning process and individual progress, organizations can mitigate these triggers.

Benefits of a Growth Mindset at Work

a) **Enhanced Employee Performance:** Employees with a growth mindset are more likely to take initiative, innovate, and strive for continuous improvement. This leads to higher overall performance and productivity.

b) **Greater Resilience:** A growth mindset equips employees with the resilience needed to handle challenges and setbacks. They are more likely to persevere and find solutions rather than becoming discouraged.

c) **Improved Employee Engagement:** When employees believe their efforts can lead to growth, they are more engaged and motivated. This increased engagement results in better job satisfaction and retention.

d) **Fostering Innovation:** A culture that values learning and adaptability encourages innovative thinking. Employees feel empowered to experiment, take risks, and contribute new ideas.

e) **Organizational Agility:** In a rapidly changing business environment, organizations with a growth mindset are better positioned to adapt and thrive. Employees' willingness to learn and grow enables the organization to pivot and respond to new opportunities and challenges effectively.

Application of Growth Mindset in Organizations:

a) **Leadership Development:** Leaders play a crucial role in fostering a growth mindset within an organization by exemplifying and promoting continuous learning. By openly discussing their own learning journeys, acknowledging their mistakes, and demonstrating a commitment to both personal and professional growth, leaders set a powerful example for employees to emulate. Additionally, they can further reinforce this mindset by providing ample opportunities for professional development, such as workshops, courses, and mentorship programs. Encouraging leaders to seek feedback and view challenges as opportunities for growth instills a culture of continuous improvement and adaptability at the highest levels of the organization.

b) **Employee Development and Training:** Organizations can cultivate a growth-oriented culture by offering a variety of learning opportunities, such as on-the-job training, cross-functional projects, and access to online learning platforms, encouraging employees to pursue new skills and knowledge. Additionally, training programs should emphasize the learning process rather than just outcomes, celebrating efforts, progress, and learning from mistakes to develop a growth mindset among employees.

c) **Performance Management:** Performance management systems should incorporate developmental goals alongside performance targets, encouraging employees to set objectives related to skill acquisition and personal growth. Providing constructive feedback that emphasizes effort, strategies, and improvement helps employees understand how they can develop and enhance their abilities, thereby fostering a growth mindset and promoting continuous improvement.

d) **Organizational Culture:** Encouraging a culture where experimentation and taking calculated risks are valued helps foster innovation and growth, as employees feel safe to try new things without fear of failure. Additionally, recognizing and celebrating instances of learning and development through awards, shout-outs in meetings, or internal communications, highlighting stories of personal and professional growth reinforces this culture, motivating employees to continue striving for improvement.

e) **Collaboration and Team Dynamics:** Creating opportunities for team members to engage in peer coaching, knowledge-sharing sessions, and collaborative projects, fosters a culture of collaborative learning, helping to embed a growth mindset within teams as they collectively seek to improve and innovate. Additionally, ensuring that teams feel psychologically safe to express ideas, ask questions, and admit mistakes encourages open dialogue and continuous learning, further strengthening team dynamics and collaboration.

f) **Recruitment:** Focusing on hiring candidates with a demonstrated ability to learn and adapt, rather than solely those with specific skills or experience, ensures the selection of individuals who are willing to take on new challenges and have a track record of personal development. Complementing this approach, growth-focused on-boarding programs should emphasize the importance of a growth mindset, introducing new hires to the organization's commitment to learning and development from day one, thereby fostering an environment conducive to continuous improvement and adaptability.

g) **Innovation and Change Management:** Supporting innovative thinking by providing resources and time for employees to explore new ideas, fosters a culture where challenges are seen as opportunities to innovate. Additionally, equipping employees with the skills and mindset to adapt to change through training on change management and resilience helps them view change as a chance for growth rather than a threat, enhancing the organization's overall adaptability and innovation capacity.

The growth mindset theory offers a powerful framework for driving organizational change and enhancing employee performance. By fostering an environment that values effort, learning, and adaptability, organizations can unlock the full potential of their workforce and achieve sustained success.

2. **Appreciative Inquiry in Organizational Development:**

Appreciative Inquiry (AI) is a strengths-based approach to organizational development that focuses on identifying and amplifying what an organization does well. Originating from positive psychology, AI seeks to shift the focus from problem-solving to recognizing and building on successes and strengths. This methodology develops a positive mindset, encouraging employees to envision and construct a future that enhances and magnifies the organization's best aspects. Here, we delve into the theory and application of Appreciative Inquiry in the workplace. The core principles of Appreciative Inquiry theory are

a) **Constructionist Principle:** This principle suggests that reality is constructed through language and conversations. By focusing on positive dialogue, organizations can create a shared vision of success. This positive construction helps in shaping the organizational culture and identity.

b) **Principle of Simultaneity:** Inquiry and change are not separate processes but occur simultaneously. Act of asking positive questions begins the change process, developing immediate improvements in the organizational climate and attitudes.

c) **Poetic Principle:** This principle suggests that organizations are like open books and can be interpreted and reinterpreted in many ways. By choosing to focus on the positive aspects, organizations can continuously reframe their narrative to highlight strengths and achievements.

d) **Anticipatory Principle:** Positive images of the future lead to positive actions. By envisioning a desired future, organizations can mobilize their efforts toward making that vision a reality. This forward-looking approach energizes and motivates employees.

e) **Positive Principle:** Sustainable change requires a focus on the positive. Positive questions and discussions lead to positive relationships and outcomes. This principle emphasizes the importance of positivity in driving long-lasting organizational change.

The 5D Cycle of Appreciative Inquiry: The AI process typically follows a 5D cycle, each phase building upon the previous one to create a comprehensive and engaging change strategy:

1. **Definition:** Clarify the focus of the inquiry. Determine what the organization wants to learn more about or improve. This phase involves setting the stage for a positive inquiry by framing the right questions.
2. **Discovery:** Identify and appreciate the best of what is. This phase involves gathering stories and examples of peak experiences and successes within the organization. By highlighting these positive instances, organizations can understand what works well.
3. **Dream:** Employees and stakeholders collectively imagine the future of the organization by dreaming big and picturing ideal outcomes. This shared vision sets a compelling direction for change.
4. **Design:** Based on the dream phase, participants design the organizational structures, processes, and strategies that will help achieve the envisioned future. This phase involves planning and strategizing actionable steps.
5. **Destiny/Delivery:** Implement and sustain the change. This final phase focuses on executing the designed strategies and ensuring the changes are embedded into the organizational culture. Continuous learning and adaptation are key aspects of this phase.

Benefits of Appreciative Inquiry

a) **Enhanced Engagement:** AI actively involves employees at all levels in the change process, fostering a sense of ownership and engagement. When employees are part of envisioning and creating the future, they are more committed to achieving it.

b) **Positive Organizational Culture:** By focusing on strengths and successes, AI helps cultivate a positive organizational culture. This positivity boosts morale, reduces resistance to change, and enhances overall job satisfaction.

c) **Improved Collaboration:** The AI process encourages open communication and collaboration. As employees share positive stories and co-create future visions, they build stronger relationships and teamwork, leading to better organizational cohesion.

d) **Sustainable Change:** The strengths-based approach of AI ensures that changes are not only implemented but are sustainable. By building on existing strengths, organizations can create lasting improvements that are aligned with their core values and competencies.

e) **Innovative Solutions:** AI's focus on positive possibilities encourages creative and innovative thinking. By imagining the best possible future, employees are more likely to come up with novel solutions and approaches to achieving organizational goals.

Application of Appreciative Inquiry in Organizations

a) **Strategic Planning:** AI can be used in strategic planning to align organizational goals with its strengths and positive core. This ensures that the strategy is grounded in what the organization does best and can realistically achieve.

b) **Leadership Development:** Appreciative Inquiry helps develop leadership skills by encouraging leaders to focus on strengths, foster positive relationships, and inspire a shared vision. Leaders trained in AI are more likely to create empowering and motivating environments.

c) **Team Building:** AI can be a powerful tool for team building, helping teams to recognize and leverage their collective strengths. This fosters a collaborative spirit and enhances team performance.

d) **Change Management:** During periods of significant change, AI provides a framework for managing transitions smoothly. By focusing on what works well, organizations can minimize disruptions and maintain positive momentum.

Appreciative Inquiry offers a transformative approach to organizational development. By emphasizing strengths, successes, and positive possibilities, AI not only fosters a positive work environment but also drives sustainable and meaningful change. This methodology aligns the organization's present capabilities with its future aspirations, creating a resilient and dynamic organization poised for continued growth and success.

Applications of Positive Psychology

1. **Cultivating High Performing Teams:** High-performing teams demonstrate key traits such as a common purpose, trust, effective communication, and skillful conflict resolution. Organizations can cultivate team unity and collaboration by engaging in team-building activities, establishing transparent communication platforms, and offering

conflict resolution training. Building an atmosphere that prioritizes and appreciates teamwork not only boosts employee morale but also increases team effectiveness. Promoting common objectives and building a culture of confidence helps teams overcome obstacles and attain mutual accomplishments.. Through these efforts, organizations can create a supportive environment favorable to both employee satisfaction and high team performance.

2. **Encouraging Strength Use:** Using the strengths of employees is instrumental in elevating job satisfaction, engagement, and overall performance. Organizations can accomplish this by implementing methods like strengths assessments, personalized development plans, and platforms for employees to utilize their strengths in their positions. Recognizing and celebrating individual strengths not only improves employee well-being but also creates a positive and inspiring work atmosphere. By acknowledging and utilizing the special talents of each employee, organizations promote a culture of appreciation and empowerment, leading to increased productivity and satisfaction among staff members.
3. **Developing Employee Resilience:** Resilience is crucial for overcoming challenges, and organizations can help employees build resilience by providing resources for managing stress, promoting a healthy work-life balance, and offering training on coping strategies. Creating a supportive workplace culture strengthens employee resilience. Also, empowering employees to adopt a growth mindset and providing opportunities for ongoing learning and development boost their ability to bounce back from setbacks.
4. **Developing Reflective Practices:** Developing reflective practices involves incorporating activities such as gratitude journaling, mindfulness meditation, and positive affirmations into employees' daily routines. These practices encourage individuals to pause and reflect on positive aspects of their lives, encouraging emotional well-being and enhancing overall performance. By dedicating time to gratitude journaling, employees cultivate appreciation for the present moment and acknowledge the good in their lives. Engaging in mindfulness meditation techniques helps individuals manage stress, regulate emotions, and maintain focus, promoting a sense of presence and clarity. Similarly, integrating positive affirmations into daily routines increases self-esteem and confidence,

building a positive mindset beneficial for personal growth and success in the workplace.

5. **Developing Positive Workplace Culture:** In cultivating a positive workplace culture, organizations can apply principles of positive psychology to enhance employee well-being and engagement. Firstly, emphasizing a sense of meaning and purpose in employees' work can boost motivation and productivity. This involves clearly communicating the organization's mission and values while providing opportunities for employees to utilize their skills in meaningful ways. Secondly, developing positive relationships among colleagues, supervisors, and subordinates promotes effective communication, trust, and collaboration, ultimately reducing stress levels. Encouraging open communication, teamwork, and creating social interaction opportunities can nurture these relationships. Lastly, integrating humor into the workplace can contribute to stress reduction, mood improvement, and overall well-being.
6. **Enhancing Workplace Engagement and Achievement:** In cultivating workplace engagement and achievement, organizations can implement various positive psychology interventions. Firstly, the practice of savoring positive experiences involves intentionally focusing on and prolonging positive emotions and moments. This can be achieved through reflection, gratitude expression, and sharing with others, leading to increased well-being and immune system enhancement. Additionally, providing positive feedback and recognition to employees for their accomplishments and strengths can significantly impact motivation, morale, and productivity. Employers can offer praise, constructive feedback, rewards, or bonuses to acknowledge employees' contributions. Moreover, incorporating goal setting into the workplace encourages employees to identify and pursue specific objectives, fostering focus, direction, and a sense of purpose.

Practical Strategies to Enhance Well-being and Motivation at Work place

The application of positive psychology in the workplace can positively impact both subjective well-being and physiological markers of health and stress. When implementing positive psychology interventions targeted at enhancing well-being, there are four critical steps to follow:

a) **Conduct a Need Assessment:** Before implementing any intervention, it is crucial to conduct a thorough needs assessment to understand the specific challenges and requirements of any organization. This data-driven approach ensures that interventions are tailored to address the unique needs of the workforce.

b) **Objective Development:** Once the needs are identified, clear objectives for the intervention must be established. These objectives should include measurable targets and metrics to track progress over time, ensuring accountability and effectiveness.

c) **Strategy Development:** The next step involves brainstorming strategies to achieve the established objectives. It is essential to generate a wide range of ideas without immediate consideration of practicality or budget constraints. This creative approach allows for innovative solutions to emerge.

d) **Implementation and Evaluation:** After selecting the most feasible strategies, the intervention is implemented and its effectiveness is evaluated. Various methods, such as surveys, feedback collection, and objective metrics analysis can be used to assess the impact of the intervention. Continuous evaluation allows for adjustments and improvements to enhance effectiveness.

Steps for Motivation Enhancement

a) **Assessing sources of Motivation:** Understanding what motivates employees is crucial for designing effective motivational interventions. By assessing intrinsic and extrinsic motivators, organizations can coordinate interventions to align with individual preferences and values.

b) **Job Crafting:** Job crafting is when employees adjust their tasks or relationships at work to make their job more meaningful and satisfying. Providing resources and support for job crafting empowers employees to shape their roles in alignment with their strengths and interests.

c) **Creating a Shared Vision:**. Sharing a strong vision that connects with employees' values and dreams is important for boosting motivation and involvement. When everyone shares the same vision, it gives a clear sense of purpose and guidance, motivating everyone to work together toward common objectives.

Summary

Applying positive psychology principles in the workplace significantly enhances employee well-being, engagement, and performance, contributing to the overall success and growth of organizations. Defining work is not just a source of income but a means of personal and professional fulfillment. This chapter explores how a positive work environment develops a culture of positivity and implements tailored interventions. The benefits of being happy at work are manifold, including increased productivity, creativity, and collaboration, as well as improved mental and physical health. Theories such as appreciative inquiry and the growth mindset offer frameworks for leveraging strengths and fostering continuous learning and adaptability. Practical positive psychology techniques, such as fostering a culture of experimentation, recognizing and celebrating growth, and providing resources for innovation, are emphasized. Leaders play a crucial role in modeling and encouraging these principles, promoting continuous learning, and ensuring psychological safety, which in turn enhances team dynamics and collaboration. By focusing on the human side of work, organizations can ensure that employees succeed, use their strengths, and add value, thus driving sustained growth and a resilient workforce. This chapter concludes that recognizing the importance of employee well-being and fulfillment directly impacts productivity, morale, and organizational outcomes, and that with the right tools and knowledge, organizations can proactively establish a workplace where both employees and the business thrive.

CHAPTER 4

APPLICATION OF POSITIVE PSYCHOLOGY IN AGING

Traditionally, aging has been associated with decline, poor emotional health, and a reduced quality of life, often leading to a loss of independence. However, the principles of positive psychology present an opportunity to redefine aging, focusing on strengths, resilience, and the capacity for continued development. This chapter overviews key concepts of positive aging and explores strategies to enhance well-being in the elderly, translating theoretical insights into practical approaches for fostering a positive aging experience.

Aging need not be a solitary or fearful journey marked by loneliness and decline. Instead, it can be a time of rich social connections, purpose, and ongoing personal growth. Positive aging encourages us to redefine, view, and accept the inevitable changes of aging with grace and optimism. This approach helps individuals navigate both expected and unexpected changes, maintaining a higher quality of life and emotional well-being.

By examining the potential of positive psychology, this chapter advocates for an active approach to aging that supports successful aging rather than suboptimal experiences. It emphasizes the importance of fostering environments where older adults can thrive, leveraging concepts like resilience, purpose, gratitude, and social engagement. Through practical interventions such as promoting lifelong learning, building strong social networks, and cultivating a positive mindset, we can help older adults maintain autonomy, dignity, and joy in their later years. Positive aging is about embracing the journey of growing old as a communal and enriching experience, ensuring that the elderly lead lives filled with purpose and connection.

Introduction

Aging is a period in the life cycle experienced by everyone. In today's world, people are enjoying longer life spans, and the older population is expanding rapidly. This is because of better healthcare and fewer children being born. However, this also brings about more challenges in assuring that older adults can live healthy and fulfilling lives. In the past, older individuals were often regarded as less important and perceived as a burden on society. But recent researches show that many older adults are quite healthy, active, and independent. They are also involved in their communities and families. Still, there are risks, especially for the very old, and how well someone ages depends on how they deal with the changes that comes with getting older.

Meaning and Types of Aging

1. **Biological Perspective:** Aging is understood as cellular and molecular deterioration in the body. Scientific research in this field has discovered methods to alleviate physical pain and potentially increase longevity. For instance, scientific advancements have led to the growth of treatments that can reduce physical discomfort and potentially extend lifespan (Smith et al., 2018).
2. **Socio cultural Factors:** Socio cultural influences shape our attitudes toward aging. Beauty commercials often perpetuate the idea that signs of aging, such as wrinkles and grey hair, are undesirable. This is evident in the prevalent messaging of beauty products, such as soaps and hair dyes, which suggest that aging features are to be avoided (Jones, 2019).
3. **Cultural Differences:** Attitudes toward aging vary across cultures. In some cultures, older individuals are revered for their wisdom, while in others, aging is viewed as undesirable. In Japan and India, older individuals are respected and considered symbols of wisdom (Yamada & Gruenewald, 2017). In contrast, individualistic societies may perceive aging as a liability (Smith & Brown, 2016).
4. **Psychological factors:** Psychological factors play an important role in how we perceive. Stereotypes related to age can influence how individuals perceive themselves and others. The adage "you are only as old as you feel" reflects the positive implications of psychological well-being on aging (Johnson, 2018). Research by Gana, Alaphilippe, and Bailly (2004) demonstrated that individuals who maintain a perceived youthful bias experience better leisure time, higher self-esteem, and improved health.
5. **Functional Classification:** Aging can also be classified based on functionality. This classification considers activity and health levels relative to chronological age. According to this classification, individuals can be categorized as young-old, old-old, or oldest-old, based on their level of activity and ability to cope with daily tasks (Smith & Jones, 2017).

6. **Psychosocial Theory:** Erikson's psychosocial theory offers insights into the psychological conflicts experienced in old age. According to this theory, individuals in old age reflect on their life experiences and may feel either a sense of integrity or despair (Williams & Smith, 2015). Research by Malone et al. (2016) suggests that feelings of accomplishment or regret influence an individual's mental health in later life.

Problems Faced by People in Old Age

1. **Social connectedness:** Social connectedness can become a significant challenge in old age, as factors such as retirement, mobility limitations, and loss of loved ones can lead to increased isolation. This isolation can have detrimental effects on mental and physical health, contributing to feelings of loneliness, depression, and anxiety. In the absence of social interaction, older adults may experience a decline in cognitive function and may become more vulnerable to develop any chronic diseases. Furthermore, social isolation can worsen existing health conditions and increase the mortality rate. Strengthening social connectedness in old age is important for improving overall well-being and holistic health among older adults.
2. **Meaning in Life:** Finding meaning in life can become a pressing challenge, as individuals reflect on their past accomplishments and future aspirations. The quest for purpose may intensify as physical abilities diminishes, leading to feelings of existential uncertainty and emotional distress. Without a sense of meaning, older adults may struggle to find fulfillment, leading to a higher likelihood of depression, isolation, and a decreased quality of life. However, discovering meaning can foster resilience and a sense of peace, guiding individuals through life's transitions with purpose and vitality.
3. **Wisdom:** In old age, wisdom can become a complex problem, as cognitive decline may challenge its solemn wisdom's realm. Memory lapses and cognitive impairments may hinder, leaving a sense of frustration and uncertainty to hinder. Effects ripple through daily life, decisions, and interactions, leaving individuals grappling with doubts and distractions. Yet, wisdom's essence persists, resilient amid the storm, Guiding through adversity, offering solace and reform.
4. **Resilience:** Resilience in old age presents a crucial challenge as the body weakens and circumstances rearrange. Adversities like health declines and loss of loved ones, test resilience, revealing its true strength in the run.

Yet, those who weather these storms with fortitude and grace often find renewed purpose, a brighter embrace. Resilience shields against despair, fostering hope's flame, and empowers older adults to triumph despite life's game.

ATTRIBUTES OF AGING ⟶	**ADVERSE IMPACTS-**	**OUTCOMES**
Loneliness	Excess stress	Decreased coping ability
Anxiety/fear	Sleep challenges	Injury risk increases
Depression	Lack of motivation	Deficient self-care
Disability	Excess disability	Dependence
Pain	Chronic pain	Opioid usage
	LOW LIFE QUALITY	**LONGEVITY DECLINE**

Schematic of anticipated aging impacts and outcomes in the presence of various negative psycho-affective attributes of cognition such as fear, depression, anxiety, and pain coupled with the absence of efforts to heighten positive thoughts and regardless of actual health status.

Role of Positive Psychology in Older Adult Well-being

- **Emergence and Focus of Positive Psychology:** Positive psychology, a relatively new branch of psychology that emerged around 2000, emphasizes the study of positive subjective experiences, individual strengths, and factors that contribute to a fulfilling life (Ranzijn, 2002). Unlike traditional psychology, which often focuses on pathology and mental illness, positive psychology seeks to understand and cultivate the aspects of life that lead to happiness and well-being. This approach centers on identifying and harnessing personal strengths and capabilities to enhance overall well-being (Stoner, 2019).
- **Definition of Well-being:** Well-being, as defined by the World Health Organization, is the interplay between positive and negative psychological processes. It reflects an individual's realization of their abilities, effective coping strategies, productivity, and contributions to their community (Momtaz et al., 2016). Positive psychology aims to elevate the quality of life by developing high levels of satisfaction and emotional well-being (Ramírez et al., 2014). This holistic understanding of well-being is critical for older adults, who often face unique challenges such as retirement, health issues, and social changes.

- **Misconceptions about Positive Psychology:** Critics sometimes misinterpret positive psychology as being overly focused on happiness, suggesting it ignores the complexities and challenges of life. However, positive psychology does not aim to disregard negative experiences but rather provides techniques to enhance well-being and build resilience against daily stressors (Proyer et al., 2014). This balanced approach ensures that individuals can better face life's difficulties while maintaining a positive outlook.
- **Key Components of Positive Psychology are:**
  a) **Flourishing:** Flourishing is living within an optimal range of human functioning, characterized by aspects such as goodness, growth, and resilience. In the context of aging, flourishing means that older adults engage in activities that promote personal growth and resilience, contributing to a sense of purpose and well-being. This can include volunteering, lifelong learning, and participating in community activities.
  b) **Hedonic Perspective:** The hedonic perspective focuses on the pursuit of pleasure and happiness. For older adults, this could involve engaging in activities that bring joy and satisfaction, such as hobbies, social gatherings, and entertainment. It emphasizes the importance of immediate, short-term happiness and enjoyment in daily life.
  c) **Eudaimonic Perspective:** The eudaimonic perspective emphasizes finding meaning and self-realization. Older adults may seek deeper fulfillment through activities that align with their values and passions, such as mentoring, creative pursuits, or spiritual practices. This approach focuses on long-term well-being and personal growth.
  d) **Positive Affect and Emotions:** Positive affect refers to the experience of positive emotions such as joy, gratitude, and contentment. Encouraging older adults to focus on positive experiences and emotions can enhance their overall health outcomes. Practices such as gratitude journaling, mindfulness, and engaging in enjoyable activities can foster positive emotions and improve life satisfaction.
  e) **Happiness:** Happiness is a state of well-being and contentment. Promoting activities that lead to happiness can improve the mental and emotional health of older adults. This includes fostering social connections, pursuing enjoyable activities, and maintaining a positive outlook on life.

f) **Cognitive Reappraisal:** Cognitive reappraisal involves changing one's interpretation of potentially stressful situations to maintain emotional equilibrium. Teaching older adults cognitive reappraisal techniques can help them handle stress and adversity more effectively. For example, viewing retirement as an opportunity for new experiences rather than a loss can lead to better emotional outcomes.

By focusing on these components, positive psychology provides a comprehensive framework to enhance the well-being of older adults, promoting a higher quality of life through balanced emotional health, meaningful engagement, and continuous personal growth.

In summary, positive psychology offers valuable insights and practical strategies to enhance the well-being of older adults. By understanding and applying its principles, individuals and communities can create supportive environments that promote resilience, happiness, and a high quality of life, redefining the aging process as a period of continued growth and fulfillment.

Successful Aging

The concept of "successful aging" was described by R. J. Havighurst as a state of inner satisfaction or happiness. Successful aging is about living well as you get older, and it involves different aspects like being healthy and physically fit, sharp in your thinking, staying active, and feeling positive emotions. It's not just about the length of your life, but the quality of it. Successful aging, also known as positive aging or healthy aging, refers to the process of maintaining a positive outlook, quality of life, and overall well-being as one grows older. It has been defined in different ways in different countries.

The UK: "A way of living rather than a state of being" (Positive Ageing, n.d.).

Australia: "The process of maintaining a positive attitude, feeling good about yourself, keeping fit and healthy, and engaging fully in life as you age" (Positive Psychology Institute, n.d.).

New Zealand: "Positive aging reflects the attitudes and experiences older people have about themselves and how younger generations view the process of aging. It takes into account the health, financial security, independence, self-fulfillment, personal safety, and living environment of older New Zealanders" (Ministry of Social Development, 2001).

The U.S: "Successful aging is multidimensional, encompassing the avoidance of disease and disability, the maintenance of high physical and cognitive function, and sustained engagement in social and productive activities" (Rowe & Kahn, 1997).

World Health Organization (WHO): "The process of developing and maintaining the functional ability that enables well-being in older age" (WHO, 2020).

Japan: "Japanese conceptions of aging are rooted in Buddhist, Confucian, and Taoist philosophical traditions that characterize aging as maturity. Old age is thus understood as a socially valuable part of life, even a time of "spring" or "rebirth" after a busy period of working and raising children" (Karasawa et al., 2011).

China: "The criteria are sufficiently inclusive, encompassing physical health, mental health, social engagement, and nutritional status, which in principle conform with both the WHO definition and the Rowe and Kahn model" (Zhou, Liu, & Yu, 2018; referencing the Chinese health criteria for the elderly).

Eastern Europe: "Successful aging is concerned with facilitating the rights of older people to remain healthy (reducing the costs of health and social care), remain in employment longer (reducing pension costs), while also participating in community and political life" (Foster & Walker, 2015).

Constituents of Successful Aging

Bowling & Dieppe, (2005), have described the following indices of successful aging.

1. **Physical Health:** Successful aging involves sustaining good physical health through regular exercise, proper nutrition, and preventive healthcare measures. This includes staying physically active, managing chronic conditions effectively, and adapting to changes in physical abilities.
2. **Mental Health:** Successful aging encompassing mental well-being, including maintaining cognitive function, emotional resilience, and psychological flexibility. Engaging in intellectually stimulating activities, staying socially connected, and looking for help for mental health issues are important aspects of positive aging.

3. **Social Engagement:** Successful aging emphasizes the importance of staying socially engaged and maintaining meaningful relationships with family, friends, and the community. Active participation in social activities, volunteering, and maintaining a support network can contribute to overall well-being and quality of life.
4. **Lifelong Learning:** Successful aging involves a commitment to lifelong learning and personal growth. This can include pursuing new interests, hobbies, or educational opportunities, which can promote mental stimulation, creativity, and a sense of purpose.
5. **Adaptability and Resilience:** Successful aging involves adapting to life changes and challenges with resilience and optimism. This may include adjusting to retirement, coping with loss or illness, and finding new sources of meaning and fulfillment in later life.
6. **Sense of Purpose:** Successful aging is often associated with having a sense of purpose or meaning in life. This can involve pursuing goals, contributing to the well-being of others, or engaging in activities that are in accordance with one's values and interests.
7. **Financial Security:** Successful aging includes planning for financial security and stability in later life. This may involve saving for retirement, managing finances responsibly, and accessing resources and support services as needed.
8. **Self-Care and Wellness Practices:** Successful aging emphasizes self-care and wellness practices that promote physical and mental health. This can include prioritizing sleep, managing stress effectively, practicing relaxation techniques, and seeking healthcare when necessary.
9. **Embracing Aging:** Successful aging involves embracing the aging process and viewing it as a natural and normal facet of life. This includes accepting changes in physical appearance, health, and abilities while focusing on the advantages of aging and celebrating life experiences.
10. **Maintaining Independence and Autonomy:** Successful aging result in maintaining independence and autonomy for an extended period. This may include accessing support services, adaptive technologies, and community resources that enable individuals to age in place and maintain their quality of life.

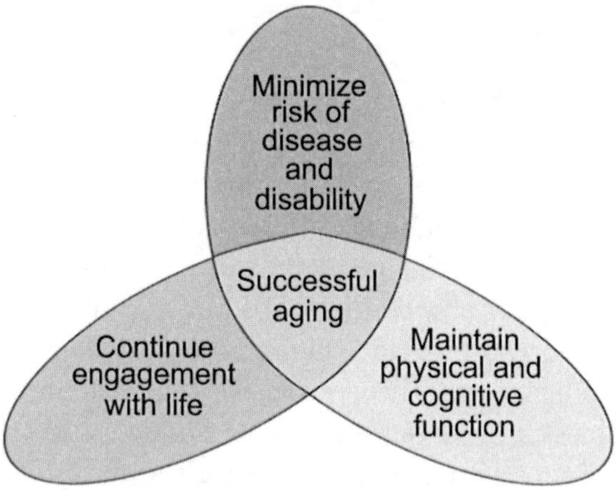

Theories of Successful Aging

1. **Activity Theory:** Activity Theory, formulated by R. Tartler in the 1960s, suggests that engagement in activities fulfills societal functions and is crucial for maintaining satisfaction in old age (Tartler, 1961, as cited in Nigg & Steidl, 2005). According to Tartler, individuals who remain inactive may experience physical and psychological decline, while those who are constantly busy may become exhausted (Tartler, 1961). The theory suggests that the ability of elderly individuals to influence events around them and contribute to society directly impacts their happiness and satisfaction in later life (Nigg & Steidl, 2005). Social roles and relationships play a significant role, as maintaining social ties and finding replacements for lost connections are crucial for optimal aging (Lehr, 2007). Upon retirement, individuals may experience a loss of social roles and connections, which can lead to feelings of loneliness (Schulz & Heckhausen, 1996). Lemon, Bengtson, and Petersen (1972) emphasize the importance of different activities linked with various social roles in shaping the self-image of elderly individuals. Informal activities, such as interactions with friends and family, are found to contribute most to life satisfaction, followed by formal activities and solitary hobbies or home-based work (Longino & Kart, 1982).

   However, it's important to acknowledge that not every elderly person has close social connections readily available which may limit the applicability of this theory (Atchley, 1989, pp. 183–190). Despite this, modern society offers numerous opportunities for elderly individuals to adapt their social roles, establish new connections, and engage in energizing activities after retirement (Nigg & Steidl, 2005).

2. **Disengagement Theory:** Old age often require a natural retreat from active roles and responsibilities. As people grow older, they might feel like taking a step back from their relationships and the world around them. This is a inherent aspect of life. Letting go and losing connections are seen as necessary steps in getting ready for the end of life. This change opens up room in society for new relationships, roles, and changes, which keeps society moving forward. (Nigg & Steidl, 2005). In contrast to the activity theory, the disengagement theory proposes that older individuals may feel greater happiness and contentment when not pressured to maintain high levels of activity or performance. Sociologists question whether a busy and active life necessarily guarantees satisfaction for older individuals, as societal expectations and stereotypes about old age can influence their outlook on life. While some older individuals may cite old age as a reason for withdrawing from challenging activities, it is not a given that they lose the capacity for active engagement (Nigg & Steidl, 2005). The disengagement theory originated from 172 interviews conducted with individuals aged 50 to 70 in the USA. It says that there is a natural need for a process of disengagement and the reduction of social relationships as individual's age. Relationships may undergo qualitative changes, with fewer social contacts and interactions, allowing aging individuals a sense of freedom from social norms (Cumming & Henry, 1979, p. 211).

   The theory postulates that some individuals desire social isolation and reduced social contacts in order to feel happier and more satisfied. In contrast to the activity theory, which emphasizes engagement and activity throughout life, the disengagement theory acknowledges the natural progression toward the end of life and death. While individuals may attempt to prolong their lives through various activities and preventative measures, mortality is an inevitable reality that cannot be denied (Lehr, 2007; Přidalová, 1998). Cumming and Henry (1979) question whether having a function or being useful contributes significantly to an older person's satisfaction. Some research conclude that individuals who have reduced social ties may actually experience greater satisfaction compared to those who remain strongly connected in social networks (Lehr, 2007).

3. **Dynamic Theories:** As people get older, they might feel like stepping back from their relationships and the world around them. This natural process is called disengagement and helps them prepare for the end of life.

It also creates space for new things to happen in society. There's a theory that suggests having personal goals is important for older adults. Even if they can't achieve all their goals, just having them can make life feel more meaningful. It's not just about reaching the goals, but also about the journey to get there (Lawton, 1985; Jung, 1994; Frankl, 1985; Tavel, 2004, 2007). In successful aging, it's not just about reaching a certain point or state, but also about how they get there. If reaching their goals is too easy, it might not feel like a real success. For example, if someone achieves financial security by doing a boring job that makes them unhappy, it might not be worth it. This dynamic approach raises questions about how long it takes to achieve goals (Freund & Riedger, 2003). Some experts argue that we can't judge a good life based only on how things are going at the moment. It's more about the long-term status in different areas of life. For example, drinking wine might make someone feel good for a short time, but if they drink too much, it can harm their health in the long run (Freund & Riedger, 2003).

A model called Selective Optimization with Compensation (SOC) suggests that successful aging involves optimizing life, focusing on important areas, and compensating for limitations. For example, older adults might use memory aids or hearing aids to compensate for age-related changes. However, some people argue that this model doesn't pay enough attention to subjective factors like happiness and optimism (Baltes & Baltes, 1989).

4. **Growth Theories:** In addition to theories that focus on the challenges of aging, some theories also highlight the potential for personal growth and wisdom as people age. C.G. Jung introduced the idea that as individuals confront the crises of aging, they can integrate their emotions and motives, leading to new opportunities for growth. Similarly, H. Thomae (1951) suggests that older individuals often reflect on their life experiences, including their failures, disappointments and ideals, as they aged. C.D. Ryff proposed a theory that outlines five conditions for healthy aging and continued development. Ryff's integrated model, which was initially known as "successful aging" and later as psychological well-being, was developed by Ryff and her colleagues. They combined ideas from different theories about how people grow and change over their lifetimes, how they develop personally, and how mental health works. This model has six parts that describe what it means to function well:

   1. **Self-acceptance:** Feeling good about yourself and accepting who you are.

2. **Positive Relations with Others:** Having good relationships with people around you, like friends and family.
3. **Autonomy:** Being independent and able to make your own choices.
4. **Environmental Mastery:** Feeling in control of your surroundings and being able to handle challenges.
5. **Purpose in Life:** Having a sense of meaning and direction in your life.
6. **Personal Growth:** Continuously learning and growing as a person throughout your life.

These dimensions of well-being and healthy mental functioning are shaped by socio-demographic characteristics (e.g., age, gender, socio-demographic status, ethnicity, and culture), as well as by individual experiences, including both unexpected life stresses and planned, normative transitions. Hedonic well-being which focuses on pleasure and the absence of pain or suffering is often associated with happiness derived from immediate gratification, enjoyment, and positive emotions, shows gains with age; that is, older adults tend to show increments in positive affect and decrements in negative affect at least until very old age. In contrast, Eudemonic well-being focuses on living in a way that fulfills one's true potential and leads to a sense of meaning and purpose in life. It's often associated with self-realization and personal growth. It is more inclined to reflect decrements in the later years, especially in terms of assessment of purpose in life and personal growth. Several psychosocial factors, including having a sense of purpose in life, maintaining strong social relationships, feeling in control of one's life (mastery), and engaging in prosocial behaviors like volunteering, have been found to positively influence various aspects of well-being as people age. This includes reporting better self-rated health, experiencing less disability, having healthier biological indicators, greater overall well-being, and maintaining better cognitive function. These effects hold true even when individuals are dealing with disabilities or chronic illnesses. Essentially, nurturing these psychosocial aspects can significantly enhance the overall health and quality of life as people grow older, despite facing health challenges.

Additionally, efforts to achieve wisdom in old age have been associated with growth theories, which emphasize the pursuit of meaning and the assimilation of life experiences. Research has also explored specific cognitive differences between individuals in varying stages of life. Studies at Duke University and in Milan, Italy, found that older adults tend to make wiser decisions than younger adults. However, perceptions of wisdom in old age vary across cultures, often reflecting traditional beliefs rather than individual wisdom. The theory of gero-transcendence suggests that human development continues into old age and is characterized by a shift toward a broader, more spiritual perspective on life. This includes a decreased focus on material possessions and superficial relationships, and an increased interest in self-reflection and solitude. However, cultural factors can influence the extent to which individuals experience gero-transcendence, with modern cultures often less supportive of this developmental process.

In recent decades, there have been changes to cognitive theories of behavior and emotions, emphasizing the importance of interpretation or representation over objective stimuli. One prominent theory in psycho-gerontology focuses on generalized expectations about human behavior (Rotter, 1975). Understanding one's personal control over a situation, known as "personal control cognition," is crucial in addressing age-related challenges (Rodin, Timko, Harris, 1985).

Lehr and Thomae suggest that the tasks individuals engage in throughout life, rather than age itself, are key in the aging process. Development is ongoing and influenced by personality traits and the environment. Successful aging involves continually adapting to new situations and challenges, a concept referred to as "re-orientating oneself" (Krohn in Otto, 1994). Both individuals and their social environments must possess the ability to adapt for successful aging to occur (Nigg, Steigl, 2005).

5. **Cognitive Theories:** In recent decades, there have been changes to cognitive theories of behavior and emotions, emphasizing the importance of interpretation or representation over objective stimuli. One prominent theory in psychogerontology focuses on generalized expectations about human behavior (Rotter, 1975). Understanding one's personal control over a situation, known as "personal control cognition," is crucial in addressing age-related challenges (Rodin, Timko, Harris, 1985). Feeling in control can fulfill a need for assistance and enhance a sense of competence, ultimately influencing overall contentment (Heckhausen & Schulz, 1995). Research conducted in retirement homes has shown that life satisfaction is more closely linked to cognitive perceptions than objective conditions (Schick, 1977). Lehr and Thomae suggest that the tasks individuals engage in throughout life, rather than age itself, are important in the aging process. Development is ongoing and influenced by personality traits and the environment. Successful aging involves continually adapting to new

situations and challenges, a concept referred to as "re-orientating oneself" (Krohn & Otto, 1994). Both individuals and their social environments must possess the ability to adapt for successful aging to occur (Nigg, Steigl, 2005).

6. **Continuity Theory:** Sociologist R.C. Atchley proposed the theory of continuity in 1989, suggesting that the best way to adapt to old age is by maintaining both inner and outer structure. Inner continuity involves preserving mental state, ideas, temperament, emotions, experiences, hobbies, and abilities, while external continuity involves maintaining social connections, familiar surroundings, and interacting with familiar people. Atchley emphasized the importance of using personal initiative and responding to environmental pressures as motivations for maintaining continuity. As individuals age, changes may threaten this continuity, affecting their sense of identity.
7. **Cultural and Anthropological Theories:** Ethnological and sociological factors play an important role in shaping the human psyche, and certain theories consider these factors in their analysis. One such theory is the modernity theory proposed by D.O. Cowgill and C.D. Holmes (Martin & Kinsella, 1994), which suggests that the status and care available for elderly individuals deteriorate as societies become more modern. According to this theory, the level of modernization is determined by factors such as industrialization, urbanization, demographic and economic conditions, medical advancements, social organization, education, religion, and climate change, all of which contribute to a decline in the status of elderly people. Despite this, elderly individuals in modern societies often hold more positive ideas and expectations about old age compared to those in less developed societies. However, critics argue that this theory may not apply universally, as evidenced by the positive perception of old age in countries like Japan, despite their high level of development. Nevertheless, studies exploring intercultural differences have shed light on the relationship between cognition and aging.
8. **Interactive Model of Longevity and Healthy Aging:** Some theories suggest that satisfactory old age and longevity are influenced by a combination of physical, mental, and social factors. Genetic, physiological, and environmental factors all play a role, but none of them alone determines longevity or satisfaction in old age. (U. Lehr,1982). Research shows that genetic, physiological, and biological factors directly affect how long someone lives and how their personality develops.

Socialization processes, such as education and family background, also shape development. Additionally, environmental factors like climate can impact longevity. Personality traits influence education, occupation, and social status, which in turn affect longevity. Eating habits, influenced by social status, personality, and environmental factors, also plays a role in how long someone lives. Lifestyle choices, including physical activity, hygiene, and preventive measures are important for longevity. Lifestyle, genetics, and personality traits all influence each other. Healthy living is influenced by factors like ecology, education, and social status. This model doesn't capture every possible influence, and further research will likely lead to adjustments and refinements.

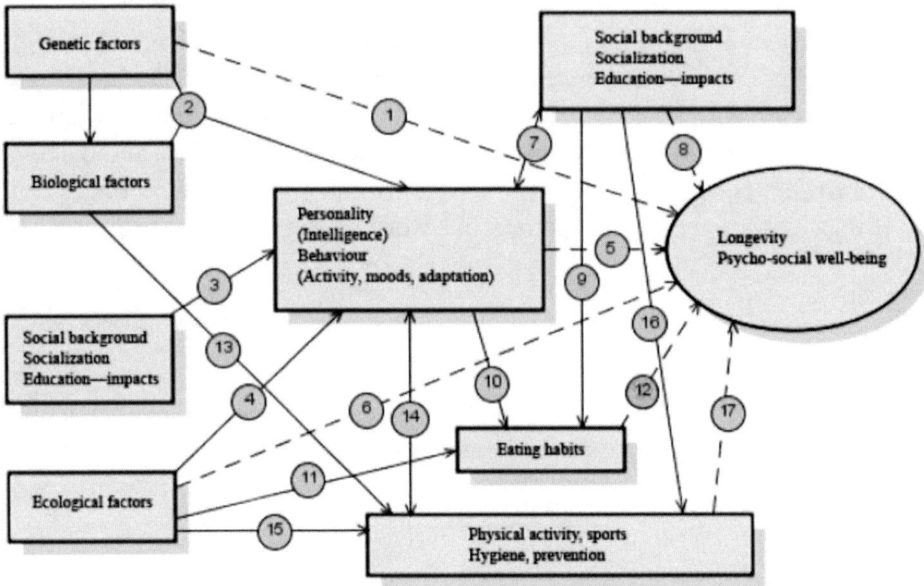

Figure 1: Factors of longevity and relations between them

At a conceptual level, successful aging can be seen as striving to maximize gains while minimizing losses. However, establishing specific and universally accepted criteria for successful aging is challenging. It's unrealistic to create a theory that comprehensively explains all aspects of aging. Instead, researchers often focus on individual factors, such as objective versus subjective measures, short-term versus long-term outcomes, specific versus universal factors, and static versus dynamic elements. While this approach may not fully explain the complexity of aging, it helps to shed light on certain aspects of the phenomenon. Successful aging can manifest in various ways, as noted by (Pulkkinen, 2000), who describes it as diverse and multifaceted. None of the existing theories offer a complete portrayal of old age and aging. If, as K. Popper suggests, a theory is like a net attempting to capture the world, then the theory of aging resembles a net with many gaps. (Freund & Riedger, 2003)

Strategies to Enhance Positive Aging

1. **Reducing Ageism:** The negative stereotypes about age, like the belief that young people can't be leaders or that old people can't be active, are made up by society. This leads to people being seen as less valuable, treated unfairly, and discriminated against because of their age. This not only harms people's mental and physical health (Stephan, Sutin, & Terraciano, 2015), but also affects how old they feel based on what they see and hear about age. Levy (2018) has suggested a PEACE model to fight ageism through positive education and contact experiences. Learning about aging with positive examples of older people can help us see getting older in a better light and understand that the negative beliefs about aging are wrong. Having positive experiences with people of different ages can bring generations closer together, like working together on a project.

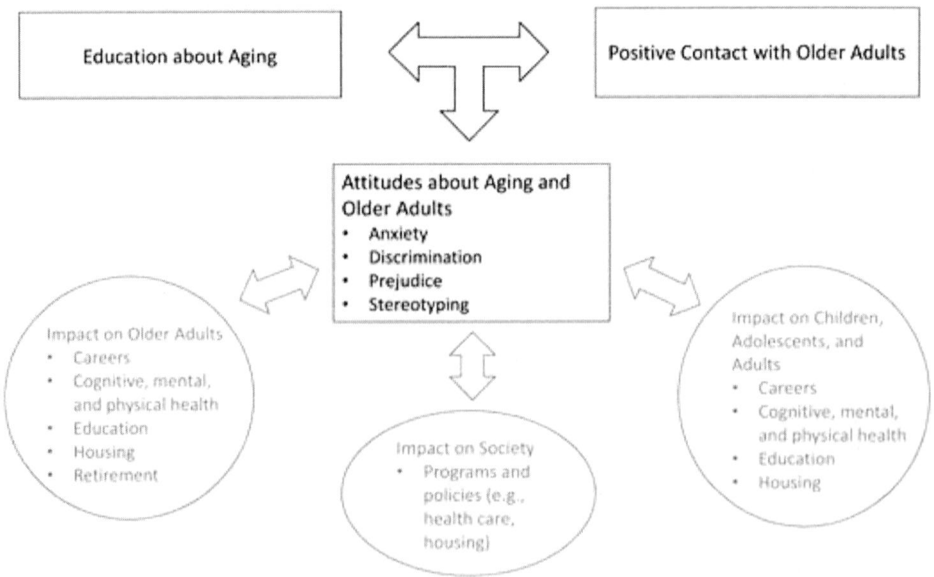

PEACE Model to Reduce Ageism (Levi, 2016)

2. **Productive Aging:** Productive aging includes the innumerable ways in which older individuals actively contribute to their own well-being and that of society beyond the narrow confines of financial gain. This concept, as articulated by scholars like Bass, Caro, and Chen (1993), and Ranzijn (2002), emphasizes that the value of older adults extends well beyond their economic output. It includes paid employment where they provide goods or services, demonstrating that seniors can still play vital roles in the workforce. Equally important, however, is their engagement in unpaid activities such as volunteering, mentoring, and imparting their accumulated wisdom and knowledge. These contributions can significantly enhance community well-being and intergenerational solidarity. Productive aging challenges the traditional perception that usefulness is solely tied to monetary productivity. Instead, it recognizes the diverse and profound ways older adults can enrich society, advocating for a broader appreciation of their roles and acknowledging the importance of their social and cultural contributions. This holistic approach to aging underscores the notion that the elderly are not merely passive recipients of care but active, valuable participants in the social fabric.
3. **Accepting Death Anxiety:** Talking about death can be scary for many people. There's often a taboo around the topic, which can make us feel anxious or fearful. As people grow older, this fear might feel more real. It can even become emotionally challenging, especially in old age. However, some experts, like Wong and Tomer (2011), suggest that accepting fear of death can actually be helpful. They believe that acknowledging this anxiety can make people stronger, give more meaning to their lives, and help them to flourish. Having a positive attitude and accepting the idea of death can also improve overall well-being. In simpler terms, facing our fear of death can be beneficial. It can make us more resilient and help us find greater purpose in life. This positive outlook can ultimately lead to a better quality of life.

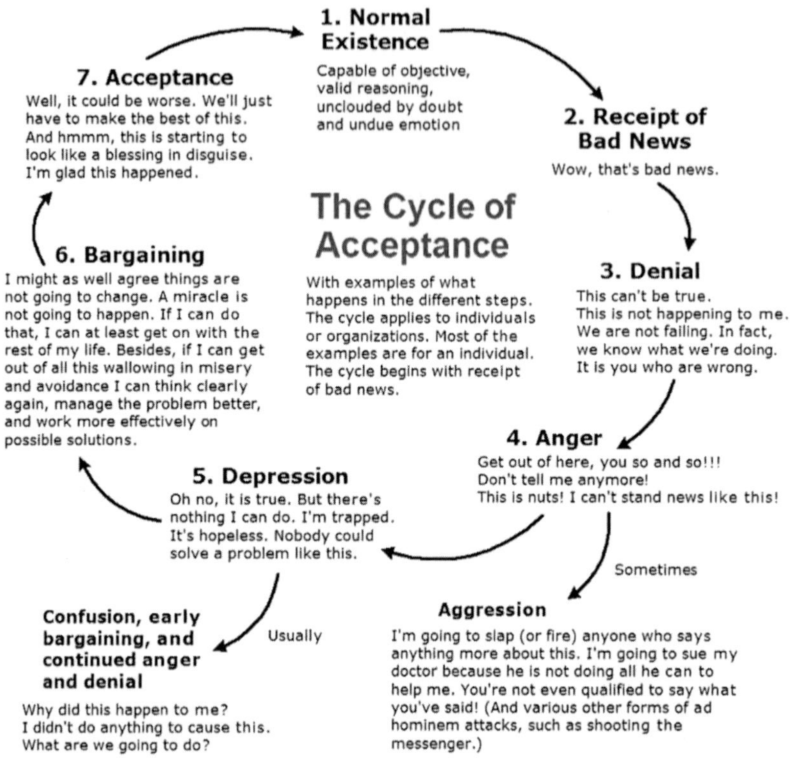

4. **Positive Health:** Subjective aging, or how one perceives oneself getting older, can have a big impact on mental and emotional well-being. It might make people feel lonely, anxious, or depressed, and even affect their physical health, like causing pain or disability. This can create a lot of stress, create sleep disturbances, and make it hard to stay motivated or take care of oneself. Positive approaches can help lessen these negative effects, like boosting ability to cope, reducing the risk of injury, and lowering reliance on pain medication. Positive psychology, a field that focuses on what makes life fulfilling and meaningful, has shown promise in helping with health issues related to aging. For example, being optimistic can improve overall health, while practices like mindfulness meditation can ease back pain, improve sleep, and even slow down the aging process. Other positive strategies, like being creative, having hope, finding humor, showing self-compassion, or connecting with spirituality, have also been found to help older adults deal with challenges like dementia and the effects of aging in a more positive way.

5. **PERMA:** The PERMA model, developed by psychologist Martin Seligman, outlines five essential elements for well-being: Positive Emotions, Engagement, Relationships, Meaning, and Accomplishment. Each component can be utilized in promoting positive aging:
    1. **Positive Emotions:** Encouraging older adults to cultivate positive emotions such as joy, gratitude, and contentment can enhance their overall well-being. This might involve engaging in activities they enjoy, spending time with loved ones, or practicing mindfulness and gratitude exercises.
    2. **Engagement:** Promoting engagement refers to helping older adults find activities that fully absorb their attention and foster a state of flow. This could include hobbies, volunteering, learning new skills, or participating in social groups and community events that align with their interests. It is also called 'Ikigai' by the Okinawans, the reason for getting up in the morning
    3. **Relationships:** Social connections are crucial for positive aging. Encouraging older adults to maintain and strengthen connection with family, friends, and community members can provide emotional support, companionship, and a sense of belonging.
    4. **Meaning:** Helping older adults find meaning and purpose in their lives is essential for positive aging. This might involve encouraging them to reflect on their values, beliefs, and personal goals, and to engage in activities that align with their sense of purpose, whether it's through volunteering, mentoring, or pursuing lifelong passions.
    5. **Accomplishment:** Supporting older adults in setting and achieving meaningful goals can contribute to their sense of accomplishment and self-esteem. This could involve setting realistic goals related to health, personal development, or contributing to the community, and celebrating their achievements along the way.

    Incorporating the PERMA model into support programs for older adults can help in developing a holistic approach to positive aging that addresses their emotional, social, and psychological well-being. By focusing on these five elements, older adults can cultivate a fulfilling and meaningful life as they age.
6. **Promoting Comprehensive Mental and Physical Well-being in Older Adults:** Many healthcare professionals overlook the holistic nature of older adults' health, focusing only on their cognitive and physical well-being. However, a thorough evaluation in mental health clinics

and centers for comprehensive care should consider various aspects of a person's life, including their social, cultural, historical, and spiritual background. This wider outlook allows for a better understanding of the individual's overall positive health. For instance, depression is widespread among older adults, yet many do not receive psychological interventions, leading to failure to diagnosis and inadequate treatment. Somatization, where psychological distress manifests as physical symptoms, contributes to missed diagnoses of depression. Additionally, older men, especially those with chronic physical illnesses or disabilities, are at heightened risk of suicide.

To tackle these challenges and encourage healthy aging, positive health programs aim to empower seniors by emphasizing their strengths and resources. These programs promote physical, cognitive, and social well-being through dietary improvements, reducing tobacco and alcohol consumption and on the other hand, increasing physical activity, and adopting stress management techniques. By following these guidelines, seniors can alleviate the impact of diseases on their health and positively influence cognitive function and mood stability. Healthcare professionals play a crucial role in implementing such interventions and reaching out to older adults in their communities to encourage participation in health promotion activities.

Shifting focus to strengths in elderly care: Instead of just looking at what's wrong with older adults, practitioners and therapists should focus more on their strengths and abilities. Instead of seeing vulnerability or low mood as the main issues, they should identify and activate the person's strengths and abilities, as well as the support from family, friends, and the community. This approach helps individuals in achieving their objectives and prevents potential problems.

Summary

In the journey of aging, one undeniable truth emerges attitude matters. Regardless of age, our perspective shapes our experience. While positive aging isn't always a picturesque path adorned with roses and daffodils, it's the lens through which we view the journey that ultimately dictates its quality. Research consistently emphasizes the profound impact of attitude on aging, affirming that our mindset reigns supreme in facing the problems and joys that come with growing older. Positive psychology is a newer realm of psychology with its interests in younger generations. However, there is a gamut of evidence to suggest that positive psychological interventions can be effective for older adults as well. Positive psychology would serve to better the well-being in a rapidly growing population. Positive psychology offers a ray of hope in this regard, providing a framework that empowers individuals to cultivate resilience, find meaning, and develop well-being as they age. It acknowledges that aging involves a diverse collection of experiences, including successes and challenges, and provides individuals with resources to cross this path with strength and dignity. At the heart of positive psychology lies the belief in the transformative power of positivity. It emphasizes the importance of nurturing positive emotions, cultivating meaningful relationships, and using one's strengths to flourish in later life. Positive Psychology offers a new science and framework to conduct research on the values and strengths of old age. Older adults are important members of society who are still capable of success and fulfillment. Aging does equate to detriment. It is time that psychology shifts the paradigm of a deficit orientation to a strengths orientation.

CHAPTER 5

APPLICATION OF POSITIVE PSYCHOLOGY IN EDUCATION

Children form the foundation of any society. Nurturing them is important for their overall growth and their contribution to the nation. Each child is different, influenced by their unique backgrounds. Parents and schools play a significant role in shaping their lives. Providing them with a solid educational foundation ensures they have the skills and knowledge needed to contribute positively to their communities and the world. Additionally, proper care and education help children develop into well-rounded individuals, leading to better outcomes for both them and society. Understanding these influences is crucial for comprehensive child development. Positive psychology, which highlights individuals' strengths and goodness, shows potential for promoting children's well-being. By focusing on what's good in children, we can help them develop. Investing in children's well-being ensures a brighter future for society as a whole.

Today's youth face increasing stress and complexity, impacting their mental health adversely (Waters, 2011). Rising levels of distress and depression among students highlight the urgent need to equip them with resilience, optimism, and hope to mitigate the risk of mental illnesses. Given that students spend a significant portion of their waking hours at school, it serves as an ideal environment for addressing their well-being. Positive schools prioritize students' subjective well-being, fostering positive emotions and attitudes toward learning (Huebner et al., 2004). Positive education, an application of positive psychology, emphasizes emotional well-being and social skills alongside academic achievement. Recognizing the importance of emotional well-being alongside cognitive abilities, schools are shifting towards a holistic approach to student development. Positive education aims to cultivate healthier individuals who contribute positively to society, focusing on nurturing talents for holistic growth. Its fundamental goal is to promote flourishing and positive mental health within the school community (Seligman et al., 2009). Evidence-based coaching, a component of positive education, enhances well-being, resilience, and goal-setting skills in both students and teachers (Green, Grant & Rynsaardt, 2007; Grant, Green, & Rynsaardt, 2010). By equipping individuals with competencies for constructive problem-solving and goal-setting, positive education develops personal development and societal contribution.

In this chapter, we explore how positive psychology principles can be applied in both school and education to foster happy, healthy, and resilient future generations. Since schools are where young people learn about who they are and how to interact with others, they're perfect for introducing positive psychology activities that make students feel better.

Introduction

A school is an educational institution where children receive instruction in various subjects, develop social skills, and engage in extracurricular activities. It serves as a foundational environment for intellectual growth, emotional development, and social interaction. Schools play a crucial role in shaping a child's future by providing structured learning experiences, developing critical thinking, and encouraging curiosity. Schools help children develop essential life skills, such as teamwork, communication, and problem-solving. Overall, a supportive school environment is vital for nurturing well-rounded individuals prepared to contribute positively to society.

The Role of Schools and Parents in Supporting Children's Development

1. **Establishing Responsive Relationships with Parents:** A strong, responsive relationship between parents and children is fundamental. Parents should actively listen to their children's concerns, validate their feelings, and provide consistent support. Schools can facilitate parental involvement through regular communication, workshops, and parent-teacher meetings, ensuring that parents are engaged in their child's academic and emotional development. Parents and educators can model positive behaviors such as empathy, patience, and resilience, which children can emulate.
2. **Strengthening Core Skills like Cognition and Emotion Regulation:** Schools should focus on enhancing cognitive skills through engaging and challenging curriculum activities that stimulate critical thinking and problem-solving abilities. Teaching children how to manage their emotions is crucial. Schools can integrate Social-Emotional Learning (SEL) programs that include mindfulness, emotional literacy, and stress

management techniques. Activities that promote self-reflection, such as journaling and group discussions, help children understand and regulate their emotions better.

3. **Reducing Sources of Stress:** Schools must create a welcoming and inclusive environment where students feel safe and supported. Anti-bullying programs and inclusive policies are vital in this regard. Incorporating regular breaks, physical activities, and creative outlets like art and music can help reduce stress. Additionally, ensuring a balanced workload can prevent academic pressure from becoming overwhelming. Providing access to counseling services, stress management workshops, and peer support groups can help students manage stress effectively. Schools can also educate parents on recognizing signs of stress and anxiety in their children and ways to address them.

By focusing on these three core principles—establishing responsive relationships with parents, strengthening core cognitive and emotional skills, and reducing sources of stress—schools and parents can create a nurturing environment that supports the holistic development of children. This comprehensive approach not only addresses immediate educational needs but also develops long-term well-being and resilience, equipping children to face the complexities of their world with confidence and competence.

Positive Education integrates Well-being and Academic Achievement

- **Bridging the Gap Between Parental Aspirations and School Focus:** Positive Education, as proposed by Seligman et al. in 2009, seeks to address the significant discrepancy between parents desires for their children and the traditional goals of schooling. Parents typically aspire for their children to be happy, healthy, and confident, whereas schools often emphasize academic achievement, discipline, and cognitive skills. While these academic goals are undeniably important, they do not encompass the holistic development of a child. Positive education aims to bridge this divide by incorporating principles from positive psychology into the educational curriculum, ensuring that the emotional and psychological well-being of students is given as much importance as academic achievement.
- **Historical Context and Philosophical Foundations:** The integration of psychological interventions in schools is not a novel concept. Since the 1930s, educational systems have implemented various psychological approaches to support students. Positive Education builds on this foundation, supplementing traditional psychological methods with the principles of positive psychology. Philosophers like Aristotle have

long underscored the importance of happiness as the ultimate goal of education, reinforcing the idea that student well-being should be a primary focus. Positive education thus aligns with historical and philosophical perspectives that advocate for the comprehensive development of individuals through education.

- **The Role of Teachers and Emotional Support:** Teachers inherently understand the connection between student well-being and effective teaching. Maslow's hierarchy of needs supports the notion that emotional support is essential for higher-order cognitive functions, such as learning. Research indicates that providing emotional support at the beginning of the school year enhances instructional quality later on. Therefore, positive education does not suggest replacing academic achievement with mental health concerns, but rather recognizes that developing mental health is crucial for academic success. This integrated approach ensures that students are emotionally supported, which in turn facilitates better learning outcomes.
- **Educational Psychology and Positive Psychology:** Educational psychology has traditionally focused on promoting self-esteem, meaning, and self-confidence among students. Positive psychology extends this focus by developing theoretical models for the good life, applicable beyond formal education and into lifelong learning. Pioneers like Martin E. P. Seligman emphasize the role of education in achieving optimal functioning and preventing mental health issues such as depression. Positive psychology challenges the deterministic view that individuals are merely products of their biology, demographics, and experiences. Instead, it highlights the agency of individuals in shaping their well-being, with education playing a pivotal role in this process.
- **A Paradigm Shift in Education:** Positive Education represents a paradigm shift in the approach to schooling. It acknowledges the importance of academic achievement while simultaneously prioritizing the mental health and well-being of students. By integrating positive psychology principles into educational practices, positive education aims to create happier, healthier, and more resilient individuals. This approach aligns with broader societal goals of promoting well-being and fulfillment. Education, therefore, extends beyond the classroom, encompassing lifelong learning and personal growth, and Positive Education offers a framework for nurturing individuals who are not only academically proficient but also emotionally resilient and psychologically empowered.

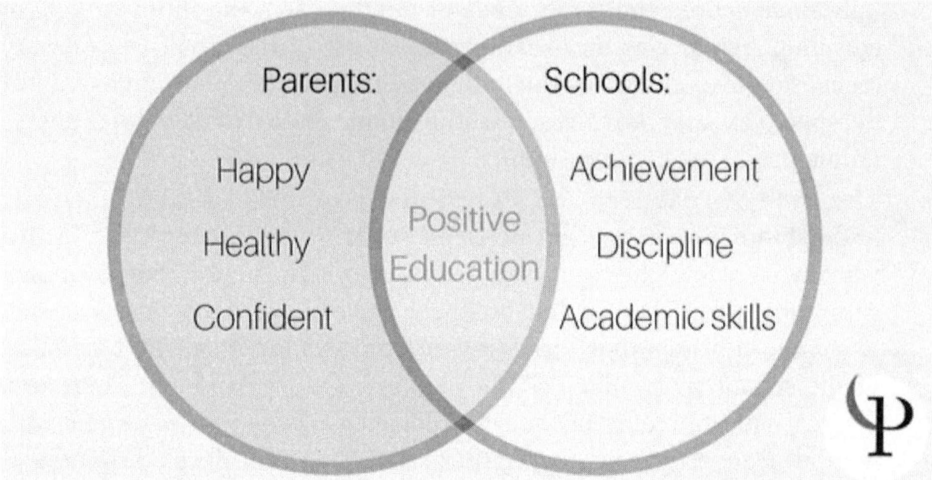

Positive Schooling

Schooling serves as the cornerstone of a child's formative years, profoundly shaping their development. The choice of educational institution, the caliber of educators, the dynamics within the school community, and the overall experiences encountered all play an important role in shaping a child's growth. A positive school environment promotes not only academic advancement but also facilitates skill acquisition, nurtures personality development, and cultivates a sense of confidence. In essence, schooling aims to provide an enriching experience that serves as a foundation for a child's journey toward self-discovery and fulfillment. Teachers, akin to second parents during the early stages of schooling, play a crucial role in providing guidance, support, and care. The educational journey should empower children, instilling within them the confidence and resilience needed to navigate life's challenges. Moreover, education should transcend the mere imparting of knowledge; it should strive to cultivate character and wisdom. The ultimate goal is to facilitate holistic development encompassing physical, mental, social, emotional, moral, and spiritual dimensions. Such a comprehensive approach not only equips children to achieve personal happiness and success but also encourages them to contribute positively to the well-being of society. When a child embark on their first day of school, they seek a nurturing environment characterized by love, care, and support. They anticipate opportunities for exploration and learning, as well as a sense of inclusion and belonging within the school community. Similarly, parents harbor expectations that their children will be nurtured, protected, and provided with the tools necessary for future success.

Crucially, developing a positive school environment requires prioritizing equity and inclusivity. Regardless of background or ability, every child should feel valued, respected, and supported within the school community. Upholding principles of fairness and inclusivity not only promotes academic success but also develops a sense of safety and belonging for all students.

Achieving a Positive School Experience Involves Addressing Three Key Dimensions:

1. **Physical Dimension:** This encompasses ensuring adequate infrastructure within classrooms and throughout the school premises. It includes provisions for essential facilities such as well-equipped laboratories, spacious playgrounds, clean drinking water, and accessible toilets, catering to the needs of all students, including those with disabilities. Schools should strive to maintain clean, green spaces that foster an inviting and stimulating atmosphere conducive to learning.
2. **Psychological Dimension:** Schools must offer opportunities to enhance both cognitive abilities and psychological well-being among students. Utilizing innovative teaching methodologies sustains students' interest in learning and nurtures their creativity. Implementing appropriate disciplinary practices fosters self-regulation and contributes to students' mental health.
3. **Socio-emotional Dimension:** Cultivating a warm and welcoming school climate is crucial. Schooling should promote self-awareness regarding emotions, attitudes, beliefs, and values, while also fostering interpersonal skills. Access to various support services ensures that the emotional and mental health needs of students are addressed effectively.

Positive schooling endeavors to establish a supportive environment where children feel safe, valued, and embraced. It actively encourages positive behaviors and interactions among students, aiming to integrate the physical, cognitive, and emotional aspects of their development comprehensively. Moreover, schooling is not solely about academic education and career preparedness; it also serves as a platform for instilling values, transmitting culture, nurturing compassion, and promoting the well-being of all individuals within the school community. By addressing these dimensions, schools play a pivotal role in shaping well-rounded individuals equipped not only with knowledge and skills but also with the moral and emotional intelligence necessary for a fulfilling life.

A Whole School Approach

In addition to focusing on the well-being of children, a comprehensive approach to positive schooling also involves addressing the needs of all stakeholders within the school community. This "whole school approach" advocates for collective action toward creating a positive climate that nurtures the development of students. It emphasizes the importance of fostering mental health and well-being as a shared responsibility among all members of the school community. Whole school thinking encourages everyone within the school environment to prioritize well-being and mental health. As highlighted by Weare (2015), it underscores that well-being and mental health are concerns that involve everyone within the school community.

Key aspects of this approach include:

- Involving students in various aspects of school life, including decision-making, and providing opportunities for them to voice their opinions.
- Actively teaching social and emotional skills, attitudes, and values to students.
- Ensuring teachers are well-trained and regularly updating their knowledge and skills through ongoing professional development.
- Offering support services and interventions to assist students facing difficulties, disabilities, or hardships.
- Engaging parents and families in school activities and fostering strong partnerships between home and school.
- Employing specialist staff to address the specific needs of students and promoting a collaborative approach among the school community.

This holistic approach to the entire school experience integrates various components to promote well-being and address mental health concerns, as supported by the National Healthy Schools Program (2006). It recognizes that the well-being of students, teachers, school leaders, staff, and parents is interconnected and essential for creating a positive school climate. An exemplary model of this approach is the Positive Education program implemented by Geelong Grammar School in Australia, as described by Seligman et al. (2009). This program, rooted in the principles of positive psychology, focuses not only on academic achievement but also on enhancing the well-being and flourishing of students and staff. By prioritizing both success and happiness, positive education offers a holistic framework that values both material prosperity and well-being, ultimately contributing to a more fulfilling and enriching educational experience.

Differences Between Positive Education and Positive Schools

Positive Education	Positive Schools
Focuses on Individual well-being	Considers the entire school community as a "Social System"
Emphasizes individual responsibility	Highlights "Contextual responsibility"
Teaches well-being as a distinct subject	Embeds well-being strategies within the cultural ethos of the school
Utilizes extrinsic motivators for positive behaviors	Emphasizes "autonomous motivation" for fostering well-being
Primarily Psychological approach	Socio-Psychological approach

These differences highlight how positive education and positive schools approach the goal of achieving well-being within the school community from distinct perspectives.

Importance of Positive Psychology in Education

In today's complex world, children are immersed in a digital landscape dominated by media and technology, profoundly shaping their interactions and experiences. While this digital reality is unavoidable, it's essential to equip children with core values and resilience to navigate this ever-changing landscape effectively. Positive psychology offers a transformative approach to enhancing the school experience, enabling children to not only succeed but also thrive. Amidst the pressures of modern society, including heightened media usage and shifting societal norms, children, and adolescents face mounting stress and anxiety. By embedding principles of positive psychology into education, schools can cultivate a supportive environment that nurtures the holistic development of children, equipping them with the tools and mindset needed to thrive amidst the challenges of the modern world. Positive psychology is helpful in education in the following ways:

1. **Enhances Mental Health and Well-Being:** Positive psychology emphasizes proactive strategies to enhance students' mental health, reducing the prevalence of anxiety, depression, and stress-related disorders. It teaches students techniques for managing their emotions, and developing a sense of stability and well-being.
2. **Builds Resilience and Coping Skills:** Students learn to bounce back from setbacks and challenges, essential for overcoming obstacles both in

school and in life. By incorporating positive psychology, schools provide students with tools to handle stress and adversity effectively.

3. **Promotes Holistic Development:** Positive psychology ensures that education addresses intellectual, emotional, social, and psychological development, producing well-rounded individuals. Students are encouraged to explore their strengths, values, and interests, leading to personal growth and fulfillment.
4. **Improves Academic Performance:** A positive mental state can improve concentration and cognitive function, leading to better academic outcomes. Students who feel good about themselves are more motivated and engaged in their studies, which can enhance learning and retention.
5. **Enhances Life Satisfaction and Happiness:** By developing positive emotions, schools help students experience greater satisfaction and happiness, which can enhance their overall quality of life. Techniques such as gratitude exercises, mindfulness, and positive thinking are incorporated into the curriculum to boost overall happiness.
6. **Encourages Social Responsibility and Empathy:** Positive psychology promotes empathy and compassion, helping students to understand and connect with others. Students are encouraged to participate in community service and social initiatives, fostering a sense of social responsibility.
7. **Nurtures Creativity and Innovation:** A supportive and positive learning environment encourages creative thinking and innovation, allowing students to explore and express new ideas. Positive psychology encourages a solution-oriented mindset, helping students develop effective problem-solving skills.
8. **Reduction of Depression and Anxiety:** Positive psychology offers preventative measures that reduce the onset of depression and anxiety, creating a healthier school environment. Schools can establish support systems and programs that promote mental health and well-being among students.
9. **Supports Lifelong Learning:** Positive psychology fosters a growth mindset, where students see challenges as opportunities for growth, leading to a lifelong love of learning. By focusing on intrinsic motivation, students are encouraged to pursue learning for personal satisfaction and growth, beyond external rewards.
10. **Aligns with Broader Societal Goals:** Positive psychology promotes values such as cooperation, respect, and kindness, contributing to a more harmonious society. The emphasis on well-being aligns with societal

goals of promoting mental health and overall life satisfaction, preparing students to be contributing members of society.

By integrating these principles, positive psychology transforms the educational experience, making it more comprehensive and conducive to the overall development of students. This approach not only prepares students academically but also equips them with the emotional and social skills necessary to thrive in an increasingly complex world.

Components of Positive Education

When applying positive psychology in the school environment, it's crucial to establish a foundation based on care, trust, and inclusivity. Snyder, Lopez, and Pedrotti (2011) propose a holistic framework for a positive schoolhouse, comprising five key components:

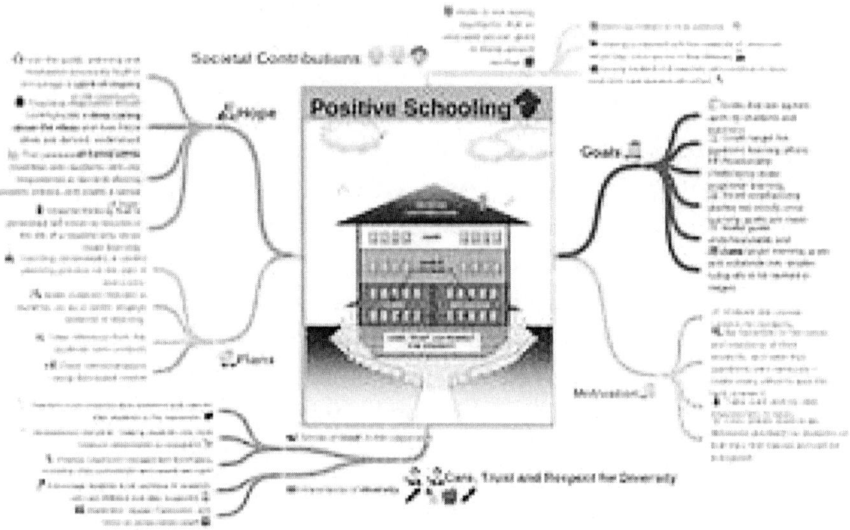

- **Foundation-Level-Care, Trust, and Respect for Diversity:** This level signifies the importance of values such as love and care in building such environments. Students look up to their teachers and make them their role models. Thus, these values are deemed important. Trust is very important and needs to start early in the younger classes. Trust has a contagion effect and that spreads to the entire class, even if the teacher starts with building trust with a few students first. Watson and Ecken (2003) stated, "The building of caring and trusting relationships becomes the most important goal in the socialization of these children. Trust can be developed amongst students by not being cynical about them but showing one's love and care for them. It is highly imperative for the teacher to have a patient ear to listen to the children's problems and understand them with empathy; trying to understand the student's perspective is equally important. Also, respecting diversity is critical. Students come from varied cultural backgrounds. Thus, understanding and respecting their diversity as teachers is appreciable. Moving away from prejudice and discrimination also paves a strong trust between the teacher and the student. Also, making other students aware of the sensitivities of people who come from different backgrounds is essential. Highlighting similarities between the students and also making them aware that differences need to be valued and respected. Encouraging students to make friends with students coming from different ages, races, ethnic backgrounds, etc. points to what positive education emphasizes. This increases their understanding of different cultures and also enhances their social skills in dealing with people from different backgrounds. This effort is inclusive. Positive psychology is dedicated to building the best in life. Thus, including the genius and showing care and love for them is equally important, rather than assuming that they are bright, and can take care of themselves.

- **First Floor-Plans and Motivation:** Planning is, of course, very important, be it in any sphere of life. Planning to keep students motivated is of the utmost importance. For example, Robert Cialdini came up with a program wherein certain mystery stories were given to the students pertaining to certain topics. By getting involved in the stories, the students automatically learn the content for which the stories were made. Motivation can also be kept alive by bringing an enthusiastic attitude to the classroom. This positive energy flows to the students and acts like a contagion. Being sensitive to the needs and questions that are raised in the class should be taken care of with sincerity. If the teacher doesn't know the answer to a question that is raised in the class, it is completely okay. But the teacher should subsequently put in every effort to know the answer and also take it up in the next class with the students. Motivation to stay alert and active in class can be brought about by making the class as interactive as possible. Asking students questions increases their motivation to read and come for the next class. Another very crucial way of motivating students is to praise them. Praise can be given privately, or it can even be given in public. Praising a student for his efforts in front of others helps in increasing competition, and thus the performance of the class can increase altogether. It has been found by Hurlock (1925) that praise is more effective for children regardless of age, ability, and gender. However, Henderlong and Lepper (2002) found that praise is proven to be positively correlated with confidence and better academic performance results.

- **Second Floor: Goal (content):** Goals that are set mutually between the teacher and the student aim at a greater probability of achieving success. Snyder, Lopez and Pedrotti (2011) state that "the most conducive targets are the stretch goals, in which the student seeks a slightly more difficult learning goal than attained previously. Reasonably challenging goals engender productive learning, especially if the goals can be tailored to particular students (or groups of students). Setting goals for daily classes is usually done by the teacher himself; however, designing the course content and setting goals according to the level and interest of the students keeps them highly engrossed and involved. The marking scheme should not be very strict. The teacher should focus on their learning inputs rather than putting in effort to get better grades. Stepping toward goals also increases the probability of achieving success, and also keeping informing the students of their progress that keeps them motivated at the task. Goals, as mentioned earlier, should be mutually agreed upon, concrete, and also understandable to the students.
- **Third Floor: Hope:** Teaching involves passion on the part of teacher or the educator. There has to be a love for the subject that the teacher is teaching. It is only through this attitude that a teacher can bring this positive zeal to the students. This perspective on learning instills a push at the end of the student to continuously acquire more and more knowledge. This instills in the students a continuous, vicious cycle of gaining knowledge. Thus, positive psychology imparts and produces a sense of hope in the students who wish to learn and gain knowledge. A hopeful student believes that she or he will continue to learn long after stepping out of the classroom (Snyder, Lopez & Pedrotti, 2011).
- **Roof: Contributions to Society:** Societal contribution indicates the social obligation that the students have for society. It is hoped that the students, as they have now gained knowledge, will pass this on and share it with other people who they continuously meet in the course of their lifetime. The students now share the knowledge that they have with other people. Thus, they are now turning into being teachers for other people.

Through this way, pupils in a way give back to society what they have learned, for its improvement.

Care and trust are fundamental in developing both academic achievement and psychological well-being among students, particularly those from disadvantaged backgrounds (Gilman, Huebner, & Buckman, 2008; Collins, 2001). Embracing diversity in attitudes, beliefs, and behaviors based on various social factors is equally essential for creating an inclusive learning environment. Setting clear goals tailored to each student's needs and involving practical, culturally relevant learning experiences are essential for achieving positive outcomes. Motivating students to engage in learning activities is vital for their academic success and overall development. Hope serves as a cornerstone of positive schooling, emphasizing the importance of instilling in students the belief that they can learn and grow throughout their lives (Snyder, Lopez, & Pedrotti, 2011). Teachers play a crucial role in nurturing students' aspirations and empowering them to pursue lifelong learning.

Models for Positive Education

Positive Education models, rooted in Seligman's PERMA model, include various approaches aimed at developing well-being and personal development. Among these models are:

1. **Eliot Aronson's 'Jigsaw Classroom':** Eliot Aronson's "Jigsaw Classroom" is an innovative cooperative learning approach designed to enhance collaboration, self-esteem, and intergroup relations among students. In this model, each student is assigned a unique piece of information that is essential for completing a group task or project. This setup ensures that every member of the group must contribute their knowledge and work together to achieve the common goal, thereby developing a sense of interdependence and collective responsibility. The Jigsaw Classroom method has been shown to promote positive social interactions and reduce stereotypes, as it encourages students to appreciate the diverse perspectives and strengths of their peers. By engaging in this cooperative learning process, students develop higher self-esteem and empathy as they realize their valuable role in the group's success and learn to respect and understand different backgrounds and viewpoints. Ultimately, the Jigsaw Classroom cultivates a supportive and inclusive educational environment where positive intergroup relations can flourish, leading to a more harmonious and effective learning experience for all students.

2) **Response to Intervention Model:** The Response to Intervention (RTI) model is a proactive, multi-tiered approach designed to identify and support students at risk of or currently experiencing academic challenges, including those with learning disabilities. The primary objective of RTI is to provide early, systematic assistance to students who demonstrate signs of academic struggle, thereby preventing minor issues from escalating into significant learning difficulties. By intervening promptly, RTI aims to address academic deficiencies before they become entrenched, ensuring that all students have the opportunity to succeed.

- **Multi-Tiered Framework of RTI:** RTI operates through a multi-tiered framework that offers varying levels of intervention based on students' specific needs.
  - ➢ The first tier, or universal tier, involves high-quality classroom instruction and regular screening of all students to identify those who may require additional support. In this tier, educators use evidence-based teaching methods and conduct frequent assessments to monitor student progress, ensuring that any academic concerns are detected early.
  - ➢ Students who do not respond adequately to tier one intervention are moved to tier two, where they receive targeted, small-group instruction. This supplemental instruction focuses on specific areas of difficulty and is delivered alongside the regular curriculum. Progress monitoring continues, allowing educators to assess the effectiveness of the interventions and make necessary adjustments.
  - ➢ For students who still struggle despite tier two support, tier three provides intensive, individualized interventions. This highest level of intervention often involves one-on-one instruction and may include special education services for students with diagnosed learning disabilities. The goal of tier three is to address severe and persistent academic challenges through personalized strategies tailored to each student's unique needs.
- **Benefits and Importance of RTI:**

  The RTI model offers several benefits that contribute to its effectiveness in supporting at-risk students.
  - ➢ First, it emphasizes early identification and intervention, reducing the likelihood of long-term academic failure. By addressing learning issues promptly, RTI helps students catch up with

their peers and avoid the negative consequences associated with prolonged academic struggles.

- Second, RTI provides a structured, data-driven approach to intervention. Regular progress monitoring ensures that educators can make informed decisions about the types and intensity of support required for each student. This systematic approach enhances the precision and effectiveness of interventions, leading to better educational outcomes.
- Furthermore, RTI develops a collaborative environment among educators, specialists, and parents. By working together to monitor and support students, these stakeholders can share insights and strategies, ensuring a comprehensive support system. This collaboration is particularly valuable for students with learning disabilities, as it ensures that they receive consistent, well-coordinated care.

The Response to Intervention model is a vital framework for supporting students who are at risk or experiencing academic challenges. By providing timely, systematic interventions through its multi-tiered approach, RTI helps address academic deficiencies and ensures that all students receive the necessary support to thrive. Through early identification, targeted instruction, and ongoing progress monitoring, the RTI model promotes academic success and equity, creating a more inclusive and effective educational environment for all learners.

3. **Positive Behavioral Support Model:** The Positive Behavioral Support (PBS) model is a comprehensive, multi-tiered approach that parallels the Response to Intervention (RTI) framework but extends its focus to include behavioral issues. This model aims to create supportive environments that develop positive behavior and address problematic behaviors through systematic, evidence-based strategies. Like RTI, PBS operates on three levels of intervention, ranging from universal strategies to individualized support.
   - **Universal Level-Promoting Positive Behavior:** At the universal level, PBS involves implementing school-wide strategies to teach and reinforce expected behaviors. This proactive approach includes clearly defining behavioral expectations, teaching these expectations for all students, and consistently reinforcing positive behavior across all school settings. By establishing a cohesive and predictable environment, schools can prevent many behavioral issues

before they arise. Universal strategies also include creating a positive school culture where good behavior is recognized and rewarded, thus encouraging students to adhere to expected norms.

- **Secondary Level-Targeted Group Interventions:** The secondary level of PBS targets students who are at risk of developing behavioral issues. These students may not respond sufficiently to universal strategies and require additional support. At this level, small-group interventions are implemented to address specific behavioral concerns. Interventions may include social skills training, group counseling, and targeted behavioral support plans. These strategies aim to address the underlying causes of at-risk behaviors and provide students with the skills and support needed to improve their conduct and prevent escalation.
- **Tertiary Level-Individualized Intensive Interventions:** For students who exhibit persistent and severe behavioral issues, the tertiary level of PBS provides individualized, intensive interventions. This level involves a thorough assessment of the student's behavior, including identifying triggers, patterns, and underlying factors contributing to the problematic behavior. Based on this assessment, personalized behavior intervention plans are developed, often incorporating collaboration with behavioral specialists, educators, and family members. These plans are designed to address the specific needs of the student, using strategies such as one-on-one support, individualized counseling, and specialized instruction. The goal is to reduce problematic behavior, teach alternative, positive behaviors, and support the student in achieving long-term behavioral improvements.

The Positive Behavioral Support model offers a structured approach to managing and improving student behavior through its three-tiered system. By incorporating strategies that range from universal prevention to individualized intervention, PBS ensures that all students receive the support they need to exhibit positive behavior. This comprehensive model not only addresses behavioral issues effectively but also contributes to a positive and conducive learning environment. Through consistent teaching of expected behaviors, targeted group interventions for at-risk students, and intensive individualized support for those with severe behavioral challenges, the PBS model promotes a holistic and proactive approach to fostering a safe and supportive school community.

4. **The Penn Resiliency Program (PRP):** The Penn Resiliency Program (PRP) is an evidence-based intervention designed to equip children with the necessary tools to manage everyday stressors effectively. By focusing on the development of key psychological skills, PRP aims to develop resilience and promote overall well-being among young people. The program's core components emphasize the enhancement of optimism, realistic problem-solving, and flexible goal-setting, which are crucial for solving life's challenges. The core components of PRP are as follows:
   a) **Enhancing Optimism:** PRP encourages children to adopt a positive outlook by teaching them to view setbacks as temporary and solvable rather than permanent and insurmountable. This optimistic thinking pattern helps reduce feelings of helplessness and develops a proactive attitude toward life's difficulties.
   b) **Realistic Problem-Solving:** The program trains children to approach problems with a realistic mindset, assessing situations accurately, and developing practical solutions. This skill is vital for effectively managing stress and avoiding the cognitive distortions that often lead to negative emotional states.
   c) **Flexible Goal-Setting:** PRP emphasizes the importance of setting flexible, achievable goals. Children learn to adapt to their goals as circumstances change, ensuring that they remain motivated and focused even when faced with obstacles.
   d) **Decision-Making and Assertiveness:** The program also aims to improve children's decision-making abilities and assertiveness. By fostering these skills, PRP helps children make informed choices and communicate their needs and boundaries effectively, reducing the likelihood of behavioral problems.

Research, including extensive meta-analyses, supports the efficacy of the Penn Resiliency Program in several key areas:

- **Reduction of Symptoms:** PRP has been shown to significantly reduce symptoms of depression and helplessness among children. By promoting optimistic thinking and problem-solving skills, the program helps to reduce the cognitive patterns that contribute to these conditions.
- **Prevention of Clinical Disorders:** The program is effective in preventing the onset of clinical levels of depression and anxiety, providing children with the tools to manage stress and emotional challenges before they increase.

- **Reduction of Behavioral Problems:** PRP also helps reduce behavioral issues by promoting assertiveness and decision-making skills, which are crucial for healthy social interactions and self-regulation.
- **Cross-Cultural Efficacy:** Importantly, research indicates that PRP is equally effective across different racial and ethnic backgrounds, demonstrating its adaptability and broad applicability.

Importance of Comprehensive Training and Supervision: The success of the Penn Resiliency Program hinges significantly on the quality of training and supervision provided to group leaders. Comprehensive training ensures that leaders are well-equipped to deliver the program effectively, adhering to its core principles and methodologies. Ongoing supervision supports leaders in maintaining program fidelity, addressing challenges, and continuously improving their facilitation skills. This focus on training and supervision is crucial for maximizing the program's positive impact on students.

The Penn Resiliency Program emerges as a reliable and effective intervention that yields substantial improvements in students' overall well-being. By enhancing optimism, promoting realistic problem-solving, and fostering flexible goal-setting, PRP equips children with the skills necessary to navigate everyday stressors successfully. The program's proven ability to reduce symptoms of depression, prevent clinical disorders, and reduce behavioral problems, combined with its effectiveness across diverse populations, underscores its value as a comprehensive tool for fostering resilience and emotional health in young people.

Theories of Positive Schooling

Two influential models informing positive schooling are the Values in Action (VIA), Classification of Strengths (Peterson & Seligman, 2004) and the PERMA model of well-being (Seligman, 2011).

1. **The VIA Classification (VIA):** It is similar to diagnostic systems for mental disorders like the DSM and ICD, and serves to identify and cultivate psychological strengths and virtues in individuals, thus reshaping traditional approaches to mental health diagnosis and treatment. The VIA classification system comprises 24 character strengths organized under six overarching virtues: Wisdom and knowledge, Courage, Humanity, Justice, Temperance, and Transcendence. Schools can leverage these character strengths to develop a positive climate and enhance students' sense of confidence, capability, and value.

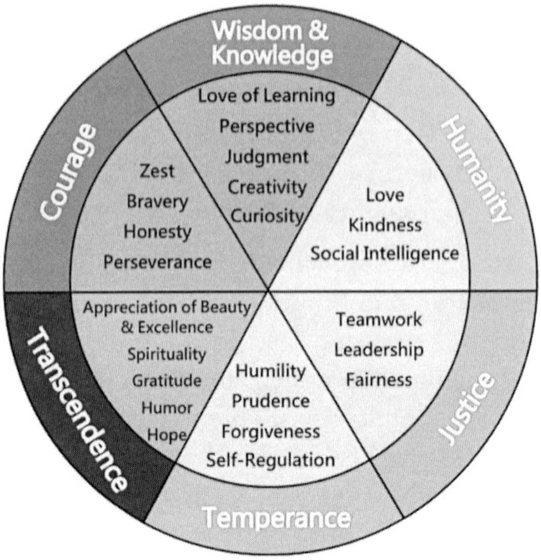

The VIA (Values in Action) Classification of Character Strengths and Virtues is a comprehensive framework developed by positive psychology to identify and classify positive traits in human beings. This classification can be instrumental in the context of Positive Schooling, which aims to create educational environments that promote not just academic learning but also the holistic development of students. Positive Schooling focuses on developing well-being, resilience, and personal growth, preparing students to lead fulfilling and meaningful lives. Let us understand how each of the six virtues and their corresponding character strengths can be integrated into the Positive Schooling concept and how they can benefit students.

1. **Wisdom and Knowledge**
   - **Curiosity:** Encouraging curiosity involves creating an inquiry-based learning environment where students are motivated to ask questions, explore topics in depth, and seek out new information. This can be achieved through project-based learning, research assignments, and field trips.
   - **Love of Learning:** This can be nurtured by providing a variety of learning experiences that cater to different interests and learning styles, encouraging students to pursue their passions, and engaging deeply with subjects they are passionate about.
   - **Judgment:** Teaching students to think critically and make well-formed decisions can be fostered through activities that require

analysis, evaluation, and synthesis of information. Debates, case studies, and problem-solving tasks can help develop this strength.

- **Creativity:** Schools can promote creativity by incorporating arts, music, and innovative projects into the curriculum. Providing opportunities for students to express themselves through various mediums and encouraging out-of-the-box thinking are key strategies.
- **Perspective:** Helping students develop perspective involves teaching them to consider multiple viewpoints and understand broader contexts. Discussions on social issues, literature, and history can cultivate this strength, encouraging empathy and global awareness.

2. **Courage**
   - **Bravery:** Bravery can be encouraged by creating a safe and supportive environment where students feel comfortable taking risks and standing up for their beliefs. Activities like public speaking, leadership roles, and community service can help students practice bravery.
   - **Perseverance:** Building perseverance involves teaching students the value of determination and resilience. Schools can promote this through goal-setting exercises, long-term projects, and celebrating effort and improvement as much as achievements.
   - **Honesty:** Honesty can be emphasized by providing a culture of integrity and openness. Schools can have clear policies against cheating and dishonesty and encourage students to express their true selves and values.
   - **Zest:** Encouraging zest means promoting a lively and energetic approach to life and learning. Schools can incorporate physical activities, enthusiasm in teaching, and an engaging curriculum that captures students' interests.
3. **Humanity**
   - **Love:** Love in the context of schooling refers to building strong, supportive relationships. Teachers can create a nurturing environment by showing genuine care for students, and peer mentoring programs can help to develop friendships and mutual support.

- **Kindness:** Promoting kindness involves encouraging acts of compassion and service. Schools can integrate community service projects, peer support programs, and recognition of kind acts to instill this virtue.
- **Social Intelligence:** Developing social intelligence involves teaching students to navigate social situations effectively. Programs on emotional intelligence, conflict resolution, and teamwork can help students understand and manage their own and others' emotions.

4. **Justice**
   - **Teamwork:** Encouraging teamwork involves collaborative projects and group activities where students learn to work together towards common goals. This fosters cooperation, communication, and a sense of community.
   - **Fairness:** Promoting fairness means ensuring that all students are treated equitably. Schools can teach the importance of justice through discussions on ethical dilemmas, democratic practices in the classroom, and fair policies.
   - **Leadership:** Leadership can be developed by providing students with opportunities to take on leadership roles. Student councils, club leadership, and classroom responsibilities can help cultivate leadership skills.
5. **Temperance**
   - **Forgiveness:** Teaching forgiveness involves encouraging students to let go of grudges and seek reconciliation. Conflict resolution programs and restorative justice practices can help students learn the value of forgiveness.
   - **Humility:** Humility can be fostered by teaching students to recognize their strengths and weaknesses without arrogance. Encouraging reflection, gratitude exercises, and discussions on the importance of humility can help.
   - **Prudence:** Prudence involves teaching students to make careful and thoughtful decisions. Schools can promote this by emphasizing the importance of planning, foreseeing consequences, and considering options before acting.
   - **Self-Regulation:** Developing self-regulation involves helping students manage their emotions and behaviors. Techniques

such as mindfulness, stress management strategies, and setting personal goals can support self-regulation.

6. **Transcendence**
   - **Appreciation of Beauty and Excellence:** Encouraging students to appreciate beauty and excellence can be achieved through exposure to the arts, nature, and celebrating achievements. This can help students recognize and value the good in the world.
   - **Gratitude:** Promoting gratitude involves encouraging students to recognize and appreciate the positive aspects of their lives. Gratitude journals, thank-you notes, and discussions on gratitude can be effective strategies.
   - **Hope:** Fostering hope means helping students develop a positive outlook and set optimistic goals. Schools can support this through motivational talks, goal-setting activities, and celebrating progress and achievements.
   - **Humor:** Incorporating humor involves creating a joyful and positive learning environment. This can be achieved by encouraging laughter, using humor in teaching, and allowing students to express themselves playfully.
   - **Spirituality:** Encouraging spirituality involves helping students explore their own beliefs and values. This can be supported through reflective practices, discussions on meaning and purpose, and providing opportunities for students to connect with their inner selves.

By integrating the VIA classification into the Positive Schooling concept, educators can help students develop a broad range of character strengths that contribute to their overall well-being, academic success, and ability to lead meaningful lives.

2. **PERMA Model:** The PERMA model, developed by Martin Seligman, is a framework for well-being that can be effectively integrated into Positive Schooling to develop a holistic educational environment. The model consists of five elements: Positive Emotion, Engagement, Relationships, Meaning, and Accomplishment. Let us understand how each element can be applied in the context of Positive Schooling:

   1. **Positive Emotion**
      - **Creating a Positive Classroom Environment:** Teachers can develop an atmosphere where students feel happy and safe by

using positive reinforcement, celebrating successes, and creating an inclusive environment.

- **Incorporating Activities:** Teachers should incorporate activities that bring joy such as art, music, games, and mindfulness practices can help students experience positive emotions.
- **Encouraging Gratitude:** Integrating gratitude exercises, such as gratitude journals or thank you notes, can help students focus on positive aspects of their lives.

2. **Engagement**
    - **Promoting Active Learning:** Engaging students through interactive lessons, hands-on projects, and collaborative activities that captivate their interest and attention.
    - **Identifying Strengths and Interests:** Helping students discover and develop their unique strengths and interests, leading to deeper engagement in their learning.
    - **Flow Experiences:** Designing activities that are challenging yet achievable, allowing students to experience flow, where they are fully absorbed and lose track of time.
3. **Relationships**
    - **Building Strong Teacher-Student Relationships:** Teachers can develop trusting and supportive relationships with students, showing genuine care and interest in their well-being.
    - **Encouraging Peer Support:** Creating opportunities for students to form positive connections with peers through group work, peer mentoring, and social activities.
    - **Community Building:** Developing a sense of community within the school through events, traditions, and collaborative projects that bring students together.
4. **Meaning**
    - **Connecting Learning to Real-World Issues:** Helping students see the relevance of their studies by linking lessons to real-world problems and encouraging them to contribute to solutions.
    - **Exploring Purpose:** Encouraging students to reflect on their values, goals, and the impact they want to make in the world, through discussions, writing assignments, and service projects.

- **Incorporating Ethics and Philosophy:** Teaching subjects that explore fundamental questions about life, purpose, and ethics, fosters a deeper sense of meaning in students.

5. **Accomplishment**
    - **Setting and Achieving Goals:** Helping students set realistic and challenging goals, and providing the support and resources they need to achieve them.
    - **Celebrating Successes:** Recognizing and celebrating both small and large achievements to boost students' confidence and motivation.
    - **Developing a Growth Mindset:** Encouraging students to view challenges as opportunities for growth, emphasizing effort and persistence over innate ability.

Integrating PERMA into School Culture

- **Professional Development for Teachers:** Training teachers to understand and apply the PERMA model in their teaching practices and interactions with students.
- **School Policies and Programs:** Designing school policies and programs that promote well-being, such as anti-bullying initiatives, mental health support, and extracurricular activities.
- **Monitoring and Evaluation:** Regularly assessing the well-being of students and staff, using surveys and feedback to continually improve the implementation of the PERMA model.

By integrating the PERMA model into the Positive Schooling approach, schools can create an environment that not only supports academic achievement but also promotes the overall well-being and personal growth of students, preparing them for a fulfilling and meaningful life.

Importance of Positive Schooling

Positive schooling endeavors to provide opportunities for students to engage in each of these aspects. By embracing the principles of PERMA, schools can offer a multidimensional approach to happiness and well-being, encouraging students to participate in activities that promote positive emotions, engagement, meaningful relationships, and a sense of accomplishment.

Applied within the schooling context, this approach involves a diverse range of activities aimed at fostering happiness and well-being, ultimately contributing to a healthy and joyful school environment. Furthermore, positive schooling encourages students to look beyond themselves and contribute meaningfully to their communities and society. By fostering a sense of altruism and social responsibility, students not only find purpose and fulfillment but also contribute to the collective progress of humanity. This reciprocity of learning and giving back enriches one's life, leading to authentic happiness and a sense of meaning and fulfillment.

Happy Teacher= Happy Class

- **Teacher Happiness Matters:** Just like it's important for students to be happy in school, it's equally crucial for teachers to feel happy too. When teachers are happy, it directly impacts how students feel about education. If teachers are joyful and satisfied with their work, it helps students see learning as something enjoyable and positive.
- **Balancing Academic and Emotional Needs:** Teachers play a big role in not just teaching subjects but also in supporting students emotionally. However, sometimes it can feel overwhelming for teachers to manage both the academic and emotional aspects of teaching. If teachers are asked to do more without proper support, it can affect their happiness and effectiveness in the classroom.
- **Teacher Happiness Affects Student Happiness:** Studies have found that when teachers are content with their pay, it reflects positively on their teaching and students' emotional well-being. Teachers who feel they're underpaid or aren't satisfied with their wages tend to have classrooms with lower emotional support, which impacts students negatively. On the

flip side, higher wages for teachers lead to more positive emotions and behaviors among students.

In essence, ensuring that teachers are happy and satisfied with their work is just as important as ensuring student happiness. Happy teachers create positive learning environments that benefit everyone involved.

Application of Positive Psychology Techniques in Education

Devi and Patra (2020) emphasize the importance of interventions in schools that promote mental health among teenagers. Keyes (2002) adds that these programs should not only focus on removing negative factors but also on building positive ones. Positive Psychology Interventions (PPIs) aim to encourage positive behavior, enhance strengths, and help students flourish by boosting their resilience and developing their cognitive, social, and emotional skills.

1. **Positive Emotions- The Three Blessings:** The theory of the broadening-and-building action of positive emotions, as proposed by Barbara Fredrickson, suggests that positive emotions not only indicate well-being but also contribute to it. This theory has significant implications for education, particularly in understanding how positive emotions can enhance learning and development in children. Research shows that children in a positive state of mind learn more quickly. Positive emotions can increase their intellectual resources, such as attention span, creativity, and intuition. They also improve social skills like empathy, cooperation, and kindness, and even boost physical fitness (Fredrickson, 1998). Positive emotions help children see new possibilities and expand their perspectives, allowing them to move beyond their usual thoughts and activities. Moreover, positive emotions indirectly help children cope with stress by increasing their available resources. The "Three Blessings" program is an example of a simple exercise designed to cultivate positive emotions in children. It involves reflecting on three things that went well during the day and exploring the reasons behind their success. This exercise has been shown to enhance happiness in children for up to six months, illustrating the practical benefits of developing positive emotions in education (Wallis, 2005).
2. **Holistic Student Development:** Scholars like Noddings (1995), Palmer (2003), and Cain & Carnellor (2008) stress the importance of nurturing the 'whole student,' encompassing social, emotional, moral, and intellectual growth. PPIs are defined as activities or programs that

cultivate positive feelings, thoughts, and actions (Sin & Lyubomirsky, 2009). Effective programs include those focusing on resilience, hope, happiness, and well-being, such as the "Bounce Back" program and the Happiness Curriculum program. The Happiness Curriculum, initiated by the Government of Delhi in 2018 for students in government schools from nursery to 8th grade, aims at holistic education. It includes a 45-minute "happiness period" comprising mindfulness, stories, activities, and expression. Studies show that students, teachers, and parents are generally satisfied with this curriculum (Devi & Patra, 2020).

3. **Positive Schooling Approach:** While many interventions target individual students, Khanna (2016) suggests the importance of broader positive schooling approaches, focusing on character strengths and well-being among both students and teachers. This approach advocates for creating a positive culture and climate within the entire school community.
   a) **Practicing Gratitude:** Gratitude is important for making people feel better overall (Emmons & McCullough, 2003). In positive psychology, one way to do this is by looking at tough times in your past and finding a way to make them helpful or positive for today and the future. Teachers can help students with this by having a daily gratitude routine in class. At the end of each day, students can think of three things they're thankful for and three things they can do better. For younger students, this could be even simpler. They could sit in a circle and share the best and hardest parts of their day. This helps them get used to being grateful, making it more likely they'll keep doing it as they grow up.
   b) **Planning Lessons Around Student Strengths:** Some children learn better when they connect with a concept they're already familiar with or when they feel confident in what they're doing because of experiences. For teachers, it's crucial to understand what their students are good at and include those strengths in their daily lessons. When students feel comfortable and confident in what they're doing, they're more likely to want to learn (Gilpin, 2008). One idea is to combine Gardner's theory of multiple intelligences with Seligman's strengths approach. Teachers can use a chart to observe students and note where they excel or show strong character traits. By doing this, teachers can plan activities that tap into each student's strengths and interests, making learning more engaging and enjoyable for everyone.

c) **Teaching Forgiveness:** Forgiveness is important for feeling better because it helps let go of negative feelings like anger and resentment (Snyder & Lopez, 2005). Teaching forgiveness might not always seem important in school. But in positive psychology, forgiveness means letting go of bad feelings about something bad that happened and the person who caused it. To teach forgiveness, students can:

1. Think about what happened without getting too upset.
2. Understand how the other person might feel.
3. Remember a time when they were forgiven and how good that felt.
4. Decide to forgive, and maybe write it down or say it.
5. Keep reminding yourself that they are forgiven, especially when they think about the bad thing again (Gilpin, 2008).

Teachers can help students with each of these steps, showing them how to forgive and when they might need to use it in their lives.

4. **Applying the Growth Mindset in Education:** Maintaining an open mindset and being willing to learn and grow is crucial in education. When students believe they can enhance their abilities through hard work and practice, they become more receptive to new experiences and less fearful of failure. According to Dweck (2007), our beliefs about our abilities shape our mindset, which can be either growing or fixed. While a fixed mindset sees abilities as set, a growth mindset believes in cultivating abilities through perseverance. Encouraging a growth mindset means nurturing the idea that individuals can improve and achieve beyond their initial potential through hard work. Before focusing on students' strengths, schools may develop a growth mindset to ensure a positive attitude toward learning. Recognizing learning as an opportunity rather than a mandatory process is a key to nurturing growth. In education, how teachers praise students significantly impacts mindset development. Praising effort rather than intelligence encourages students to tackle more challenging tasks. Thus, educators should praise students for their effort, fostering the belief that improvement is possible through hard work and encouraging them to embrace challenges.

5. **Integrating CASEL and Panchakosha Model for Holistic Well-being in Schools:** The Collaborative for Academic, Social, and Emotional Learning (CASEL) advocates for systemic Social and Emotional Learning (SEL) alongside academics in schools across all grades. It emphasizes Goleman's five competencies of emotional intelligence: self-awareness,

self-management, social awareness, relationship skills, and responsible decision-making. Through CASEL's school-wide program, the entire school community collaborates to foster a caring and supportive environment where students can thrive academically and emotionally.

In parallel, the Panchakosha model from Indian scriptures offers a holistic approach to well-being, consisting of five layers, or "koshas." Schools can utilize this model to promote holistic development among students. The Annamaya kosha focuses on proper nutrition and exercise; the Pranamaya kosha emphasizes breathing techniques; and the Manomaya kosha involves training the mind. By integrating practices based on the Panchakosha model, schools can nurture students' physical, mental, and emotional well-being, complementing the efforts of CASEL's SEL program. Together, these approaches create a comprehensive framework for promoting holistic well-being in educational settings.

Challenges in Indian Schools

While the concept of positive schooling is universal, it faces many challenges in execution in India. The challenges are:

1. **Socio-Cultural Context and Demographic Variables:** Indian schools serve a wide range of socio-economic backgrounds, making it challenging to implement a one-size-fits-all approach to positive schooling. Cultural values and societal norms influence educational priorities and methods, requiring adaptations to align with local contexts.
2. **Focus on Cognitive Development vs. Holistic Development:** The current education system often prioritizes cognitive development and academic achievement over social-emotional learning and mental health. Emotional aspects are crucial for learning. According to Krathwohl's taxonomy, affective knowledge significantly impacts cognitive learning, suggesting the need for balanced educational approaches.
3. **Infrastructure and Facility Deficiencies:** Many Indian schools suffer from inadequate infrastructure, including insufficient classrooms, lack of libraries, and poor sanitation facilities. Overcrowded classrooms hinder effective teaching and personalized attention, affecting student engagement and learning outcomes.
4. **Examination-Driven System:** The current system places undue emphasis on grades and examinations, which can lead to stress and neglect of holistic development. The curriculum often lacks practical

application and fails to connect with the students' real-life contexts, reducing engagement and interest in learning.

5. **National Education Policy (NEP) 2020:** NEP 2020 aims to promote multidisciplinary education, but its implementation faces challenges such as outdated infrastructure and resistance to change. Proper training for teachers is essential to adapting to new educational methodologies and developing a supportive and effective learning environment.
6. **Mental Health and Well-Being:** There is a growing need to address mental health concerns among students, teachers, and staff to create a positive school culture. Developing supportive disciplinary methods and a caring school environment is crucial for the overall well-being and development of students.
7. **Parent-School Partnerships:** Strengthening parent-school partnerships is vital for the successful implementation of positive schooling. Involving parents in the educational process enhances support for students. Collaboration among various stakeholders, including educators, parents, policymakers, and community members, is essential for comprehensive educational reform.
8. **Budgetary Provisions and Policy Changes:** Sufficient budgetary provisions are necessary to improve infrastructure, resources, and training programs. Implementing policy changes that focus on holistic development, practical curriculum, and mental health support can lead to the creation of thriving, happy schools.

To successfully implement positive schooling in India, it is essential to address these multifaceted challenges. By considering the socio-cultural context, balancing cognitive and social-emotional learning, improving infrastructure, reforming the examination-driven system, and ensuring adequate training and support for teachers, Indian schools can create conducive learning environments. Additionally, fostering mental health, strengthening parent-school partnerships, and ensuring adequate funding and policy support are crucial steps towards achieving holistic educational outcomes and developing well-rounded, resilient students.

Summary

Psychology has long been applied to education, and positive psychology naturally finds its place in this realm. Positive education isn't entirely new; it's a replication of the age-old belief that the ultimate goal of education is to ensure student happiness. This idea traces back to ancient thinkers like Aristotle, who emphasized the importance of happiness in education. Studies consistently show that happy and emotionally supported children perform better both academically and emotionally. Therefore, it's crucial for schools to integrate positive psychology principles into their classrooms. By prioritizing student happiness, schools can significantly impact the overall well-being and success of their students. However, as schools adopt these principles, they must be mindful not to overload their teachers. Research indicates that the well-being of teachers directly influences the emotional and academic outcomes of their students. Hence, it's essential to consider both student and teacher happiness as primary objectives in positive education initiatives. Positive schools prioritize both academic outcomes and students' satisfaction and well-being. Positive emotions and experiences, such as satisfaction with school, are important indicators of students' mental health in these environments. Therefore, there is a growing need to build positive schools that enhance the positive health attributes of both students and teachers. Assessing students' positive emotions and attitudes, such as school satisfaction and positive attitudes toward learning, provides valuable information for promoting positive health and implementing intervention strategies. Positive psychology interventions in schools also extend to adults responsible for educating children and adolescents. Teachers, staff, educators, and parents should be familiar with positive psychology concepts and skills to model positive behaviors for students. Therefore, training programs for teachers often include positive psychology principles and models to systematically integrate them into teaching activities.

Many educational institutions are increasingly implementing targeted programs and interventions, including curriculum changes, to promote positive mental health, social and emotional skills, character strengths, well-being, and learning achievement. This focus on positive psychology in schools benefits both students and educators, developing a supportive and enriching learning environment. In essence, positive education builds upon historical foundations and aims to prioritize student happiness, recognizing its profound impact on academic and emotional outcomes. Additionally, it emphasizes the importance of maintaining teacher well-being to create a supportive learning environment for all.

CHAPTER 6

APPLICATION OF POSITIVE PSYCHOLOGY IN PARENTING

Parenting is an extraordinary journey, filled with moments of joy, wonder, and love. Yet, it also comes with its fair share of challenges and uncertainties. Parents go through various developmental stages, from the early years of infancy to the chaotic teenage years, constantly seeking the best ways to support their children's growth and well-being. In this journey, positive parenting stands out as an important belief. It's like a light that helps us know how to raise strong, caring, and successful people. At its core, positive parenting is more than just a set of techniques; it is a holistic approach including care, guidance, communication, and unconditional support. Rooted in attachment theory, behavioral principles, and social learning, positive parenting emphasizes the importance of developing secure attachments, promoting adaptive behaviors, and developing children's self-esteem and creativity.

The foundation of positive parenting rests on the belief that every child has the innate potential for growth and development. By creating a supportive environment, parents can empower their children to flourish emotionally, socially, and academically. Research shows the profound impact of positive parenting on children's adaptive outcomes, ranging from enhanced self-esteem and strength to improved social skills and academic achievement.

In this book chapter, we will learn about positive parenting, exploring its meaning, benefits, and applications across different developmental stages and situations.

Introduction

Parents always try to give their best for the proper development of their children. They want their child to be happy, healthy, and successful. However, along with having the intention to see our children flourish, it is also important to know the strategies and know-how for achieving that goal. Since each child is uniquely placed in a particular sociocultural context, parenting practices, and methods need to be understood. However, there are common grounds and principles, which need to be ensured for parenting to be effective and help children reach their optimum development and flourish in their lives. As stated by Patra (2022), "the larger goals of parenting are usually neglected in the competitive world where every parent wants their child to be the best amongst others, not the best of her/him. As a result, the child may gain wide knowledge, acquire various skills and achieve a lot, but may not develop self-awareness, self-connection, and self-realization that will give a true purpose to one's life.

Positive psychology principles offer a transformative approach to parenting, enabling parents to break free from negative patterns and cultivate a nurturing environment favorable to their children's well-being and growth. Despite the challenges parents face, integrating gratitude, mindfulness, optimism, and a growth mindset into parenting practices can yield remarkable benefits for both parents and children. Research emphasizes the effectiveness of a strengths-based approach in enhancing parent-child relationships and promoting child well-being. By focusing on their children's strengths and talents, parents not only develop a sense of competence and self-worth in their children but also reduce their stress levels, leading to a more positive family dynamic. When parents approach their role with kindness and understanding towards themselves, they are better equipped to respond to their children's needs empathetically, creating a supportive environment.

The impact of parents' attitudes towards failure on their children's mindset emphasizes the importance of adopting a growth mindset in parenting. When parents prioritize learning and personal development over performance, they instill in their children resilience to setbacks and a motivation to face challenges, leading to higher levels of psychological well-being and academic achievement. The shift in focus from criticism and overprotection to encouragement and growth develops strength, happiness, and a strong sense of self-worth in children, laying the foundation for a fulfilling and meaningful life. The integration of positive psychology principles into parenting practices offers a holistic and empowering approach to child-rearing.

Parenting Styles

There are four parenting styles:

1. **Authoritative Parenting Style:** Authoritative parents are warm and nurturing while maintaining clear rules and expectations. They explain reasons for rules and consequences and listen to their child's opinions while making the final decisions. Example: At mealtimes, authoritative

parents involve their children in meal preparation and allow them to choose certain aspects of the meal, promoting a healthy relationship with food and encouraging autonomy.

2. **Permissive Parenting Style:** Permissive parents are warm and nurturing, but have low expectations and use discipline sparingly. They allow children to make their own choices and often bail them out of the consequences. Example: Permissive parents may allow their children to eat whatever they want, even if it means making a special meal, leading to picky eating habits and unhealthy diet choices.
3. **Authoritarian Parenting Style:** Authoritarian parents enforce strict rules, high standards, and punishment to regulate their child's behavior. They have high expectations and are inflexible in their rules. Example: Authoritarian parents might enforce rules at mealtimes, such as finishing everything on their plate, without discussing the reasons behind the rules or the importance of certain foods.
4. **Neglectful Parenting Style:** Neglectful parents fulfill basic needs but pay little attention to their child's emotional or developmental needs. They offer minimal nurturing and have few expectations or limitations. Example: Neglectful parents may not consistently buy groceries or plan meals, leaving the child uncertain about when they will eat next and leading to preoccupation with food and potential overeating.

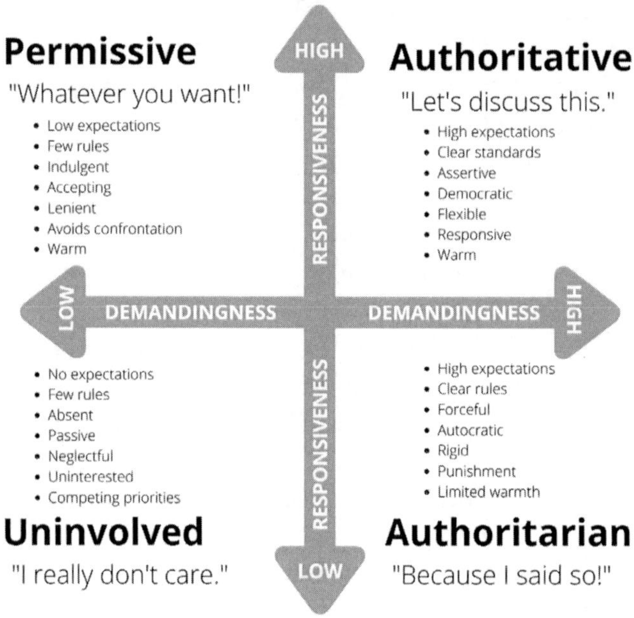

Theories of Parenting

The six theories of Parenting are as follows:

1. **Evolutionary Theory:** Evolutionary theory suggests that parenting behaviors have developed over time because they increase the survival and reproductive success of offspring. This theory is grounded in the principles of natural selection, where traits and behaviors that enhance an individual's fitness—meaning their ability to survive and reproduce—are more likely to be passed on to subsequent generations. In the context of parenting, evolutionary theory suggests that certain caregiving practices are instinctual, having been shaped by centuries of human evolution to ensure that children reach adulthood and can reproduce. These behaviors include nurturing, protecting, and teaching offspring essential survival skills. For example, a parent's instinct to respond to a crying baby serves the critical function of ensuring the child's immediate needs are met, thereby increasing the likelihood of the child's survival.

   Parental investment is another key concept within this theory. It refers to the time and resources parents devote to raising their children, which is seen as a compromise with their ability to invest in other potential offspring. Evolutionary theory explains that humans have developed a high level of parental investment compared to many other species, resulting in prolonged childhoods during which parents provide extensive care and learning opportunities. This extended period allows children to acquire complex skills and social behaviors necessary for survival in human societies. Overall, evolutionary theory provides a framework for understanding why certain parenting behaviors are universal and deep-rooted. These behaviors have been naturally selected because they enhance the chances of children surviving, flourishing, and eventually passing on their genes to the next generation.

2. **Attachment Theory:** Attachment theory, developed by John Bowlby and expanded by Mary Ainsworth, emphasizes the critical role of the emotional bond between a parent and child in the child's development. According to this theory, a secure attachment is formed when a caregiver is consistently responsive and available to the child's needs. This reliable presence provides the child with a sense of safety and security, which is essential for healthy development. John Bowlby proposed that attachment behaviors are biologically programmed and have evolved to ensure the survival of the infant. He observed that children who maintain proximity to their caregivers are more likely to be protected from dangers, thus

increasing their chances of survival. The attachment system is activated in times of distress or uncertainty, prompting the child to seek comfort and security from the caregiver.

Mary Ainsworth's "Strange Situation" study further elaborated on attachment theory by identifying different attachment styles: secure, anxious-ambivalent, and avoidant. Securely attached, children feel confident exploring their environment because they trust that their caregiver will be there for them if they need reassurance or help. This secure base allows them to develop independence and resilience. Conversely, children with insecure attachments may exhibit anxiety, fearfulness, or indifference in relationships, potentially hindering their social and emotional development.

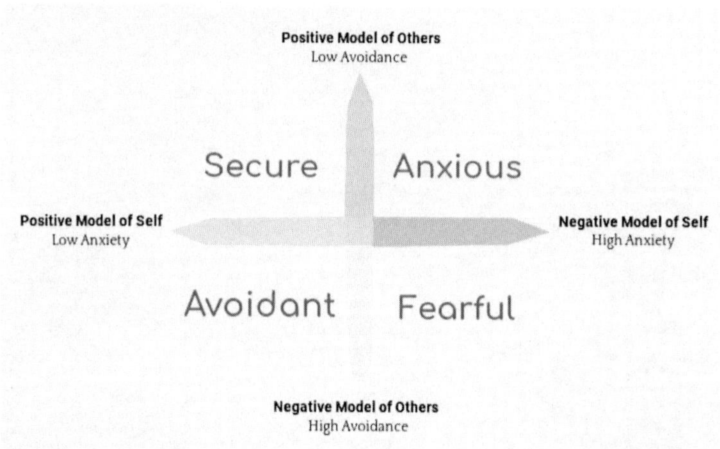

Attachment theory highlights that the quality of the early parent-child relationship has long-term implications for a child's emotional health, social relationships, and cognitive development. Securely attached children are more likely to develop positive self-esteem, effective coping skills, and healthy interpersonal relationships. Thus, consistent and responsive caregiving that develops secure attachment is fundamental to a child's overall well-being and developmental pathway.

3. **Socialization Theory:** Socialization theory examines the process by which parents and caregivers impart the norms, values, and behaviors necessary for children to function within their culture. This theory highlights the critical role of social interactions in shaping a child's understanding of societal expectations and appropriate conduct. Through everyday interactions, children learn the language, customs, moral values,

and social roles that are integral to their culture. Parents and caregivers serve as primary agents of socialization, modeling behaviors and setting expectations that guide the child's development. For instance, through positive reinforcement and discipline, parents teach children what is considered acceptable behavior. This process begins early in life and continues as children grow, with each stage bringing new social skills and knowledge. Peer interactions, educational systems, and media also contribute significantly to socialization. As children engage with peers, they learn cooperation, conflict resolution, and other social skills. Schools provide structured environments where children are exposed to societal norms and academic knowledge, while the media influences children's perceptions of the world and societal standards.

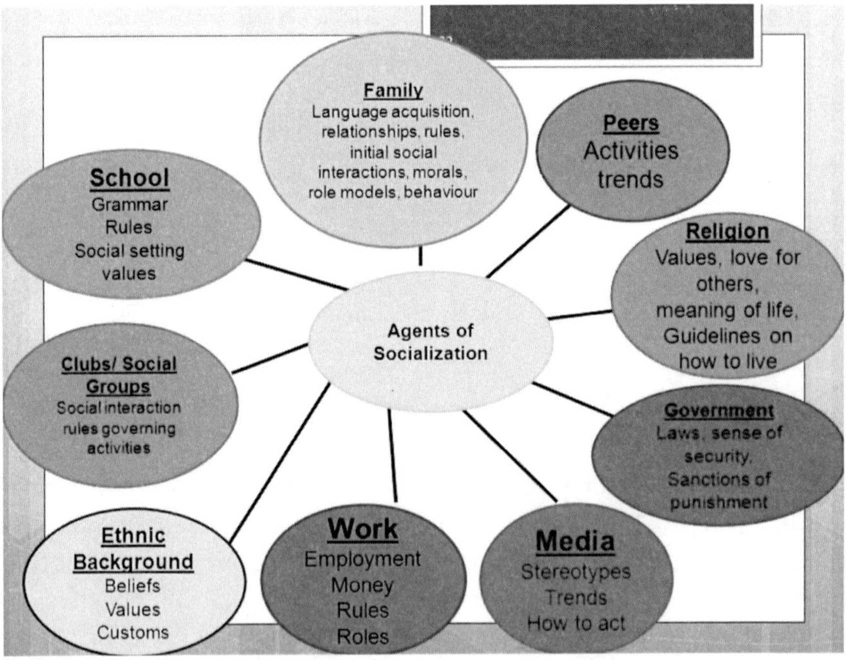

The effects of socialization on children are profound. Proper socialization equips children with the tools needed to face social situations, form relationships, and contribute to society. Well-socialized children tend to exhibit better communication skills, higher self-esteem, and a stronger sense of identity. They are also more likely to succeed academically and professionally.

Conversely, inadequate socialization can lead to difficulties in social interactions, behavioral problems, and challenges in adapting to societal norms. Children who do not receive consistent guidance and support may struggle with self-regulation, empathy, and establishing healthy relationships.

4. **Behavioral Genetics:** Behavioral genetics examines the influence of both genetic and environmental factors on behaviors, including parenting. This theory seeks to understand the extent to which inherited traits and environmental conditions shape a child's development. Researchers in this field utilize twin studies, family studies, and adoption studies to understand the relative contributions of genetics (nature) and environment (nurture). Genetic predispositions play a significant role in influencing a child's temperament, personality, and susceptibility to certain behaviors. For example, children may inherit tendencies towards extraversion or introversion, which can shape their social interactions and emotional responses. These inherited traits often interact with the child's environment, affecting how they develop over time.

   Parenting styles are also influenced by genetic factors. Parents may adapt their parenting strategies based on the individual needs of their children, which can vary according to each child's genetic makeup. For instance, a parent might employ more structured routines for a child who has a genetic predisposition for high activity levels, while a more emotionally sensitive child might receive gentler and more nurturing care. This dynamic interaction highlights how parenting is not a one-size-fits-all approach but is tailored to the unique genetic traits of each child.

   The nature versus nurture debate is central to behavioral genetics, emphasizing that both genetics and environment play crucial roles in development. Understanding how these factors interact helps explain why children from the same family can exhibit different developmental paths despite shared genetics and upbringing. This comprehensive perspective emphasizes the complexity of human development and the importance of considering both inherited traits and environmental influences in shaping behaviors and outcomes.

5. **Social Cognition Theory:** Social cognition theory, prominently associated with Albert Bandura, emphasizes the importance of observational learning, imitation, and modeling in child development. According to this theory, children acquire behaviors, attitudes, and emotional responses by watching and imitating the actions of others, particularly those of their parents and caregivers. Bandura's concept of the "Bobo doll experiment" famously demonstrated that children are likely to imitate aggressive

behaviors observed in adults. This observational learning is not limited to direct imitation; children also learn the consequences of behaviors by seeing how others are rewarded or punished, which Bandura termed "vicarious reinforcement."

Through this process, parents and caregivers serve as primary models for behavior. Children observe and internalize their parents' ways of interacting with others, managing emotions, and handling various situations. For example, a child who sees their parent calmly solving conflicts is more likely to adopt similar strategies in their interactions. Additionally, parents' attitudes towards tasks like education and chores can shape a child's approach to these activities.

The influence of social cognition theory on child development is profound, as it highlights the crucial role of the environment and social context in shaping a child's learning and behavior. By observing and imitating positive behaviors and coping mechanisms, children develop social skills, self-regulation, and problem-solving abilities. Conversely, exposure to negative behaviors can lead to the adoption of undesirable actions. Thus, understanding the principles of social cognition theory helps in creating nurturing environments where positive modeling can promote healthy development.

6. **Systems Theory:** Systems theory, when applied to family dynamics, conceptualizes the family as an interconnected and interdependent system. Each family member plays a role, and their behaviors and interactions influence and are influenced by other members. This perspective emphasizes that the family is more than just a collection of individuals; it is a cohesive unit where each person's actions and emotions impact the whole family dynamic.

   One of the core principles of systems theory is that changes in any part of the system can lead to changes in the entire system. For instance, if a parent experiences stress at work, it may affect their mood and behavior at home, which in turn can influence the child's emotional well-being and behavior. Similarly, a child's behavioral issues or achievements can affect the overall family atmosphere, potentially altering parenting practices and sibling relationships.

   The theory also highlights the importance of boundaries within the family system. Healthy families typically have clear but flexible boundaries, allowing for individual autonomy while maintaining close familial connections. Disruptions in these boundaries, such as overly involved or disengaged relationships can lead to developmental challenges for children. For example, overprotective families might hinder a child's ability to develop independence, while neglectful families might fail to provide the necessary emotional support.

Systems theory emphasizes the complexity of these interactions by considering external influences on the family, such as social, economic, and cultural factors. For example, a family's socioeconomic status can affect parenting styles, the availability of resources, and stress levels, all of which can influence a child's development. The impact of systems theory on child development is significant. By understanding that a child's development is not isolated but deeply embedded within the family system, this theory advocates for holistic approaches to address developmental issues. Interventions based on systems theory often focus on improving family dynamics, enhancing communication, and establishing healthy boundaries. This systemic approach can develop a supportive environment that promotes the child's emotional, social, and cognitive development, highlighting the essential role of a well-functioning family unit in nurturing healthy development.

Positive Parenting

Positive parenting refers to the use of positive psychology principles and techniques in child-rearing practices. Thus, instead of focusing on what is wrong in the child, it emphasizes what is right and good in the child. It also focuses on the parents themselves — being self-aware, being mindful, and learning to see the larger goal of parenting. Listening to the child, understanding the needs of the child, and being a good role model will help the child feel loved and confident.

According to Seay et al. (2014): Positive parenting is the continual relationship between a parent(s) and a child or children that includes caring, teaching, leading, communicating, and providing for the needs of a child consistently and unconditionally."

The Committee of Ministers of the Council of Europe (2006) similarly defined positive parenting as "... nurturing, empowering, nonviolent..." and "provides recognition and guidance which involves setting boundaries to enable the full development of the child" (in Rodrigo et al., 2012).

On the basis of the above definition, characteristics of Positive Parenting are as follows:

- It involves guiding
- It involves leading
- It involves teaching
- It is caring
- It is empowering
- It is nurturing
- It is sensitive to the child's needs
- It is consistent
- It is always non-violent
- It provides regular open communication
- It provides affection
- It provides emotional security
- It provides emotional warmth
- It provides unconditional love
- It recognizes the positive
- It respects the child's developmental stage
- It rewards accomplishments
- It sets boundaries
- It shows empathy for the child's feelings
- It supports the child's best interests

Along with these characteristics, Godfrey (2019) proposes that the underlying assumption of positive parenting is that "... all children are born good, are altruistic and desire to do the right thing ..." Godfrey further adds that the objective of positive parenting is to teach discipline in a way that builds a child's self-esteem and supports a mutually respectful parent-child relationship without breaking the child's spirit (2019).

The Pillars of Positive Parenting Techniques

1. **Establishing Unconditional Love and Support:** One of the fundamental pillars of positive parenting is unconditional love and support. Children thrive in an environment where they feel loved, cherished, and accepted for who they are, irrespective of their strengths and weaknesses. Expressing affection and offering encouragement can significantly impact a child's self-esteem and overall well-being.
2. **Practicing Effective Communication:** Communication is the cornerstone of any healthy relationship, including the one between

parents and children. Positive parenting emphasizes active listening and empathetic communication. By genuinely understanding a child's emotions and thoughts, parents can build a stronger connection and resolve conflicts more effectively.

3. **Setting Clear and Consistent Boundaries:** While positive parenting encourages a nurturing environment, it also recognizes the importance of boundaries. Clear and consistent boundaries provide children with a sense of structure and security. By setting reasonable limits, parents can help their children develop self-discipline and responsible decision-making skills.
4. **Encouraging Independence with Guidance:** Encouraging independence is a vital aspect of positive parenting. Allowing children to make age-appropriate choices and opinions nurtures their sense of autonomy and tone- confidence. Parents act as attendants, offering support and advice while empowering their children to explore the world around them.
5. **Developing Emotional Intelligence:** Emotional intelligence plays a pivotal role in a child's social and emotional development. Positive parenthood teaches children to embrace and manage their feelings, as well as empathize with others. This foundation of emotional intelligence equips children to make healthier connections and manage life's challenges more effectively.

Benefits of Positive Parenting

- **Building Stronger Parent-Child Relationships:** Positive parenting strengthens the bond between parents and their children. When children feel loved, admired, and supported, they're more likely to trust their parents and entrust them during times of joy or torture. This open communication develops a deeper understanding of each other's passions and perspectives.
- **Nurturing Self-Esteem and Confidence:** By providing unconditional love and stimulation, positive parenthood boosts children's attitude and confidence. When children believe in their capacities and worth, they're more willing to take on challenges and explore their interests without fear of failure.
- **Reducing Behavioral Issues:** Positive parenting emphasizes positive reinforcement and effective communication rather than disciplinary measures. This approach reduces the likelihood of aggressive or defiant

behavior in children. Instead, children learn to express themselves constructively and develop a sense of responsibility for their actions.

- **Creating a Positive Learning Environment:** Positive parenting helps children to feel safe to explore and learn. When they are not afraid of harsh punishments or criticism, they are more inclined to take risks and engage in activities that promote their cognitive and creative development.
- **Promoting Mental and Emotional Well-being:** Emotionally harmonized parenthood contributes to a child's internal well- being. When parents validate their child's feelings and offer support during challenging times, it helps children learn adaptability and manage the problems of life more effectively.

Positive Parenting Techniques

1. **Safe and Stimulating Environment:** Creating a safe and stimulating environment for children is a fundamental positive psychology technique in parenting, aimed at developing their psychological growth and well-being. A safe environment provides children with a sense of security and stability, allowing them to explore, learn, and grow without fear or anxiety. When children feel safe, they are more likely to take risks, try new things, and engage in meaningful experiences. This sense of security is essential for healthy psychological development, as it enables children to build trust in their surroundings and develop a strong sense of self-esteem and confidence.

   Moreover, a stimulating environment provides children with opportunities for cognitive, emotional, and social growth. Stimulating environments are rich in sensory experiences, educational materials, and social interactions that encourage curiosity, creativity, and exploration. These environments challenge children to think critically, solve problems, and develop important skills such as communication, collaboration, and empathy. In a safe and stimulating environment, children are encouraged to express themselves freely and engage in activities that interest them. Positive parenting involves creating a balance between providing structure and guidance, while also allowing children the freedom to explore and discover at their own pace. This approach helps children develop a sense of autonomy and independence while still feeling supported and cared for by their parents.
2. **Positive Discipline:** The effectiveness of positive discipline as a positive psychology intervention technique lies in its emphasis on nurturing a

supportive and respectful parent-child relationship while developing healthy behavioral patterns. Positive discipline focuses on clear and open communication between parents and children. By maintaining transparent communication channels, parents can express expectations, boundaries, and consequences constructively, facilitating mutual understanding and cooperation. Moreover, positive discipline encourages parents to behave assertively yet empathetically. Assertive behavior involves setting firm and consistent boundaries, while empathy allows parents to understand and validate their child's feelings and needs. This balanced approach helps children feel understood and supported, while also learning the importance of respecting boundaries and considering others' perspectives. Positive discipline emphasizes the use of positive reinforcement to encourage desirable behavior. Instead of solely focusing on punishing negative behavior, parents actively recognize and reinforce positive actions through praise, rewards, and encouragement. This approach motivates children to repeat positive behaviors, ultimately shaping their overall conduct in a positive direction.

3. **Realistic Expectations:** Understanding and adopting the concept of realistic expectations in parenting is a crucial positive psychology intervention technique that promotes healthy child development and nurtures positive parent-child relationships. It involves recognizing that children are unique individuals with their personalities, strengths, and challenges. They are not mere extensions of their parents' desires or expectations. As Kahlil Gibran beautifully expresses, children are what life desires and hopes for, and while they come through their parents, they do not belong to them. This perspective encourages parents to respect their children's autonomy and individuality, allowing them to grow and flourish in their way.

   Furthermore, adopting realistic expectations involves understanding the influence of various ecological systems on a child's development, as proposed by Bronfenbrenner's Ecological theory. This theory emphasizes the interconnectedness between the child and their immediate and larger environments, including family, school, community, society, and culture. These environments shape the child's experiences, beliefs, and behaviors, influencing their development in profound ways. By recognizing the complexity of these environmental influences, parents can better understand their child's behavior and adjust their expectations accordingly. For example, a child growing up in a high-pressure academic environment may experience different stressors and challenges compared to a child in a more relaxed setting. Understanding these contextual factors helps parents set realistic goals and expectations that take into account their child's unique circumstances.

Moreover, accepting realistic expectations involves acknowledging the dynamic nature of development across different stages of childhood. Children undergo significant changes in cognitive, emotional, and social development as they grow, and their needs and abilities evolve accordingly. Parents who understand these developmental processes are better equipped to provide appropriate support and guidance, adjusting their expectations based on their child's stage of development.

4. **Self Care:** Prioritizing self-care enables parents to cultivate self-awareness and regulate their emotions. By taking the time to attend to their own needs and emotions, parents can develop a deeper understanding of themselves and their reactions to various parenting challenges. This self-awareness allows them to respond to their child's behavior in a more calm, thoughtful, and constructive manner, rather than reacting impulsively out of stress or frustration. Moreover, practicing self-care develops empathy, kindness, and compassion towards oneself. Parenting is demanding and exhausting, and parents often experience feelings of guilt, inadequacy, or burnout. By engaging in self-care activities that promote relaxation, rejuvenation, and self-compassion, parents can replenish their emotional reserves and cultivate a more nurturing and compassionate attitude towards themselves. This, in turn, enables them to extend empathy, kindness, and understanding towards their child, developing a supportive and loving parent-child relationship.
5. **Mindfulness in Parenting:** Mindful parenting is a practice rooted in applying mindfulness to the role of being a parent, developing a sense of presence and centeredness in each moment with one's child. As Jon Kabat-Zinn, the founder of mindfulness-based stress reduction describes, mindfulness is about "befriending our-selves and our experience," and mindful parenting extends this principle to the parent-child relationship and the journey of parenting itself. Unlike following specific steps or procedures, mindful parenting revolves around adopting the dynamic relationship between parent and child. It involves being fully present and attentive to both one's own emotions and those of the child, cultivating awareness and acceptance of the present moment. This allows parents to engage with their children with calmness and intentionality, even during

routine or challenging moments. Parenting inherently carries stress and frustration, compounded by the daily demands of children. This stress can manifest in reactive behaviors such as yelling, impulsive rule-setting, or withdrawing, followed by feelings of remorse or guilt. Mindful parenting seeks to interrupt this cycle by promoting awareness of stressful situations and emotions, enabling parents to pause and respond thoughtfully rather than reactively. As such, mindful parenting is a pathway to developing connection, understanding, and mutual growth within the family dynamics. Key concepts of mindful parenting:

a) **Attention and Focus:** Mindful parenting facilitates presence because parents remain focused on the current moment with their child. Mindfulness techniques, such as deep breathing, can help parents provide their undivided attention rather than being distant and distracted.

b) **Awareness:** Noticing and catching emotions before they grow out of control is essential in mindful parenting. This includes being aware of and paying attention to stressful situations and complicated emotions (whether the parent's, the child's, or both). Parents who are fully present and aware at the moment can more easily notice when their kids (and they) are becoming frustrated or upset. Then, they can help kids recognize their emotions, name them, and deal with them positively.

c) **Acceptance and Non-Judgment:** In mindful parenting, parents learn to be present with all emotions and situations, accepting them as they are rather than judging them as "bad" and something to avoid, fix, or struggle against. This does not mean that parents accept all behavior. Instead, parents accept the emotion driving the behavior to help kids through the experience. Mindful parenting also means parents accept their range of emotions without judging themselves harshly for feeling frustrated, angry, or bored. Acceptance and non-judgment allow parents to be open to what happens in any given moment with their kids, and this openness helps prevent automatic reactions and impulsive words or actions.

d) **Empathy and Compassion:** Rather than berating kids for their words or feelings, parents help kids understand their emotions and accept themselves fully by approaching them with deep understanding. This involves being attentive and listening to kids as they share their feelings. When parents calmly reflect their kids' feelings to them, kids feel heard and can begin to understand their complex emotions. Empathy also involves openly forgiving them for mistakes. Parents also admit their parenting mistakes (even those who practice mindful parenting slip up) and ask for forgiveness. In this way, mindful parenting teaches kids that everyone makes mistakes and is still lovable and worthy of forgiveness and respect. This helps kids be compassionate with themselves and others.

e) **Creative Problem Solving:** Parents who practice mindful parenting refrain from stepping in to solve kids' problems for them. Rather than rushing in with a solution, they stay present, express empathy and understanding, and guide them in exploring how to address problems and stressful situations. Openness may include asking questions such as, "Can you remember something you did before that worked," or "Is there something you can say to let your friend know how you feel without hurting their feelings?"

f) **Appreciation and Gratitude:** With mindful parenting, the emphasis is on what is right rather than wrong. Parents convey appreciation for their kids' positive behaviors and openly express gratitude for positive aspects of life. These concepts combine to assist parents in being present with their kids in a way that aligns with their values and visions for their family. Together, they help work toward the ultimate goal of mindful parenting.

6. **Active Listening and Empathy:** Active listening and empathy serve as foundational pillars of positive parenting. These practices involve truly understanding and empathizing with a child's thoughts and emotions, which can profoundly impact their emotional well-being. When the child expresses himself/herself, it's crucial to genuinely grasp their perspective without judgment. Empathy acts as a validating force, showing the child that their emotions matter and are understood, thus developing trust in the parent-child relationship.

7. **Setting Clear and Consistent Boundaries:** In an environment where boundaries are clearly defined, children develop a sense of clarity and understanding of the consequences of their actions. Positive parenting emphasizes gentle guidance and explanations to help children understand the reasons behind rules, avoiding strict disciplinary measures. This approach develops self-discipline and encourages children to take responsibility for their actions.

8. **Praise and Encouragement:** Offering praise and recognition for children's efforts and achievements is a powerful way to boost their self-esteem and confidence. Rather than focusing solely on the result, parents should celebrate the journey and the perseverance they demonstrate along the way. In moments of difficulty, parents should give encouragement, which acts as a source of strength and helps develop a positive attitude towards overcoming challenges.
9. **Quality Time and Bonding:** An invaluable network of emotionally connections forms when parents spend meaningful time and emotional bonds with their children. Participating in activities tailored to their interests, whether it's reading, playing games, or having simple conversations, strengthens this unbreakable bond. Removing distractions and giving undivided attention to the child during these special moments, not only deepens the parent-child relationship but also creates opportunities for honest conversations and a deeper understanding of your child's needs.
10. **Safe and Stimulating Environment:** Creating a safe and stimulating environment for children is a fundamental positive psychology technique in parenting, aimed at developing their psychological growth and well-being. A safe environment provides children with a sense of security and stability, allowing them to explore, learn, and grow without fear or anxiety. When children feel safe, they are more likely to take risks, try new things, and engage in meaningful experiences. This sense of security is essential for healthy psychological development, as it enables children to build trust in their surroundings and develop a strong sense of self-esteem and confidence.

Summary

Positive parenting, informed by principles of positive psychology, transforms the challenging journey of parenting into a deeply satisfying and rewarding experience for both parents and children. This approach emphasizes the emotional well-being of children, ensuring they feel loved, respected, and valued. By fostering sensitivity, mindfulness, and responsiveness, positive parenting creates a solid foundation for healthy development and growth. It equips children with crucial skills such as self-regulation, responsibility, and self-confidence. Essential techniques of positive parenting include active listening, empathy, clear boundaries, praise, positive discipline, and quality time. These practices help build a nurturing environment where children can thrive and flourish.

Positive parenting recognizes the uniqueness of each child, acknowledging that there is no universal approach that works for all. It requires time, patience, and a willingness to adapt techniques to fit the specific dynamics of each family. Parents who embark on this journey need to be patient with both themselves and their children, understanding that cultivating a harmonious parent-child relationship is a gradual process.

The application of positive psychology in parenting fosters resilience, strength, and joy within families. It creates a supportive and loving environment that enables children to reach their full potential. By emphasizing the positive aspects of behavior and development, parents can help their children build a strong emotional foundation, essential for facing life's challenges. Ultimately, positive parenting not only enhances the child's growth but also enriches the overall family dynamic, leading to stronger, happier relationships and a more fulfilling parenting experience. Through positive psychology, parents, and children alike can achieve a sense of well-being and mutual respect, paving the way for a brighter future.

CHAPTER 7

APPLICATION OF POSITIVE PSYCHOLOGY IN SOCIAL RELATIONSHIPS

In an era marked by increasing digital connectivity but also rising feelings of isolation, the significance of positive social relationships cannot be overstated. Social relationships include a broad spectrum of connections, ranging from intimate partnerships and familial bonds to friendships and community networks. At their core, these relationships serve as the cornerstone of human existence, providing avenues for emotional support, companionship, and shared experiences. However, the quality of these relationships is important, as positive interactions develop resilience, happiness, and overall life satisfaction. Drawing upon foundational theories of positive psychology, the chapter explains the mechanisms through which individuals can cultivate and strengthen their social connections. Key concepts such as empathy, gratitude, and forgiveness serve as building blocks for nurturing meaningful relationships and fostering trust and intimacy. Additionally, the exploration of character strengths and virtues highlights the role of authenticity and altruism in fostering genuine connections.

The chapter examines the psychological benefits derived from positive social interactions, including enhanced emotional regulation, stress reduction, and increased resilience in the face of adversity. By developing a sense of belonging and social support, individuals are better equipped to handle life's challenges and pursue personal growth and fulfillment.

Moreover, the application of positive psychology extends beyond individual relationships to broader societal contexts, emphasizing the importance of promoting inclusive communities and promoting social cohesion. Through collective efforts to cultivate empathy, kindness, and compassion, societies can create environments that nurture positive social norms and values, ultimately supporting greater well-being for all members.

Introduction

Social connection is a fundamental aspect of human existence, including a deep sense of belonging and emotional closeness with others. Pavey et al. (2011) argue that this intrinsic need for connection is important in shaping our overall life satisfaction, underscoring its significance from early infancy to adulthood. Our innate drive for connection compels us to direct the complexities of social interactions, utilizing both verbal and non-verbal cues to promote bonds and ensure communal survival.

From the moment of birth, humans are wired to seek and maintain connections with others. Through intricate systems of communication, including vocalizations, touch, and facial expressions, we establish rapport and convey our emotions and intentions. These non-verbal signals serve as vital tools in our collection, enabling us to nurture and care for members of our social groups, thereby enhancing our collective resilience and ensuring the continuation of our species. Consider the innumerable non-verbal behaviors that play a crucial role in promoting pro-social relationships. Head tilts, direct gazes, and genuine smiles signify social engagement, facilitating rapport and mutual understanding. Conversely, head nods may signal deference or submissiveness, encouraging harmonious interactions within social hierarchies. Blushes and displays of embarrassment reveal our concern for social evaluation, prompting efforts to pacify and reconcile with others. Even subtle cues like oblique eyebrows can convey empathy and concern for the well-being of others, developing a sense of connection and relationship. Moreover, laughter emerges as a universal language of warmth and cooperativeness, exceeding cultural boundaries and developing a sense of shared humanity. These non-verbal expressions serve as the basis of social cohesion, facilitating cooperation, empathy, and mutual support within our social networks.

In essence, the intricate interplay of non-verbal communication emphasizes the profound significance of social connection in human life. By utilizing these subtle cues and gestures, we affirm our shared humanity and produce bonds that sustain us through life's challenges, enriching our existence with meaning and fulfillment.

Importance of Positive Relationships

In the past two decades, the positive psychology movement has yielded an unprecedented growth of empirical investigations into advancing optimal human functioning and improving well-being (Fowler, Seligman, & Koocher,

1999; Lyubomirsky & Layous, 2013). Research conducted in the area of positive psychology emphazises the significant role of positive human connections in promoting emotional, physical, and psychological well-being, especially amid challenging circumstances. The importance of relationships can be summarized as follows:

1. **Emotional Support and Stability:** Relationships provide emotional support, helping individuals feel understood, valued, and cared for. Emotional support from positive relationships enhances stability and resilience, especially during tough times.
2. **Mental Health Benefits:** Positive relationships reduce symptoms of depression and anxiety. Supportive connections promote a sense of purpose and improve overall mental health.
3. **Physical Health Improvements:** Strong relationships are linked to better physical health outcomes, such as lower stress levels and improved immune function. Positive social connections can lead to reduced blood pressure and better cardiovascular health.
4. **Facilitation of Personal Growth:** Supportive relationships encourage personal development by providing motivation and emotional backing. These connections help individuals pursue goals, overcome challenges, and grow beyond previous levels of functioning.
5. **Increased Resilience:** Positive relationships help individuals bounce back from adversity more effectively. Supportive connections not only aid in returning to baseline but also facilitate growth beyond prior levels.
6. **Stress Reduction:** Relationships that provide responsive and sensitive support help mitigate the effects of stress. Lower stress levels contribute to overall well-being and health.
7. **Social Well-Being and Sense of Belonging:** Reciprocal, caring connections foster a sense of community and belonging. Positive relationships enhance social networks, promoting a supportive environment.
8. **Longevity and Life Expectancy:** Research shows that individuals with strong social connections tend to live longer. Positive relationships contribute to healthier behaviors and better stress management, which can increase life expectancy.
9. **Enhanced Coping Mechanisms:** Supportive relationships help individuals develop better strategies for coping with life's challenges. These connections provide practical advice, encouragement, and perspective during difficult times.

10. **Increased Happiness and Life Satisfaction:** Positive relationships are strongly linked to higher levels of happiness and life satisfaction. Feeling connected and supported contributes to a sense of fulfillment and well-being.
11. **Academic and Professional Success:** Supportive relationships provide the encouragement and resources needed to succeed in educational and career endeavors. Positive social connections can enhance motivation, focus, and performance.
12. **Strengthening Community and Social Fabric:** Relationships extend their benefits beyond individuals to strengthen communities. Positive social connections promote social cohesion, cooperation, and mutual support, benefiting society as a whole.

By recognizing and nurturing the importance of relationships, individuals can enhance their emotional, physical, and psychological well-being, creating a more resilient and thriving society.

Feeney and Collins identified two key ways in which positive relationships contribute to thriving. Firstly, supportive connections empower individuals to grab opportunities for personal growth, enhance well-being, and cultivate a sense of purpose and meaning in life. These relationships help enhance prior levels of functioning, emphasizing growth and improvement through life's opportunities and challenges. Secondly, amidst adversity, positive support not only protects individuals from stress but also enables them to flourish. Relationships play an important role in not only helping individuals return to baseline but also facilitating growth beyond prior levels of functioning.

The effectiveness of support depends not only on its arrangement, but also on how it is delivered. Responsive and sensitive support is essential, ensuring that recipients feel understood, validated, and cared for. Conversely, support that induces feelings of weakness, guilt, or inadequacy, or that restricts autonomy, can be detrimental. Establishing reciprocal caring connections is fundamental for encouraging emotional, physical, and social well-being in individuals

Characteristics of Close Relationships

Close relationships can indeed be distinguished from casual relationships by several key characteristics:

1. **Trust:** In close relationships, there is a high level of trust between individuals, meaning they feel safe and secure sharing personal information and vulnerabilities without fear of judgment or betrayal.

2. **Knowledge:** Close relationships involve a deep mutual understanding of preferences, beliefs, values, and life experiences. Individuals in close relationships often get to know each other on a profound level.
3. **Care:** Close relationships are characterized by care and concern for each other's well-being. Individuals in these relationships demonstrate empathy, support, and a sense of responsibility for each other's happiness and success.
4. **Interdependence:** Close relationships involve a high degree of interdependence, where the lives of the individuals are intertwined. They rely on each other for emotional support, practical assistance, and companionship.
5. **Commitment:** Close relationships involve dedication and commitment, even during challenging times. Individuals in these relationships are willing to invest time, effort, and resources to nurture and sustain the relationship.
6. **Intimacy:** Close relationships feature emotional intimacy, which involves sharing thoughts, feelings, and experiences in a deep and meaningful way. This emotional connection encourages closeness and strengthens the bond between individuals.

Close relationships can manifest in various forms, including platonic friendships and romantic relationships. Romantic relationships typically involve elements of passion and sexual intimacy, along with the characteristics mentioned above. These relationships often involve a strong attachment to one person at a time, characterized by exclusivity and a deep emotional connection. Understanding the processes of love, attachment, and friendships can provide further insights into the nature and significance of close relationships in individuals' lives. These relationships contribute significantly to psychological well-being by providing support, fulfillment, and a sense of belonging. Applying principles from positive psychology can further enhance the quality and satisfaction of close relationships, promoting greater happiness and resilience in individuals' lives.

Theories of Relationships

1. **Social Exchange Theory:** Social exchange theory, which views social behavior as an exchange process, suggests that individuals evaluate the benefits and costs of their relationships to maximize rewards and minimize risks. This theory provides a comprehensive framework for understanding relationship dynamics by highlighting several key elements. First,

individuals conduct a costs vs. benefits evaluation, where costs include investments of time, money, and emotional energy, while benefits include companionship, support, and shared experiences. Positive relationships occur when benefits outweigh costs, whereas negative relationships emerge when costs surpass benefits. Moreover, individuals' expectations and comparison levels, shaped by their experiences, play a significant role in how they perceive and assess their current relationships. These prior experiences create a framework within which people evaluate the quality and dynamics of their interactions with others. Consequently, the way individuals view and judge their relationships is heavily influenced by the attachment patterns and interactions they experienced earlier in life. High expectations from previous relationships can lead to dissatisfaction if current experiences do not measure up.

The theory also addresses the "honeymoon phase" of relationships, a period during which individuals tend to overlook costs and exaggerate benefits. As the relationship matures, individuals become more aware of the true exchange balance, adjusting their perceptions accordingly. Furthermore, individuals continually evaluate alternatives, assessing whether their current relationship is more fulfilling than potential other options. This ongoing comparison can affect the stability and longevity of the relationship.

Equity plays a crucial role in relationship health. Perceived fairness or equity in the exchange within a relationship is essential for maintaining satisfaction and stability. When exchanges are perceived as inequitable, feelings of resentment or guilt may develop, potentially leading to conflict or dissolution. Overall, social exchange theory explains how individuals face the complexities of relationships by weighing costs and benefits, considering expectations and alternatives, and striving for equity from initial attraction to long-term commitment.

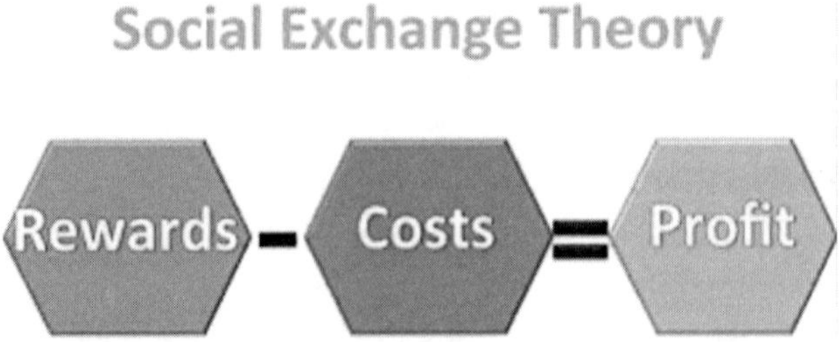

2. **Attachment Theory:** John Bowlby's attachment theory suggests that attachment is an innate biological process essential for survival, focusing on the emotional bond formed between an infant and their primary caregiver. According to Bowlby, this bond is critical for the infant's development and well-being. He outlined four stages of attachment development. In the pre-attachment stage (birth to 6 weeks), infants are naturally sociable and use behaviors such as crying and smiling to engage caregivers, though they have not yet formed a clear attachment. During the attachment in the making phase (6 weeks to 6-8 months), infants begin to show preferences for familiar caregivers and exhibit discomfort when separated from them, marking the early signs of attachment. The clear-cut attachment stage (6-8 months to 18 months to 2 years) is characterized by strong attachment behaviors, including seeking proximity to the primary caregiver and experiencing separation anxiety. In the final stage, the formation of reciprocal relationships (18 months to 2 years and onwards), children develop a more sophisticated understanding of their caregiver's behavior, actively participating in the attachment relationship and seeking comfort and support as needed.

   Bowlby also introduced the concept of internal working models, suggesting that early attachment experiences shape mental representations of the self, others, and relationships. These models influence an individual's future expectations and behaviors in relationships. The notion of the caregiver as a secure base is central to Bowlby's theory; a secure attachment provides a sense of safety and confidence, allowing the child to explore their environment while knowing they can return to the caregiver for reassurance. This secure base supports a healthy developmental path, allowing the child to manage social and emotional challenges successfully. The impact of early attachment experiences extends into adulthood, with securely attached individuals generally forming healthier, more trusting relationships. In contrast, those with insecure attachments might struggle with intimacy and trust issues. Bowlby's theory emphasizes the profound influence of early caregiver-infant interactions on social and emotional development, highlighting the long-lasting effects of attachment on future relationships.

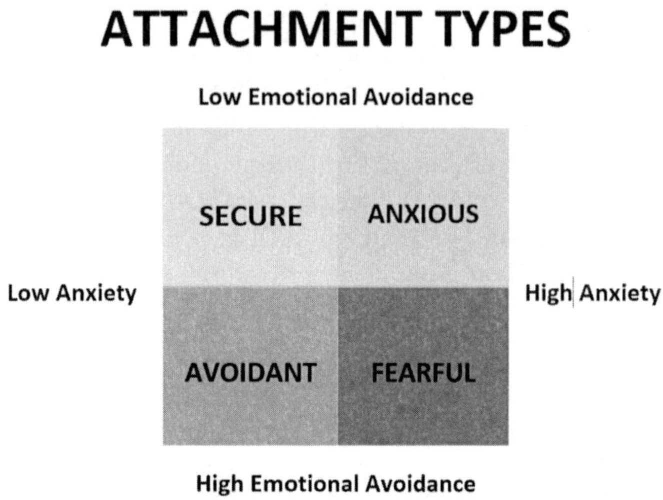

3. **Interdependence Theory:** Interdependence theory provides a comprehensive framework for understanding social relationships by examining both the structural properties and psychological processes that characterize interactions between individuals. This theory, primarily developed by Harold Kelley and John Thibaut, emphasizes how the mutual influence between people shapes their social experiences and outcomes.

   Interdependence theory identifies six key structural dimensions that shape social situations:

   - **Level of Dependence:** This dimension assesses the extent to which one person's outcomes are dependent on another's actions. High dependence means that an individual's satisfaction or well-being is significantly influenced by the partner's behavior.
   - **Mutuality of Dependence:** This examines whether the dependence in the relationship is equally shared. In mutually dependent relationships, both individuals have a similar level of reliance on each other, developing a sense of balance and reciprocity.
   - **Basis of Dependence:** Dependence can arise from either unilateral or joint control over outcomes. Unilateral control means one person predominantly influences the outcomes, while joint control indicates that both parties contribute to and influence each other's outcomes.
   - **Association of Interests:** This dimension considers how the partners' outcomes coordinate, ranging from mutually beneficial (positive correlation) to conflicting interests (negative correlation).

When interests align, cooperation and shared goals are more prevalent, whereas conflicting interests can lead to competition or conflict.

- **Temporal Structure:** Interactions and their consequences evolve. The temporal structure recognizes that past interactions influence present behavior and future outcomes, highlighting the importance of considering the dynamic nature of relationships.
- **Availability of Information:** Adequate information about each other's outcomes, motives, and potential future actions is crucial. When individuals have clear and accurate information, they can better predict and understand their partner's behavior, leading to more effective interactions.

Interdependence theory also outlines several psychological processes that help explain how individuals direct social interactions:

- **Affordance:** Situations afford specific motives and behaviors based on their structural properties. For example, in cooperative tasks with shared goals, the situation promotes cooperation and teamwork.
- **Transformation:** Individuals often prioritize broader, long-term considerations over immediate desires, leading to adaptive and sometimes altruistic responses. For instance, in a team brainstorming session, members may prioritize the group's success over personal recognition, developing collaborative problem-solving.
- **Attribution Processes:** People interpret the implications of others' actions, distinguishing between situational factors (e.g., external circumstances) and intentional factors (e.g., deliberate choices). Accurate attributions help in understanding motives and maintaining trust.
- **Self-Presentation:** Individuals convey their motives and intentions through their actions, which influences how trustworthy and reliable they appear to others. Effective self-presentation can enhance mutual trust and cooperation.
- **Interpersonal Dispositions:** These are actor-specific inclinations shaped by experiences and adaptations, which influence how individuals respond to various situations. For example, a person who has experienced consistent support in past relationships may be more trusting in new relationships.
- **Relationship-Specific Motives:** These motives pertain to how individuals respond uniquely to specific partners, influencing trust

and commitment levels. Strong, positive relationship-specific motives can enhance the stability and quality of the relationship.

- **Social Norms:** These are rule-based inclinations that regulate behavior within social interactions, promoting cooperative and predictable behavior. Social norms help to maintain order and mutual expectations in relationships.

Interdependence theory offers valuable insights into the dynamics of social relationships across various facets. It sheds light on power dynamics by revealing how dependence and mutuality influence the distribution of power within relationships. Moreover, it examines cooperation, explaining how shared interests and social norms foster cooperative behaviors among individuals. When conflicts arise, interdependence theory aids in identifying effective resolution strategies by comprehending the underlying structural and psychological factors at play. Furthermore, it explores the intricate mechanisms of trust and commitment, highlighting how factors like accurate information, adept self-presentation, and positive relationship-specific motives contribute to their development. By examining the relationship between structural dimensions and psychological processes, interdependence theory offers insight into relationship dynamics, empowering individuals to guide and enrich their social interactions skillfully.

4. **Social Penetration Theory:**

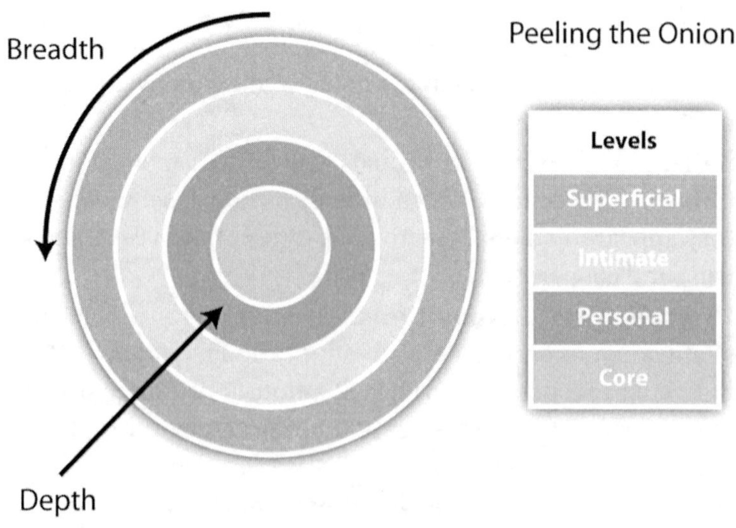

This theory, proposed by Irwin Altman and Dalmas Taylor (1973), suggests that relationships develop through gradual self-disclosure, leading to deeper levels of intimacy and understanding. At its core, the theory emphasizes self-disclosure as the primary mechanism through which relationships progress from superficial to deep levels of connection. The metaphor of the onion model clearly illustrates how individuals gradually reveal their inner selves over time. Just as one peels back the layers of an onion to reach its core, interpersonal interactions involve the gradual unveiling of personal information, moving from the public image to the private self. This process includes various layers of disclosure, ranging from superficial details like preferences in clothing to deeper aspects such as spiritual values and intimate fears.

Central to social penetration is the concept of breadth and depth in communication. Breadth refers to the variety of topics discussed, while depth pertains to the intimacy and vulnerability inherent in these discussions. As individuals engage in reciprocal self-disclosure, they operate through stages of social penetration, from orientation to stable exchange. Each stage represents a progression towards greater intimacy, characterized by increased openness and honesty.

However, the theory acknowledges that relationships can also experience de-penetration or dissolution. Social de-penetration occurs when individuals retract or withhold personal information due to interpersonal conflict or relational stressors. This process may signify a breakdown in trust or a need for relationship renegotiation. Moreover, social penetration theory integrates elements of social exchange theory, which emphasizes the exchange of rewards and costs in relationships. Individuals weigh the potential benefits of self-disclosure against the perceived risks, influencing the pace and depth of relationship development. Relationships are more likely to flourish when the rewards of disclosure outweigh the costs, developing trust and intimacy.

Social penetration theory provides an understanding of the interaction of interpersonal relationships, throwing light on the gradual process of self-disclosure and intimacy. By understanding how individuals go through various stages of disclosure, researchers and practitioners can better comprehend the factors influencing relationship development and maintenance.

5. **Social Identity Theory:** Social Identity Theory (SIT) offers a compelling framework for understanding how social relationships are formed and

maintained based on group affiliations. At its core, SIT suggests that individuals derive a significant portion of their identity from the groups to which they belong. These groups include various dimensions such as ethnicity, nationality, religion, profession, or even more informal categories like hobbies or interests. Let us understand how social identity theory is applied to social relationships.

- **Formation of Social Relationships:** SIT suggests that social relationships often originate within the context of shared group memberships. When individuals identify with the same group, whether it's a cultural community, a workplace team, or a group of friends with similar interests, they are more likely to form connections with each other. This initial identification with a common group develops a sense of belonging and shared identity, providing a foundation for building relationships.
- **Group Norms and Values:** Within social groups, there are often established norms, values, and behaviors that members follow. These norms serve as guidelines for interaction within the group and help to shape social relationships. Individuals are more likely to connect with others who exhibit similar beliefs and behaviors consistent with the group's norms. This shared adherence to group values reinforces social cohesion and strengthens interpersonal bonds.
- **In-Group Favoritism:** SIT highlights the phenomenon of in-group favoritism, wherein individuals show preference towards members of their group over those outside the group. This bias can influence social relationships by promoting solidarity and cooperation within the in-group, while potentially leading to competition or hostility towards out-groups. In-group favoritism contributes to the formation of close-knit social networks and can influence decisions regarding trust, cooperation, and support within these networks.
- **Social Comparison and Identity Enhancement:** Social comparison is an essential aspect of SIT, wherein individuals evaluate their group in comparison to other groups. This process of comparison can influence social relationships by shaping perceptions of group superiority or inferiority. Individuals may seek to enhance their social identity by associating with groups perceived as prestigious or advantageous, thereby influencing the types of relationships they form and the status they attain within social networks.

- **Intersecting Social Identities:** It's crucial to acknowledge that individuals often possess multiple social identities that intersect and interact with each other. These intersecting identities can influence the complexity of social relationships by creating overlapping or intersecting group memberships. For example, an individual may belong to multiple groups based on factors such as race, gender, religion, and profession, each contributing to their social identity and the relationships they form.

SIT provides a valuable insight of the dynamics of social relationships by emphasizing the role of group affiliations in shaping individual identity and interaction. By understanding how social identity influences the formation, maintenance, and dynamics of social relationships, we can gain a deeper understanding of human behavior and foster inclusive and supportive social environments.

6. **Triangular Theory of Love:** The theory was introduced by Robert Sternberg (1986) in a paper titled "A Triangular Theory of Love." Within Sternberg's triangular theory of love, he explains that there are three components of love:

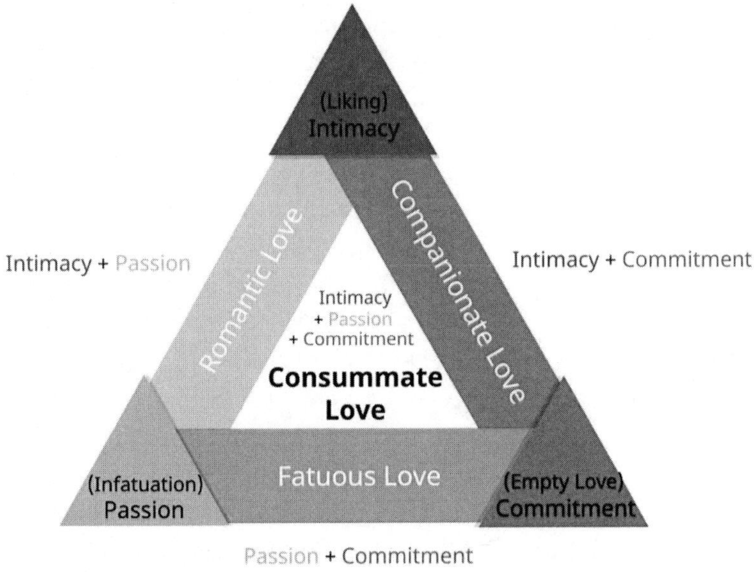

- **Intimacy:** the closeness each partner feels to the other and the strength of the bond that binds them together. Partners high in intimacy value and understand their partners.

- **Passion:** based on romantic feelings, physical attraction, and sexual intimacy with the partner.
- **Decision/Commitment:** represents cognitive factors such as acknowledging that one is in love and committed to maintaining the relationship.

According to Sternberg, these components are fundamental to what love is and interact in different ways to create various kinds of love.

There are seven types of love.

1. **Non-love:** The first type of love that Sternberg introduces is non-love, which is when none of the three components of love are present in a relationship (Sternberg, 1986). According to Sternberg, non-love can be seen in the "casual interactions" in our everyday lives and characterizes the large majority of our relationships. These relationships and interactions contain a complete lack of love, as none of the components of love are involved. This makes sense, as people would not typically express any sort of feeling of love for any brief encounter in their lives.
2. **Liking (also called friendship):** The second type of love that Sternberg introduces is liking, which is when the intimacy component of love is present in a relationship, but the passion and decision/commitment components are not. According to Sternberg, liking involves feelings of closeness, bondedness, and warmth toward the other, without feelings of intense passion or long-term commitment. Liking can be seen in the relationships in our lives that we refer to as friendships (Sternberg, 1986). Friendships can exist at different levels, and according to Sternberg, if any other components of love are present in a friendship, then it is not considered liking but is considered a different kind of love. Therefore, only friendships that lack the passion and decision/commitment components of love are considered to be the kind of love labeled as liking.
3. **Infatuation:** The third type of love that Sternberg introduces is infatuated love, which is when the passion component of love is present in a relationship, but the intimacy and decision/commitment components are not Sternberg's Fatuous Love. It is a type of love that combines Passion (physical and romantic attraction) and Commitment (decision to maintain the relationship) but lacks Intimacy (deep connection and understanding). This love type is often characterized by whirlwind romances driven by passion but lacking true depth. Sternberg places "love at first sight" in this category of love, which according to him, involves "a high degree of

psycho-physiological arousal, manifested in somatic symptoms such as increased heartbeat or even palpitations of the heart, increased hormonal secretions, erection of genitals, and so on. This kind of love develops very quickly, without time for any intimate feelings to grow or for a commitment to be made.

4. **Empty Love:** The fourth type of love that Sternberg introduces is empty love, which is when the decision/commitment component of love is present in a relationship but the intimacy and passion components are not. This type of love can commonly be found in some long-term relationships where the couple has lost feelings for one another. In Indian society, empty love may be the first stage of long-term relationship, such as in arranged marriages, while in Western societies, empty love occurs as the final or near-final stage of a long-term relationship.
5. **Romantic Love:** The fifth type of love that Sternberg introduces is romantic love, which is when the intimacy and passion components of love are present in a relationship, but the decision/commitment component is not. This kind of love can also be thought of as "liking with an added element, namely, the arousal brought about by physical attraction and its concomitants". For a popular literary example of this kind of love, one can look at "Romeo and Juliet," where the couple shares both intimate and passionate feelings towards one another but have made no real commitment to one another. Romantic love can also be found towards the beginning of some long-term relationships before the involved parties have committed to a long-term relationship with the other person.
6. **Companionate Love:** The sixth type of love that Sternberg introduces is companionate love, when the intimacy and decision/commitment components of love are present in a relationship but the passion component is not. Sternberg's Consummate Love refers to the ideal form of love that combines three components: Intimacy (deep connection and understanding), passion (physical and romantic attraction), and commitment (the decision to maintain love in the long term). It's considered the most complete and balanced form of love. This type of love is like a long-term, committed friendship, the kind that frequently occurs in marriages in which the physical attraction (a major source of passion) has died down. Because marriages typically involve such large amounts of the intimacy and decision/commitment components of love, they can often become forms of companionate love when the passion in the relationship is lost, commonly over time.

7. **Fatuous Love:** The seventh type of love that Sternberg has introduced is fatuous love, which is when the passion and decision/commitment components of love are present in a relationship but the intimacy component is not. According to Sternberg, fatuous love is where a commitment is made based on passion without the stabilizing element of intimate involvement. Because the intimate component of love takes time to develop, these relationships lack that aspect of love, and their relationship may therefore be more likely to fail.
8. **Consummate Love:** Finally, the eighth type of love that Sternberg has introduced is consummate love, which is when all three components of love are present in a relationship. Nowadays, when one thinks of love, they are most likely thinking about consummate love. Additionally, consummate love is seemingly the type of love that most people aim to find. An example of consummate love can be found in parents' love for their children, often called unconditional love.

Understanding Friendship: Friendship, as defined by Hays (1988), is a voluntary interdependence between two individuals over time, aimed at fulfilling socio-emotional goals through companionship, intimacy, affection, and mutual assistance. Friends play a crucial role in our micro-system, offering mutual respect, appreciation, and companionship. The social support hypothesis emphasizes the protective function of supportive interactions during times of stress. The dynamic nature of friendships means they can be transient, yet the level of proximity or emotional closeness often reflects our need for emotional connection and combats emotional loneliness (Cacioppo & Patrick, 2008). Two key criteria for friendship are:

a) Quality, indicating the depth of intimacy; and
b) Conflict, referring to the frequency of psychologically distressing situations.

Oswald (2017) identified four essential factors that contribute to the maintenance of friendships:

1. **Emphatic Happiness:** Sharing positive news or events develops emotional connection and strengthens the bond between friends.
2. **Availability of Social Support:** Being there for one another during challenging times cultivates trust and solidarity.
3. **Non-judgmental Acceptance:** Providing a safe space for open and honest communication without fear of criticism or rejection increases mutual understanding and acceptance.

4. **Quality and Quantity of Time Spent Together:** Investing time in each other's company allows for meaningful interactions and strengthens the friendship bond.

Numerous studies have highlighted the positive effects of these friendship qualities on happiness, satisfaction, well-being, and feelings of trust (Mikulincer & Shaver, 2013; Braithwaite & Holt-Lunstad, 2017; Keltner et al., 2018). Overall, friendships contribute significantly to our emotional and social fulfillment, serving as pillars of support and sources of joy in our lives.

Benefits of Practicing Positive Psychology in Social Relationships

a) **Enhanced Relationship Satisfaction:** Positive psychology encourages partners to recognize and appreciate each other's strengths, developing a deeper sense of respect and admiration. By concentrating on the positive elements of the relationship, couples can reduce conflicts and enhance their overall satisfaction and harmony.

b) **Stronger Bonds and Connections:** Sharing positive experiences and expressing gratitude strengthens emotional bonds, making relationships more resilient. Positive psychology promotes supportive behaviors, encouraging partners to be more empathetic and understanding towards each other's needs.

c) **Improved Communication:** Techniques such as active listening help partners feel heard and valued, reducing misunderstandings and fostering open communication. Emphasizing constructive feedback over criticism helps maintain a positive dialogue, leading to healthier interactions.

d) **Reduction in Negative Behaviors:** Focusing on positive interactions and reframing negative situations reduces the frequency and intensity of conflicts. Implementing positive discipline strategies helps manage disagreements without resorting to harmful behaviors.

e) **Greater Emotional Resilience:** Positive relationships act as a shield against stress, providing emotional support that helps individuals cope better with life's challenges. Positive psychology develops resilience, enabling individuals and couples to recover more quickly from setbacks.

f) **Enhanced Overall Well-Being:** Practices such as gratitude, optimism, and mindfulness contribute to better mental health, reducing anxiety and depression. Positive social interactions and emotional support have been linked to improved physical health outcomes, including lower blood pressure and stronger immune function.

g) **Longevity and Life Satisfaction:** Positive relationships contribute to longer life expectancy by providing emotional and social support. Individuals who practice positive psychology report higher levels of life satisfaction and happiness.

h) **Professional and Financial Benefits:** Positive psychology enhances workplace relationships, leading to improved teamwork, collaboration, and job satisfaction. Positive attitudes and behaviors can lead to better job performance and career advancement, potentially increasing income levels.

i) **Holistic Personal Growth:** By focusing on strengths and positive traits, individuals can achieve personal growth and self-actualization. Positive psychology helps individuals find meaning and purpose in their relationships and lives, contributing to overall fulfillment.

j) **Community and Social Impact:** Positive relationships and behaviors extend beyond individual interactions, contributing to more supportive and cohesive communities. Individuals who practice positive psychology are more likely to engage in pro-social behaviors, such as volunteering and helping others, enhancing the social system.

By integrating positive psychology into social relationships, individuals can cultivate a supportive and nurturing environment that promotes personal growth, resilience, and happiness. This holistic approach not only improves interpersonal connections but also contributes to overall well-being and life satisfaction.

Application of Positive Psychology in Social Relationships

1. **Recognizing Positive Attributes:** When experiencing anger towards someone, it's common for negative thoughts or criticisms to surface, such as "She is always indecisive" or "He is always temperamental." However, positive psychology encourages us to shift our focus towards spotting strengths in our relationships. Strengths, as defined by Linley (2008), are preexisting capacities for authentic and energizing behaviors, thoughts, or feelings that enable optimal functioning and performance. Research by Kashdan et al. (2018) indicates that perceiving strengths in our partners predicts better daily relationship satisfaction. Here are some tips that help in recognizing positive attributes.

1. By listening with passion and energy when people discuss topics that excite them.
2. By noticing the energy and engagement people show during conversation.
3. By reflecting on our strengths, recognizing them in oneself increases the likelihood of noticing strengths in others.

2. **Strengths and fulfillment Dreams Genogram:** Creating a family strengths tree as a technique of positive psychology can significantly increase social relationships in several ways:
    1. **Promoting Appreciation:** By outlining the strengths of each family tree, individuals can develop a deeper appreciation for the positive qualities present in their partner's family and their own. This exercise encourages a shift in focus from potential shortcomings to the strengths and resilience that exist within each family lineage.
    2. **Developing Understanding:** The process of constructing a family strengths tree allows couples to gain insight into each other's backgrounds and the factors that have shaped their personalities and values. Understanding the positive characteristics and achievements within each family helps individuals understand their partner's upbringing and influences, developing empathy and mutual understanding.
    3. **Encouraging Communication:** Discussing the strengths identified in each family tree promotes open and meaningful communication between partners. Sharing stories and experiences related to family strengths can deepen emotional connection and intimacy, creating a supportive environment for discussing challenges and goals within the relationship.
    4. **Building Resilience:** Recognizing the resilience and positive attributes within one's family history can inspire individuals to face challenges more effectively. By acknowledging the strengths that have helped family members overcome hardships; individuals can cultivate a sense of optimism in their own lives and relationships.
    5. **Empowering Problem-Solving:** Utilizing the strengths identified in the family strengths tree, couples can approach relationship issues with a solution-focused mindset. Positive psychology techniques encourage individuals to use their strengths to face challenges collaboratively, developing a sense of empowerment and efficacy in managing relationship dynamics.

The family strengths tree technique is an effective way to enhance social relationships by promoting appreciation, understanding, communication, and problem-solving skills within couples. By focusing on the positive aspects of family history, individuals can cultivate stronger connections and more supportive, fulfilling relationship dynamics.

3. **Sound Relationship House:** The Sound Relationship House theory, developed by John Gottman and Julie Schwartz Gottman, is indeed a powerful framework for enhancing social relationships through positive psychology techniques. Sound Relationship House contributes to strengthening relationships in the following ways:
    1. **Build Love Maps:** This involves deep understanding and empathy by actively learning about the partner's inner world. It increases emotional intimacy and connection, which are crucial for maintaining a strong bond.
    2. **Share Fondness and Admiration:** Expressing appreciation and respect increases a positive atmosphere in the relationship. By focusing on each other's strengths and qualities, couples reinforce their love and admiration, promoting feelings of security and validation.
    3. **Turn Towards, Not Away:** Being attentive and responsive to your partner's gestures for connection builds trust and closeness. This floor emphasizes the importance of emotional responsiveness and support, which are foundational for healthy communication and intimacy.
    4. **The Positive Perspective:** Adopting a positive outlook enables couples to approach challenges with resilience and understanding. By reframing negative situations and attributing positive intentions to each other, couples develop goodwill and mutual respect, which strengthens their bond during difficult times.
    5. **Manage Conflict:** Learning constructive conflict management skills is essential for resolving differences without damaging the relationship. By prioritizing empathy, active listening, and emotional regulation, couples can resolve disagreements and emerge with greater understanding and cohesion.
    6. **Make Life Dreams Come True:** Supporting each other's goals and aspirations increases a sense of partnership and mutual growth. By advocating for each other's dreams, couples deepen their emotional connection and create shared experiences that enrich their relationship.

7. **Create Shared Meaning:** Establishing shared rituals, traditions, and goals reinforces the couple's identity and sense of belonging. By co-creating meaningful experiences and narratives, couples strengthen their bond and create a sense of purpose and unity.
8. **Trust and Commitment:** The weight-bearing walls provide stability and security in the relationship. Trust and commitment enable couples to face challenges and uncertainties with confidence, knowing that they can rely on each other and are committed to the relationship's growth and well-being.

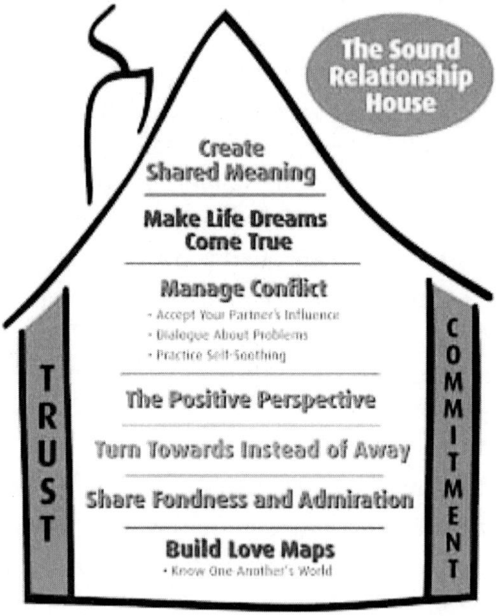

The Sound Relationship House theory offers a comprehensive roadmap for building and maintaining healthy, fulfilling relationships. By incorporating positive psychology principles such as empathy, gratitude, resilience, and a growth mindset, couples can cultivate deeper connections, navigate challenges effectively, and sustain long-term happiness and satisfaction in their relationships.

4. **Emotional Reservoir:** The concept of the emotional reservoir is analogous to that of a bank account where we store our savings; however, in this case, we reserve our emotions. The concept is rooted in the Gottman Relationship model, which serves as a powerful positive psychology technique for enhancing social relationships by developing intimacy, managing conflicts, and reducing emotional distance. Positive

interactions, such as expressions of appreciation, acts of kindness, and empathetic responses, constitute deposits, while negative interactions, like criticism, defensiveness, and contempt, represent withdrawals. By understanding and implementing the principles of the Emotional Bank Account, couples can cultivate a culture of emotional responsiveness, support, and validation within their relationship. The steps are as follows:

1. **Building Intimacy:** Making consistent deposits into the Emotional Bank Account strengthens the emotional bond between partners. Expressing appreciation, showing affection, and empathizing with each other's experiences deepen intimacy and foster a sense of closeness and connection.
2. **Managing Conflicts:** Maintaining a positive balance in the Emotional Bank Account serves as a safeguard during conflicts. When partners have built up a reserve of positive interactions, they are more likely to approach disagreements with goodwill, understanding, and empathy, reducing the likelihood of conflicts and increasing the chances of resolving them constructively.
3. **Reducing Emotional Distance:** Regular deposits into the Emotional Bank Account help to resolve emotional distance between partners. By consistently demonstrating care, respect, and support, couples create a foundation of trust and security, which develops open communication and vulnerability, thereby bridging emotional gaps and strengthening the relationship.

Investing in the Emotional Bank Account involves mindfulness, appreciation, empathy, and affection, all of which are fundamental aspects of positive psychology. By actively cultivating emotional connections and prioritizing positivity, couples can create a supportive and fulfilling relationship environment that increases growth, resilience, and long-term happiness.

5. **Three Good Things Technique:** It is a powerful tool for enhancing social relationships, particularly in the context of conflicted relationships. It involves reflecting on and writing down three positive events or experiences that occurred during the day, along with why each of these things happened, and expressing gratitude either silently or by sharing with someone else if appropriate. The technique enhances social relationships in the following ways:

   1. **Develops Positivity:** By focusing on positive aspects of each other's behavior, partners shift their attention away from negative

thoughts and focus on appreciation and gratitude. This helps in the development of a more positive atmosphere within the relationship, where both partners feel valued and validated.

2. **Increases Appreciation:** Frequently, in conflicted relationships, partners may fall into negative patterns of thinking where they overlook each other's positive actions. Participating in the "three good things" exercise encourages partners to actively seek out and acknowledge positive behaviors, developing increased appreciation for each other's efforts and contributions.
3. **Enhances Communication:** This activity encourages open and constructive communication between partners. By verbalizing and reflecting on positive behaviors, partners have the opportunity to express their appreciation directly to each other. This can strengthen emotional bonds and build trust, as both partners feel heard and understood.
4. **Promotes Self-Reflection:** Additionally, the exercise encourages partners to reflect on their contributions to the positive aspects of the relationship. This self-reflection builds self-awareness and personal growth, as individuals become more conscious of how their actions impact their partner and the relationship as a whole.
5. **Reduces Negativity Bias:** Negativity bias is the tendency to focus more on negative experiences than positive ones, which can be detrimental to relationships. The "three good things" technique helps to counteract this bias by deliberately focusing attention on positive aspects of the relationship. Over time, this can help partners reframe their perspectives and cultivate a more balanced view of the relationship.

By promoting positivity, appreciation, communication, self-reflection, and combating negativity bias, the "three good things" technique serves as a valuable tool for enhancing social relationships, particularly in the face of conflict and tension.

6. **Encouraging Hope:** Encouraging Hope through Positive Psychology in Relationships involves linking hope with the achievement of goals. Snyder (2002) conceptualized hope as a belief system that includes both the identification of pathways toward a goal and the determination to achieve that goal (agency). In relationships, individuals with high levels of hope can find out personally meaningful goals and have confidence in their abilities to attain them. For instance, consider an example where a

husband, characterized by high hope, aims to resolve a conflict with his partner. He not only recognizes potential strategies to defuse the anger (identifying pathways) but also possesses the motivation and courage to implement them (identifying agency). Depending on whether an individual exhibits extremely low levels of pathway or agency, a positive psychologist may customize therapy to address these specific needs, such as developing individualized goals, identifying resources, and developing both pathways and agency.

7. **Caring for Relationships:** Caring for Relationships: Harvey and Omarzu (1997) proposed that minding in relationships is crucial for the development of emotional closeness. It aims to facilitate the exchange of thoughts, feelings, and behaviors between individuals in a relationship. The fundamental principles of this theory include:
   - **Understanding Each other:** This involves actively seeking and understanding each other's preferences, vulnerabilities, and secrets.
   - **Positive Attribution in Relationships:** This approach attributes positive behaviors to internal dispositions and negative behaviors to external factors.
   - **Embracing Acceptance and Mutual Respect:** This includes recognizing both the positive and negative traits in one's partner, and developing empathy and social skills.
   - **Reciprocity:** Both partners are required to share an equal share of responsibility in the relationship to enhance its quality.

Summary

Social relationships, defined as the connections we have with others, are crucial for mental and emotional health, offering support, companionship, and a sense of belonging. These relationships include familial bonds, friendships, romantic partnerships, and professional associations, each contributing uniquely to our social structure and psychological resilience.

The benefits of strong social relationships are manifold. They provide emotional support, protect against stress, and contribute to higher levels of happiness and life satisfaction. Social connections also develop a sense of identity and self-worth, enabling individuals to flourish. In terms of physical health, strong social ties have been linked to lower risks of chronic diseases, faster recovery from illness, and increased longevity. The absence of these connections, conversely, can lead to loneliness, depression, and a host of negative health outcomes. The importance of social relationships is emphasized by various theoretical perspectives. Various positive psychology intervention techniques are discussed in the chapter, for the enhancement of social relationships.

The chapter explains the critical importance of social relationships for overall well-being and demonstrates how positive psychology can offer practical tools and interventions to nurture and enhance these connections. By utilizing the principles of positive psychology, individuals can build stronger, more fulfilling relationships, ultimately contributing to their happiness and health.

CHAPTER 8

APPLICATION OF POSITIVE PSYCHOLOGY IN DISABILITY

In the field of psychology, there has historically been a prevailing focus on deficits, limitations, and pathologies, particularly concerning individuals with disabilities. The narrative is often centered on what people with disabilities can't do rather than acknowledging their strengths and capacity for growth. However, in recent decades, there has been a notable paradigm shift towards a more inclusive and empowering approach—one that acknowledges the inherent worth and potential for flourishing among individuals with disabilities. Rather than viewing disability solely through the viewpoint of impairment and incapacity, this chapter explores how the application of positive psychology can shed light on the strengths, capabilities, and inherent value of individuals with disabilities. According to positive psychology, self-determination plays an important role in the development of well-being and optimal functioning among individuals with disabilities. This emphasizes the significance of autonomy, competence, and relatedness in the development of a sense of empowerment and agency.

This chapter will address the challenges and opportunities inherent in applying positive psychology principles to disability. It will explore how the concept of "optimal human functioning" can be reframed to be more inclusive and accommodating of diverse abilities. Additionally, it will discuss the necessity for greater inclusivity within the field of positive psychology, advocating for the active involvement and representation of individuals with disabilities in research, practice, and policymaking. The chapter serves as a call to action—to shift the discussion surrounding disability towards one that celebrates strengths promotes well-being, and adopts the inherent dignity and worth of every individual, regardless of ability.

Introduction

Before we study disability and its impact on an individual's functioning, let us define the concept and understand what it means. In this field, there are three words that are used interchangeably, but all three have different meanings. Let us define and understand the concept.

The World Health Organization (WHO) has defined impairment, disability, and handicap as the following:

Impairment: Any temporary or permanent loss or abnormality of a body structure or function, whether physiological or psychological. An impairment is a disturbance affecting functions that can be mental (memory, consciousness) or sensory, internal (heart, kidney), or external (the head, the trunk, or the limbs). It is an abnormality of structure and/or function at the organ level. At this stage, an affected individual becomes aware that he or she is unhealthy." Because of autism, the student has trouble communicating the same way other people do.

Disability: A restriction or inability to perform an activity in the manner or within the range considered normal for a human being, mostly resulting from impairment.

- A disability is a condition or function judged to be significantly impaired relative to the usual standard of an individual or group. The term is used to refer to individual functioning, including physical impairment, sensory impairment, cognitive impairment, intellectual impairment, mental illness, and various types of chronic disease.
- Disability is conceptualized as a multidimensional experience for the person involved. There may be effects on organs or body parts, and there may be effects on a person's participation in areas of life.

Handicap: This is the result of an impairment or disability that limits or prevents the fulfillment of one or several roles regarded as normal, depending on age, sex, and social and cultural factors. A handicap is a disadvantage resulting from impairment or a disability that limits or prevents the fulfillment of a role that is normal (depending on age, sex, and social and cultural factors) for the affected individual. Measured as such, handicaps largely reflect societal attitudes toward people with disabilities." The student with autism has a significant handicap because the school has not provided him with an alternative communication system.

The Evolution of Disability Perception and Services: From Pathology to Positive Psychology

- **Post-World War II Shifts in Disability Perception:** In the wake of World War II, disability began to be viewed not solely as a medical pathology, but as a condition requiring broader social and psychological consideration. The aftermath of the war saw an increase in demands from parents and families advocating for alternatives to the institutionalization and isolation of individuals with disabilities (Abeson and Davis, 2000). This grassroots movement led to significant legislative measures and civil protections aimed at ensuring access to education, rehabilitation, and community integration for people with disabilities (Thompson et al., 2017). The transition from a medical-institutional paradigm to a normalization-community services paradigm marked an important moment in the evolution of disability services, emphasizing the importance of community inclusion and typical daily routines. Despite these efforts, services largely remained segregated, rooted in a pathology-centric view of disability.

- **Paradigmatic Shifts in the Medical Field:** The latter part of the 20th century witnessed a paradigmatic shift within the medical field itself. Recognizing the limitations of viewing chronic health conditions, including disability, solely through a pathological lens, new conceptualizations emerged (World Health Organization, 2001). The World Health Organization's International Classification of Functioning, Disability, and Health (ICF) in 2001 reframed disability as the result of interactions among health conditions, personal factors, and environmental influences. This groundbreaking approach introduced models of person-environment fit, emphasizing the dynamic interplay between individual abilities and the supportive context in which they operate.
- **The Emergence of Positive Psychology:** Concurrently, the emergence of positive psychology, with its focus on individual strengths and well-being, provided synergistic momentum to these new conceptualizations (Seligman and Csikszentmihalyi, 2000; Peterson, 2009). The ICF, for the first time, offered a language for a strength-based approach to disability, aligning seamlessly with the principles of positive psychology (Wehmeyer, 2013b). This approach encouraged a focus on the strengths and capabilities of individuals with disabilities rather than solely on their limitations.
- **Advocacy for Value-Laden Beliefs:** Amidst these transformative shifts, the work of Wright (1972) advocated for embracing a set of value-laden beliefs and principles that affirm the worth and dignity of individuals with disabilities (Dunn & Elliott, 2005). These principles laid the groundwork for a constructive and positive perception of disability, fostering a supportive environment conducive to personal growth. Psychology, traditionally focused on the negative aspects of human

experiences, began to shift towards studying the positive growth that can follow acquired disabilities.

- **Resilience and Subjective Well-Being:** Physical disabilities can arise from various causes, such as trauma or disease, resulting in reduced function or the loss of a body part. While restricted activity or physical loss due to disability can lead to negative psychological consequences of depressive symptoms and problem behaviors, many individuals with disabilities demonstrate remarkable resilience and report high levels of Subjective Well-being (SWB). Positive psychologists examine individuals whose lives remain positive despite their disabilities, offering scientific insights that equip sufferers with skills to focus on the positive aspects of their lives. It is crucial to recognize that physical disabilities present diverse challenges, not only intrapersonal but also interpersonal.

Perspectives on Disability

- **Psychological Perspectives on Disability:** Psychological perspectives on disability offer complex insights into the lived experiences, coping mechanisms, and potential for growth among individuals facing various impairments. These perspectives include a range of theoretical frameworks and approaches, each shedding light on different aspects of disability.
- **Biomedical Perspective of Disability:** This focuses on disability purely in terms of the impairment that it gives the individual. The biomedical model is often contrasted with the biopsychological model. The medical model of disability is presented as viewing disability as a problem of the person, directly caused by disease, trauma, or other health condition, which therefore requires sustained medical care provided in the form of individual treatment by professionals.

  In the medical model, management of the disability is aimed at a "cure," or the individual's adjustment and behavioral change that would lead to an "almost-cure" or effective cure. In the medical model, medical care is viewed as the main issue, and at the political level, the principal response is that of modifying or reforming healthcare policy.
- **Social Model of disability:** The social model of disability sees the issue of "disability" as a socially created problem and a matter of the full integration of individuals into society. In this model, disability is not an attribute of an individual but rather a complex collection of conditions, many of which are created by the social environment. Hence, the management of the problem requires social action and is the collective

responsibility of society at large to make the environmental modifications necessary for the full participation of people with disabilities in all areas of social life. The Social Model of Disability asserts that individuals possess impairments, not disabilities. According to this model, the term "people with disabilities" can be misleading as it conflates impairment and disability, implying that the disability is solely caused by the individual rather than society. In reality, disability is the result of society's failure to accommodate the needs of individuals with impairments. Hence, the term "disabled people" is used to describe individuals with impairments who experience disability due to societal barriers.

- **Bio-psycho-social Model of Disability:** The Bio-psycho-social Model integrates biological, psychological, and social factors to understand disability. It recognizes how biological predispositions, psychological processes, and social context interact to shape the experience and consequences of disability. This approach moves beyond simplistic explanations that focus solely on biological or psychological factors, acknowledging the complex interplay between various aspects of an individual's life. By considering the multifaceted nature of disability, the bio-psycho-social model provides a comprehensive framework for understanding and addressing the challenges faced by individuals with disabilities.
- **Existential and Phenomenological Model of Disability:** Existential and phenomenological perspectives within psychology offer a deep understanding of the subjective experiences of disability. By exploring themes of identity, meaning-making, and existential struggle, these perspectives acknowledge the profound impact disability has on an individual's sense of self and worldview. Moreover, they recognize the potential for transformative growth and self-discovery amidst the challenges posed by disability. This approach emphasizes the importance of understanding the personal narratives and lived experiences of individuals with disabilities, highlighting their resilience and capacity for profound psychological growth.
- **Ecological Model of Disability:** This perspective analyzes the individual's experiences in the context of family dynamics, community structures, and broader societal norms. By emphasizing the dynamic interaction between the individual and their environment, it highlights how various factors influence the opportunities and challenges faced by people with disabilities. This approach emphasizes the importance of

understanding the complex interplay between individual characteristics and environmental influences, ultimately shaping the experiences and outcomes of individuals living with disabilities.

- **Positive Psychology Model of Disability:** Positive psychology, as a perspective within psychology on disability, focuses on a strength-based approach. It directs attention to personal strength, adaptive coping mechanisms, and the pursuit of well-being in the face of adversity. By highlighting strengths rather than deficits, positive psychology aims to empower individuals with disabilities, developing a sense of self-determination and agency. Moreover, it seeks to facilitate psychological growth, emphasizing the potential for individuals to flourish despite their challenges. Through interventions that promote positivity, optimism, and personal growth, Positive Psychology offers a pathway toward developing the overall well-being and quality of life of individuals living with disabilities.

Theories of Disability

- **Functionalist Theory:** Functionalist theory, one of the core perspectives in sociology, views society as a complex system whose parts work together to promote solidarity and stability. Within this framework, disability is perceived through the perspective of the "sick role," a concept introduced by Talcott Parsons. The sick role implies that individuals who are ill are temporarily exempt from their usual roles and are expected to seek treatment to return to normal functioning. However, this perspective becomes problematic when applied to chronic conditions and disabilities that do not conform to the temporary nature of the sick role. Disabled individuals, whose conditions are often permanent and not treatable, are seen as deviating from societal norms. This view influences healthcare policies, leading to an emphasis on professional control and efforts to normalize disabled individuals, often ignoring their autonomy and unique needs. For instance, more than 70% of welfare spending is directed towards the salaries of professionals rather than direct support for disabled people, highlighting the systemic preference for professional management over self-determined care.
- **Normalization Theory:** A variant of functionalism, normalization theory seeks to integrate disabled individuals into mainstream society by promoting their engagement in culturally valued activities. This approach aims to reduce the stigma associated with disability by encouraging

conformity to societal norms. However, normalization theory can lead to controversial practices, such as cosmetic surgery for individuals with Down's syndrome, intended to make them appear more "normal." While the intention is to improve social acceptance, these efforts often reinforce the idea that disabled individuals need to change to fit societal standards rather than society adapting to include diverse forms of human existence. This approach can marginalize those who cannot or do not wish to conform to these norms, increasing discrimination and failing to address the broader social and structural barriers that disabled people face.

- **Social Constructionism Theory:** Social constructionism offers a contrasting perspective, focusing on how disability is defined and understood within different cultural and social contexts. This theory emphasizes that disability is not just a medical condition but is significantly shaped by societal attitudes, policies, and economic factors. For instance, blindness is experienced differently across countries: as a loss requiring counseling in the U.S., a support issue in Sweden, a technical problem in Britain, and a spiritual matter in Italy. This diversity highlights that disability is a social construct that varies widely depending on cultural and societal norms. Furthermore, in industrialized societies like the U.S., the concept of disability has been co-modified, turning it into a business that generates income for a range of professionals. This commoditization can lead to an overemphasis on individual treatment and rehabilitation rather than addressing systemic issues that create barriers for disabled people.
- **Postmodernism Theory:** Postmodernism challenges traditional, rigid structures of understanding, emphasizing the complexity and fragmented nature of society. It rejects universal truths and embraces multiple perspectives, suggesting that what constitutes health or normality is subjective and context-dependent. In terms of disability, postmodernism critiques the conventional association of impairments with illness and unhealthiness. It argues that having an impairment does not necessarily equate to being unhealthy, and that societal concepts of health can themselves be disabling when they impose unrealistic and oppressive standards. This perspective encourages a more nuanced understanding of disability, recognizing that disabled individuals can lead healthy, fulfilling lives despite their impairments and that societal attitudes and structures often create more barriers than the impairments themselves.
- **Critical Theory:** Critical theory examines disability through the lens of social oppression and inequality, arguing that the primary source of

disability is not the individual's impairment, but the societal structures and ideologies that discriminate and exclude. According to this theory, societal barriers, such as inaccessible public transportation or discriminatory employment practices, are the real issues that disable individuals. Critical theory advocates for social change and action to address these systemic barriers. It has helped raise political awareness and empower disabled individuals, challenging the medical model that views disability as a personal tragedy or a purely medical issue. By highlighting the role of social oppression and advocating for structural changes, critical theory promotes a shift towards recognizing and addressing the social, economic, and political factors that contribute to disability, thereby fostering a more inclusive and equitable society.

Problems Faced by Disabled

- **Stigma:** Stigma, by definition, is a mark of disgrace associated with a particular circumstance, quality, or person. In the context of disabilities, stigmas arise from misconceptions and a lack of understanding. Many people view individuals living with disabilities as "different," grouping them all into one category without considering their unique strengths and capabilities. Stigma towards disability includes exclusion, rejection, and devaluation due to perceived differences. This societal attitude supports structural and interactional discrimination, leading to lower status assignments and exclusion in educational and social settings. Stigmatization often results in adverse effects on various domains, including educational and labor market attainment, psychological well-being, and health. For disabled individuals, stigma manifests in structural barriers to inclusive education, such as limited access to resources and insufficient support. Moreover, it develops a sense of shame and withdrawal, known as stigma consciousness, impacting their experiences and interactions within society.
- **Discrimination:** Discrimination based on disability" means any distinction, exclusion, or restriction based on disability which has the purpose or effect of impairing or nullifying the recognition, enjoyment or exercise, on an equal basis with others, of all human rights and fundamental freedoms in the political, economic, social, cultural, civil or any other field. It includes all forms of discrimination, including denial of reasonable accommodation. Constant exposure to discrimination can lead to devastating effects on one's mental well-being. Some of these effects

include low self-esteem, social withdrawal, and even clinical conditions such as anxiety and depression. In a nutshell, common psychological effects of discrimination in disabled individuals include:

- Lowered self-esteem
- Increased social isolation
- Higher levels of stress and anxiety
- Development or worsening of existing depressive symptoms
- Heightened feelings of loneliness and fear
- Reduced quality of life and overall well-being

- **Oppression:** Oppression against individuals with disabilities persists as a complex interplay of historical legacies and contemporary societal norms. This systemic oppression leaves out and takes away opportunities from disabled individuals, keeping in place barriers in institutions, limited ways to access things and unfair treatment by the law. This means they feel even more left out and without power in society. This ongoing oppression makes social differences stronger, making it harder for them to join in fully and have the same rights, things, and chances as others. It keeps them stuck in situations where they don't have as much as others and aren't included as much, continuing the cycle of being at a disadvantage and not being included.
- **Social Exclusion:** Social exclusion refers to the systematic disadvantage faced by certain groups due to discrimination based on various factors such as ethnicity, disability, or gender. For individuals with disabilities, social exclusion manifests as being left out of social activities and public spaces due to physical barriers or stigma. This exclusion often results in feelings of loneliness, isolation, and alienation from society. Such experiences can profoundly impact the psychology of disabled individuals, leading to decreased self-esteem, increased feelings of worthlessness, and a sense of being disconnected from the broader community.

Application of Positive Psychology Techniques

1. **Quality of Life:** Quality of life, within the context of positive psychology, refers to a multidimensional construct that includes various aspects of an individual's well-being, including physical, emotional, social, and psychological domains. It serves as an outcomes-based evaluation framework that considers personally valued life outcomes and guides the design of support systems for individuals, particularly those with disabilities. For example, a person with a disability who receives

comprehensive support services designed to their specific needs and preferences, enabling them to lead a fulfilling and meaningful life, and exemplify a high quality of life. As conceptualized by Schalock and Verdugo (2013), quality of life is not merely a static condition but a dynamic meta-construct, incorporating core dimensions such as self-determination, financial, physical, and mental well-being, as well as outcomes related to social inclusion, personal development, and interpersonal relationships. By emphasizing values of dignity, equality, empowerment, and inclusion, quality of life interventions promote holistic well-being and enhance the overall quality-of-life for individuals.

2. **Self-Determination:** Self-determination, as defined by Causal Agency Theory, is a dispositional characteristic wherein individuals act as the causal agents in their own lives. It involves pursuing freely chosen goals and adopting self-directed, empowered behavior to achieve them. For individuals with disabilities, self-determination means being able to make choices and decisions that affect their lives, rather than having decisions made for them by others. For example, a student with a disability who struggles with his own educational needs and preferences, actively participates in setting his learning goals, and takes steps to achieve them, demonstrates self-determination. Research has shown that individuals with disabilities who are more self-determined tend to achieve better outcomes in various domains, including education, employment, and quality of life.
3. **PERMA:** The PERMA model, introduced by psychologist Martin Seligman, outlines five key elements that contribute to overall well-being and happiness
   - **Positive Emotions:** In the context of individuals with disabilities, developing positive emotions involves promoting activities and practices that enhance their mood and overall well-being. For individuals facing physical or cognitive challenges, experiencing positive emotions can serve as a powerful coping mechanism and contribute to their overall resilience. For example, gratitude journaling can be a beneficial technique for individuals with disabilities. By regularly writing down things they are grateful for, they can shift their focus from their limitations to the positive aspects of their lives, developing a sense of appreciation and contentment. Similarly, mindfulness practices, such as meditation or deep breathing exercises, can help individuals with disabilities manage stress, anxiety, and negative emotions. By

focusing on the present moment and cultivating awareness, they can develop greater emotional resilience and a more positive outlook on life. Engaging in enjoyable hobbies or activities designed according to their interests and abilities can also uplift their spirits and enhance their overall well-being. Whether it's painting, gardening, listening to music, or participating in adaptive sports, finding activities that bring joy and fulfillment can have a profound impact on individuals with disabilities.

- **Engagement:** In the context of individuals with disabilities, engagement refers to helping them find activities and activities that not only suit their interests and strengths but also provide a sense of flow and fulfillment. This involves recognizing their unique abilities and preferences and facilitating opportunities for meaningful participation in various activities. For example, individuals with physical disabilities may find fulfillment in adaptive sports or recreational activities in accordance with their abilities. Similarly, those with intellectual disabilities may engage in artistic pursuits, such as painting or music, which allow them to express themselves creatively and experience a sense of achievement. Furthermore, engagement for individuals with disabilities can extend to skill-building exercises or vocational training programs that enhance their abilities and provide avenues for personal growth and development. By identifying and supporting activities that are in accordance with their interests and strengths, individuals with disabilities can experience a greater sense of fulfillment and satisfaction.
- **Relationships:** In the context of individuals with disabilities, developing positive relationships and social connections is crucial for their overall well-being and quality of life. Building supportive networks and meaningful connections can offer a range of benefits that are particularly impactful for individuals facing physical or cognitive challenges.
  a) **Emotional Support:** Positive relationships provide a source of emotional support for individuals with disabilities, helping them to face the ups and downs of life with greater resilience. Having someone to confide in, depend on during difficult times, and share their experiences with can alleviate feelings of loneliness and isolation.

b) **Companionship:** Social connections offer companionship and brotherhood, allowing individuals with disabilities to engage in social activities, outings, and shared experiences with others. Having companionship can enhance their sense of belonging and inclusion in social settings.

c) **Sense of Belonging:** Meaningful connections with others develop a sense of belonging and acceptance within communities. When individuals with disabilities feel valued and accepted by their peers, they are more likely to participate actively in social interactions and feel a sense of pride in their identity.

d) **Practical Support:** Positive relationships can also provide practical support, such as assistance with daily tasks, transportation, or moving in public spaces. Having a supportive network of friends, family members, or caregivers can enhance individuals' independence and overall quality of life.

Overall, developing positive relationships and social connections is essential for individuals with disabilities to thrive emotionally, socially, and psychologically. By building supportive networks and meaningful connections, they can experience greater happiness, fulfillment, and a sense of belonging within their communities.

➢ **Meaning:** In the context of individuals with disabilities, finding meaning in life is essential for promoting their overall well-being and enhancing their quality of life. For individuals facing physical or cognitive challenges, discovering purpose and meaning can provide a sense of direction and motivation, empowering them to overcome obstacles and live fulfilling lives. Encouraging individuals with disabilities to explore their values helps them identify what is important and meaningful to them. This process involves reflecting on their beliefs, interests, and priorities, and coordinating their actions with these values.

a) **Setting Meaningful Goals:** Setting meaningful goals provides individuals with disabilities a sense of purpose and direction. Whether it's pursuing educational achievements, career aspirations, or personal milestones, having goals to pursue provides a sense of meaning and accomplishment.

b) **Engaging in Purposeful Activities:** Engaging the disabled in purposeful activities that match his sense of purpose and identity enables him to experience fulfillment and satisfaction.

This might include volunteering, advocating for causes, pursuing creative endeavors, or making meaningful contributions to their community.

By helping individuals with disabilities find purpose and meaning in their lives, we empower them to live with greater intentionality and fulfillment. Supporting individuals in setting and achieving goals, no matter how small can boost their self-esteem and sense of competence. Celebrating accomplishments and milestones can further reinforce feelings of success and achievement.

- **Accomplishment:** Assisting individuals with disabilities in establishing and attaining goals, regardless of their size, can significantly increase their self-esteem and feelings of competence. By breaking down tasks into manageable steps and providing support along the way, individuals with disabilities can build confidence in their abilities to overcome challenges and accomplish their objectives. Moreover, acknowledging and celebrating their achievements and milestones serves to reinforce their sense of success and fulfillment. This recognition not only validates their efforts but also encourages continued progress and growth. For individuals with disabilities, each accomplishment, no matter how small, represents a significant triumph.

4. **Strength-Based Approaches:** Strengths-based approaches emphasize identifying and utilizing individuals' inherent strengths and talents, developing a sense of empowerment and self-efficacy, particularly beneficial for those with disabilities. For instance, a person with physical disabilities may possess exceptional resilience and determination, traits that can be used to face daily obstacles and pursue personal aspirations. By recognizing and nurturing these strengths, individuals can develop a positive self-concept, contributing to their overall well-being. This approach coordinates with the strengths and virtues framework in positive psychology, focusing on character strengths such as courage, perseverance, and adaptability to facilitate growth and success despite challenges.
5. **Instilling Hope and Optimism:** Hope and optimism are integral components of positive psychology that can greatly benefit individuals with disabilities. Hope refers to the belief in the possibility of positive outcomes and the expectation that goals can be achieved, even in the face of challenges. For individuals with disabilities, maintaining hope can provide a sense of purpose and motivation to overcome obstacles and pursue their aspirations.

Optimism, on the other hand, is the tendency to expect favorable outcomes and to interpret events in a positive light. Optimistic individuals with disabilities tend to approach difficulties with a positive mindset, viewing setbacks as temporary and conquerable. For example, consider a person who has recently acquired a physical disability due to an accident. Despite facing significant physical limitations, they maintain hope for their future and remain optimistic about their ability to adapt and thrive. They may set goals for rehabilitation, engage in adaptive sports, and seek out support networks to facilitate their recovery process. These positive psychology techniques empower individuals to focus on possibilities rather than limitations, promoting psychological well-being and a sense of agency in their lives.

6. **Practicing Mindfulness:** Mindfulness is a positive psychology technique that can be immensely beneficial for individuals with disabilities. It involves being present and fully engaged in the current moment, without judgment or attachment to past or future events. For individuals with disabilities, mindfulness can provide a variety of benefits, including:
   a) **Stress Reduction:** Mindfulness techniques such as deep breathing, body scans, and mindful meditation can help individuals with disabilities manage stress more effectively. By focusing their attention on the present moment, they can alleviate anxiety and promote relaxation.
   b) **Pain Management:** Mindfulness practices have been shown to reduce pain perception and improve pain tolerance. For individuals with chronic pain conditions or physical disabilities, mindfulness techniques can offer relief and enhance their overall well-being.
   c) **Emotional Regulation:** Mindfulness helps individuals become more aware of their thoughts, feelings, and bodily sensations, allowing them to respond to challenging situations with greater composure and strength. This can be particularly helpful for individuals with disabilities who may experience heightened emotional reactivity or mood disturbances.
   d) **Enhanced Self-Awareness:** Through mindfulness practices, individuals with disabilities can develop a deeper understanding of themselves and their experiences. This self-awareness can lead to greater acceptance of their limitations and strengths, developing a sense of self-compassion and self-empowerment.

Consider a person with a physical disability who experiences chronic pain. Through mindfulness meditation practices, they learn to focus their attention on their breath and bodily sensations, gradually becoming more attuned to their pain without judgment. Over time, they develop greater resilience to pain, learning to acknowledge it without becoming overwhelmed by it. As a result, they experience reduced stress levels, improved mood, and a greater sense of control over their pain management.

7. **Coping Techniques:** Coping techniques or mechanisms are essential positive psychology intervention techniques for individuals with disabilities, helping them to face challenges, manage stress, and maintain psychological well-being. These strategies empower individuals to cope effectively with the demands of their disability and life circumstances.

   One example of a coping technique is problem-focused coping, which involves taking direct action to address the stressor or problem at hand. For instance, a person with a physical disability may encounter barriers to accessibility in their environment. Instead of feeling helpless, they may employ problem-focused coping by advocating for accommodations, such as wheelchair ramps or accessible transportation. By taking proactive steps to address the issue, they regain a sense of control and agency over their situation.

   Another example is emotion-focused coping, which involves regulating emotional responses to stressors. For instance, a person with a disability may experience feelings of frustration or sadness related to their limitations. **To cope, they may engage in emotion-focused coping strategies such as mindfulness** meditation or journaling to process their emotions and cultivate resilience. By acknowledging and validating their feelings, they can reduce emotional distress and enhance their psychological well-being.

   These strategies empower individuals to adapt to their circumstances, maintain a positive outlook, and flourish despite their disability.

8. **Positive Affirmations and Self-Compassion:** Positive affirmations and self-compassion techniques are powerful positive psychology techniques that can greatly benefit individuals with disabilities by developing resilience, self-esteem, and emotional well-being. Positive affirmations involve the practice of repeating positive statements about oneself or one's circumstances. For individuals with disabilities, affirmations can counteract negative self-talk and cultivate a more positive self-image. By affirming their strengths, capabilities, and worth,

individuals with disabilities can boost their self-esteem and confidence, enabling them to face challenges with greater resilience and optimism.

Self-compassion, on the other hand, involves treating oneself with kindness, understanding, and acceptance, particularly in the face of difficulties or setbacks. For individuals with disabilities, self-compassion allows them to acknowledge their limitations and challenges without judgment or self-criticism. Instead of thinking about perceived shortcomings, they learn to offer themselves compassion and support, developing a sense of inner strength and resilience.

Together, positive affirmations and self-compassion techniques help individuals with disabilities cultivate a more positive and compassionate relationship with them. By nurturing self-esteem, strength, and emotional well-being, these techniques empower individuals to face the ups and downs of life with greater ease and grace.

Summary

The application of positive psychology in the area of disability holds immense promise for enhancing the well-being and quality of life of individuals facing physical, cognitive, or psychological challenges. By shifting the focus from deficits to strengths, positive psychology approaches empower individuals with disabilities to cultivate resilience, optimism, and a sense of agency in their lives. Techniques such as strengths-based interventions, mindfulness practices, and positive affirmations offer valuable tools for promoting psychological well-being, coping skills, and adaptive strategies. Moreover, positive psychology interventions recognize the importance of social support, meaningful engagement, and self-compassion in fostering a sense of belonging and fulfillment for individuals with disabilities. By developing positive relationships, facilitating opportunities for meaningful participation, and promoting self-acceptance, these interventions contribute to a more inclusive and supportive environment for people with disabilities.

However, it is essential to acknowledge the complex and multifaceted nature of disability and the need for customized and context-specific interventions that address the unique needs and experiences of individuals with disabilities. Continued research, collaboration, and advocacy are crucial for advancing the application of positive psychology in disability settings and ensuring that all individuals have the opportunity to flourish and lead fulfilling lives, regardless of their abilities.

CHAPTER 9

APPLICATION OF POSITIVE PSYCHOLOGY IN COMMUNITIES

Positive psychology, an influential movement within the broader field of psychology, emphasizes the enhancement of individual strengths and the cultivation of well-being. While much of the research and application in positive psychology has traditionally focused on individual outcomes, there is a growing recognition of the profound impact this approach can have on communities. This chapter explores the application of positive psychology at the community level, highlighting its potential to develop collective well-being, resilience, and social cohesion.

Communities are more than mere collections of individuals; they are dynamic systems with unique strengths, challenges, and potentials. By applying the principles of positive psychology to communities, we can shift from a deficit-oriented perspective, which focuses on problems and deficiencies, to one that increases the positive attributes and inherent strengths within these groups. This strengths-based approach is by the broader definition of mental health, which encompasses more than just the absence of illness and includes the presence of positive attributes such as resilience, purpose, and social connection.

This chapter suggests various strategies and examples of how positive psychology principles can be effectively applied within communities. By extending the focus of positive psychology beyond the individual to include groups and communities, environments can be developed where everyone has the opportunity to grow and flourish.

Introduction

Community psychology is a specialty area within psychology that examines the intricate relationships between individuals and their communities. This field is concerned with how societal factors influence personal well-being and how individuals can actively contribute to and shape their communities Community Psychology can be defined as

"A strong, global impact on enhancing well-being and promoting social justice for all people by fostering collaboration where there is division, and empowerment where there is oppression."

"Community psychologists investigate the cultural, economic, social, political, and environmental forces that impact people's lives globally, aiming to improve overall quality of life through collaborative research and action.

One of the distinctive features of community psychology is its multidisciplinary nature. It integrates concepts and methods from various fields such as sociology, political science, public health, cross-cultural psychology, social psychology, social work, environmental psychology, and ecological psychology. This broad perspective allows community psychologists to address complex societal issues that span multiple domains.

Community psychology differs from traditional psychology by emphasizing the community as the primary unit of analysis rather than focusing solely on the individual. It studies the community as both a context for individuals and as an entity in itself, exploring how community dynamics influence individual behavior and well-being. This field applies an ecological perspective, considering the person-environment fit as a crucial factor in understanding and addressing problems. Rather than attempting to change an individual's personality or isolate environmental issues, community psychology seeks to create harmonious interactions between people and their surroundings.

The field of community psychology is both theoretical and applied. While some community psychologists engage in theoretical research to understand underlying principles, others apply these findings to real-world settings to identify issues and develop practical solutions. This dual focus allows for a comprehensive approach to addressing community problems, enhancing both theoretical knowledge and practical interventions. Community psychologists work to improve the functioning and quality of life within groups, organizations, institutions, and broader society. They employ collaborative and participatory methods, often involving community members in the research process, to ensure that interventions are culturally relevant and effectively address local needs.

Historical Development of Community Psychology

Community psychology's historical development reflects a growing awareness of the limitations of traditional psychology in addressing broad social issues and the need for a more comprehensive, community-focused approach to mental health and well-being. This evolution has been influenced by various social, political, and professional factors over several decades.

- **Early Influences and Preceding Movements:** In the early to mid-20th century, several developments laid the groundwork for community psychology. The progressive era in the early 1900s saw the rise of social reform movements that emphasized public health and social welfare. Pioneering work by social psychologists and public health experts began to highlight the importance of environmental and social factors in influencing individual behavior and well-being.
- **Post-World War II Era:** After World War II, there was a significant shift in healthcare practices. The traditional, individual-focused approach in psychology and health care gave way to more progressive practices that considered public health, prevention, and social change. This period saw an increasing recognition of the social determinants of health and the importance of addressing broader social issues such as racial and religious prejudice, poverty, and inequality.
- **1950s and 1960s:** The Roots of Community Psychology: Several key factors in the 1950s and 1960s contributed to the emergence of community psychology:
    1. **Social Changes and Movements:** The civil rights movement, anti-war protests, and other social movements highlighted the need for social change and justice. Psychologists began to see the importance of addressing these broader societal issues.
    2. **Deinstitutionalization:** The movement to deinstitutionalize people with mental illnesses and the establishment of community mental health centers underscored the need for community-based approaches to mental health care.
    3. **Critique of Clinical Psychology:** There was growing dissatisfaction with the ability of clinical psychology to address widespread mental health problems, especially the treatment needs of veterans and other large populations.
    4. **The Swampscott Conference:** A defining moment for community psychology was the Swampscott Conference in 1965. Psychologists gathered to discuss the future of community mental health and recognized the need for a new approach that emphasized community and social change. This conference is considered the birthplace of community psychology, as it called for psychologists to become political

activists and agents of social change, focusing on community-level interventions rather than individual treatment alone.

- **Establishment and Growth:** Following the Swampscott Conference, the field of community psychology began to take formal shape:
  1. **American Psychological Association (APA) Division 27:** The Society for Community Research and Action (SCRA), APA's Division 27, was established to promote the field of community psychology. It provided a professional home for community psychologists and facilitated the exchange of research and ideas.
  2. **Academic Journals:** The creation of academic journals such as the American Journal of Community Psychology, the Journal of Community Psychology, and the Journal of Community & Applied Social Psychology helped to disseminate research and theoretical developments in the field.
  3. **Evolving Focus and Contemporary Developments:** Over the years, community psychology has evolved continuously, using insights from various disciplines and broadening its focus to address a wide range of contemporary issues. This includes perspectives from sociology, political science, public health, social work, environmental psychology, and more, reflecting its broad and integrative nature. The field has increasingly recognized the importance of cultural, economic, and political contexts in shaping community well-being, leading to a more global and cross-cultural focus.

The historical development of community psychology reflects a shift from individual-focused, clinical approaches to a broader, more integrative perspective that emphasizes community well-being, social justice, and systemic change. From its roots in the social movements of the mid-20th century to its contemporary focus on multidisciplinary and global issues, community psychology continues to evolve and expand its impact on improving mental health and promoting social change.

Levels of Change

Community psychologists often work on social issues, striving to create positive social change. Watzlawick et al. (1974) differentiated between first-order and second-order change, noting that second-order change is frequently the focus of community psychology.

- **First-order Change:** Positively changing individuals within a setting to try to fix a problem.
- **Second-order Change:** Addressing the systems and structures involved with the problem to improve the person-environment fit.

For example, consider homelessness. A first-order change to "fix" homelessness would involve providing shelter to one or many homeless individuals. In contrast, a second-order change would involve addressing policy issues related to affordable housing.

Goals of Community Psychology

- **Empowerment:** Community psychology aims to empower marginalized individuals and communities. Empowerment is defined as an ongoing, community-centered process that promotes mutual respect, reflection, and participation, allowing people greater access to and control over resources. While integral to community psychology, empowerment has faced criticism for being vague and paradoxical. In the 1990s, Racino proposed the support and empowerment paradigm to complement or replace the rehabilitation paradigm, recognizing diverse groups and community-based efforts.
- **Diversity:** Another core value of community psychology is embracing diversity. Rappaport highlights diversity as a defining aspect of the field, advocating for research that benefits diverse populations in their pursuit of equality and justice. This commitment is reflected in research conducted with communities of various ethnicities, cultures, sexual orientations, disability statuses, socioeconomic statuses, genders, and ages.
- **Civic Participation:** Citizen Participation involves individuals' ability to contribute to decision-making processes, problem definition, problem-solving, and the dissemination of gathered information about them. This forms the foundation for the utilization of participatory action research in community psychology, where community members often collaborate with researchers, sharing their unique knowledge and experiences as co-researchers. Conversely, citizen participation is sought by community developers and planners, such as public administrators, to ensure that governmental funds effectively meet local needs. Three key values of participation include fostering support for governmental planning, increasing political awareness, and promoting democratic principles. Citizen participation in policymaking has a longstanding history,

particularly evident in neighborhood action, poverty programs, and other activist-led initiatives.

- **Building a Sense of Community:** The concept of a psychological sense of community, pioneered by Seymour Sarason in 1974, gained significant traction in 1986 when David McMillan and David Chavis introduced their "Theory of Sense of Community," followed by the development of the "Sense of Community Index" in 1990. Initially focused on neighborhoods, the Sense of Community Index (SCI) has since been adapted to explore other communities, such as workplaces, schools, religious groups, and communities of interest. In the context of community psychology, understanding and developing a sense of community is vital for promoting social cohesion, well-being, and collective action within diverse community settings.
- **Social Justice:** At the heart of community psychology is a fundamental commitment to pursuing social justice through both research and action. Community psychologists serve as staunch advocates for equality and policies that promote the well-being of all individuals, with a particular focus on marginalized populations. For instance, events like "Unframed Lives" in the City of Brighton and Hove in May 2019, which addressed homelessness and austerity. These events exemplify the field's dedication to understanding and addressing the systemic factors contributing to social inequities and striving to create positive change within communities.
- **Health Promotion:** Health promotion stands as a central aim of community psychology, focusing on enhancing well-being and preventing illness within communities. Community psychologists collaborate with residents, organizations, and policymakers to develop interventions that promote healthy behaviors, improve access to healthcare, and create supportive environments. By addressing social determinants of health and advocating for equitable healthcare policies, community psychology endeavors to empower individuals and communities to lead healthier lives.
- **Individual Wellness:** Community psychology aims to enhance individual wellness, encompassing both physical and psychological well-being for all individuals. Research within the field is dedicated to developing methods that promote and sustain individual wellness, with a particular emphasis on prevention strategies and facilitating second-order change to address systemic factors influencing wellness outcomes.

Theories of Community Psychology

- **Behavior Setting Theory:** Behavior Setting Theory, developed by Roger Barker in 1968, emphasizes the significant influence of ecological environments on behavior. This theory suggests that stable social structures within specific settings shape individual behaviors dynamically. Each behavior setting, such as a school, workplace, or prison, comprises specific patterns of behavior that are typical within that context. These settings have predictable outcomes due to their structured social environments. For instance, prisons tend to produce similar adverse outcomes because of their rigid social structures and rules. Understanding the relationship between dynamic individual behaviors and stable social structures helps to explain why certain environments consistently yield specific behavioral patterns.
- **Ecological Theory:** James Kelly's Ecological Theory, introduced in 1966, emphasizes the vital role environmental factors play in shaping human interactions. This theory is structured around four core principles: interdependence, adaptation, cycling of resources, and succession. Interdependence refers to the interconnectedness of all system components, meaning a change in one aspect affects the entire system. Adaptation explains why behavior that is effective in one environment might not be effective in another. The cycling of resources involves the development and utilization of various resources, such as skills, expertise, and social support, that contribute to community advancement. Succession addresses the constant changes within communities and how these changes necessitate ongoing adaptation. These principles guide the development and evaluation of community interventions aimed at prevention and positive change.
- **Sense of Community Theory:** Sense of Community Theory, proposed by Seymour Sarason in 1974, captures the essence of belonging to a larger, dependable group. This sense of community is measured through four factors: membership, influence, integration, and fulfillment of needs, and shared emotional connection. Membership defines who belongs to the community, creating a sense of personal investment. Influence refers to the ability of individuals to impact community practices, fostering a sense of empowerment. Integration and fulfillment of needs highlight the exchange of resources and the meeting of communal needs, reinforcing shared values. A shared emotional connection involves participation in collective activities like rituals and celebrations, strengthening the community bond.

This theory emphasizes the importance of social cohesion and emotional bonds in fostering a sense of belonging and mutual support.

- **Social Climate Theory:** Social Climate Theory, developed by Rudolf Moos in 2003, explores the reciprocal adaptation between individuals and their social environments. This theory is essential for understanding people's experiences within various settings by focusing on how these settings shape individuals' perceptions of social relationships, support the maintenance of norms, and facilitate change processes. The theory also examines how environments support personal development. Social climate assessment scores, which measure these aspects, are strong indicators of individual well-being. This theory highlights how the environment influences and is influenced by the people within it, emphasizing the importance of creating supportive and adaptive social settings that promote individual and communal well-being.
- **Liberation Psychology:** Liberation Psychology, developed in Latin America during the 1970s, addresses well-being within oppressed and impoverished societies. This theory focuses on empowering individuals to gain control over their lives, especially in contexts where power dynamics are unequal. Core components of Liberation Psychology include praxis and dialectics. Praxis involves the integration of theory with practice to create more grounded and effective interventions. Dialectics refers to the process of developing knowledge of the world while simultaneously working to enact social change. Liberation Psychology emphasizes that meaningful change can only occur through dialogue between the oppressed and those in power, advocating for social justice and the dismantling of oppressive structures. This approach seeks to transform the status quo by empowering marginalized groups and promoting equitable social conditions.

Community psychology theories provide robust frameworks for analyzing social problems and developing interventions that consider individuals within their environmental and community contexts. By promoting a social justice agenda, these theories offer practical ways to understand and address the needs of marginalized populations. Whether through understanding behavior settings, ecological interdependencies, sense of community, social climates, or liberation psychology, these theories collectively enhance our capacity to foster inclusive, supportive, and dynamic communities.

Individualism and Collectivism

Individualism and collectivism represent contrasting sets of values and norms that vary across cultures.

- **Individualism:** Individualism is a social and cultural philosophy that emphasizes the moral worth of the individual. It is grounded in the belief that each person is a distinct and autonomous entity with unique personal differences that set them apart from their group. This philosophy places a greater focus on internal processes such as personal goals, values, needs, preferences, rights, and identity, guiding and motivating an individual's behavior and thoughts irrespective of group conformity. Individualists tend to prioritize their personal goals over the goals of the group, behaving according to their own attitudes rather than adhering to the norms and mentality of their group. This emphasis on personal autonomy, self-reliance, and individual achievement develops a culture where creativity, personal differences, and liberty from others are highly valued.

Key Aspects of Individualistic Societies

- **Sense of Independence:** Individuals see themselves as autonomous and separate from their groups, focusing on personal goals and desires.
- **Need for Uniqueness:** There is a strong desire to be distinct and special, differentiating oneself from others through unique attributes and possessions.
- **Self as the Unit of Analysis:** Personal identity, success, and satisfaction are centered on the individual rather than the group, with goals and achievements measured at a personal level.
- **Focus on Self over Group:** Personal success and satisfaction are prioritized over the welfare of the group, with individuals pursuing what they find enjoyable and beneficial for themselves.
- **Pleasure and Self-Esteem in Relationships:** Relationships are valued for the personal benefits they provide, with an emphasis on personal pleasure and self-esteem.
- **Expression of Uniqueness Through Possessions:** Unique commodities and personal attributes serve as markers of individuality, with people defining themselves through possessions like clothes, cars, and vacations.

These aspects collectively highlight the core principles of individualism, where personal autonomy, distinctiveness, and self-focused goals are important.

- **Collectivism:** Collectivism is a social and cultural orientation that prioritizes the group over the individual. It emphasizes the interconnectedness of individuals within a group, where personal identity, values, behaviors, and needs are shaped by the collective entity. In collectivist societies, individuals view themselves primarily as part of a group, using collective pronouns and adhering to group norms and values. This interconnectedness, established from birth, creates a strong sense of duty and obligation among members to support and protect one another. The well-being of the group is important, often requiring personal sacrifices for the greater good. Hierarchical structures and communal sharing are common, with group harmony and cohesion being central to social interactions.

Key Features of Collectivist Societies

- **Dependency:** Individuals rely on the group for support, protection, and survival.
- **Conformity:** Social norms and behaviors are dictated by the group, and members obey to these norms to maintain group harmony.
- **Group as the Fundamental Unit of Analysis:** The group's interests and goals take priority over individual desires and achievements.
- **Goal of Group Harmony:** Maintaining harmony within the group is a primary objective, often requiring personal sacrifices.
- **Types of Collectivism:** There are two types of collectivism vertical and horizontal. In vertical collectivism, individuals within the group accept a hierarchical structure, with specific roles and duties assigned based on rank. On the other hand, horizontal collectivism emphasizes equality among group members with minimal hierarchy. Everyone is considered equal, sharing resources and responsibilities.
- **Interpersonal Relationships:** Strong emphasis on maintaining relationships that contribute to group cohesion, even if there is no direct personal benefit.
- **Limited Emotionality and Creativity:** Conformity and hierarchy can limit individual emotional expression and creative search.
- **Class Differences:** More pronounced class differences are often present, affecting social dynamics and resource distribution.

ME+WE=US: The Positive Psychology of US

ME+WE=US represents a balanced integration of individualism (ME) and collectivism (WE), proposing that optimal well-being and productivity arise from harmonizing personal and group-oriented values. This concept is rooted in Positive Psychology, which emphasizes strengths, well-being, and flourishing in both individuals and communities.

According to traditional views, individualism and collectivism are mutually exclusive, leading to cultural stereotypes and misunderstandings. However, these perspectives can coexist and complement each other. Cultures are not static or easily categorized as solely individualist or collectivist. Instead, they are dynamic and multifaceted, containing elements of both.

- **Balancing ME and WE:** Positive Psychology suggests that a balanced integration of individual and group orientations leads to greater well-being. This balance allows individuals to address their own needs (ME) while also contributing to the group's well-being (WE).
- **Benefits of ME+WE Integration:**
    1. **Enhanced Well-being:** Balancing personal and collective needs promotes psychological well-being and life satisfaction.
    2. **Productivity and Harmony:** Integrating individual and group goals develops a productive environment where personal achievements contribute to collective success, and vice versa.
    3. **Resilience and Adaptability:** Individuals and groups that balance ME and WE are more resilient and adaptable, effectively facing challenges by utilizing both personal strengths and collective support.
    4. **Reduced Conflict:** Emphasizing both individual and collective values can reduce conflicts arising from rigid cultural stereotypes and promote mutual understanding and cooperation.
    5. **Holistic Growth:** This approach supports holistic growth by encouraging self-improvement and community development simultaneously, leading to a more balanced and fulfilling life.

The "ME+WE=US" approach in Positive Psychology emphasizes the importance of integrating individual and collective values. By developing a balanced perspective, it enhances well-being, productivity, and harmony, ultimately leading to a more satisfying and successful life for both individuals and communities.

Community Wellness

Community wellness is the collective state of health and well-being of a community, including social, economic, environmental, cultural, and political conditions. It reflects how these factors interact to help individuals and communities flourish and reach their potential.

Community wellness and positive psychology are deeply interconnected, emphasizing the importance of empowering individuals and developing personal growth. Strength-based interventions identify and enhance both individual and communal strengths, contributing to resilience and supportive networks. Integrating an ecological perspective allows positive psychology to consider the broader context, such as workplaces and schools, for a comprehensive approach to well-being. Active community participation in wellness initiatives, through empowerment evaluation and participatory research, ensures a sense of ownership and effectiveness. Promoting positive relationships and social cohesion enhances social trust and civic engagement, ultimately creating a harmonious and resilient society.

Individual Wellness and Community Change: Individual wellness and community change are deeply interconnected, particularly within the framework of positive psychology. Positive psychology emphasizes the importance of developing individual strengths and well-being, which, in turn, can drive broader community transformation. When individuals achieve a higher state of well-being, their increased resources and resilience often contribute to heightened expectations and aspirations. This personal growth can lead to more significant community engagement and the fulfillment of collective goals.

The role of positive psychology in this dynamic is crucial. By focusing on psychological resources—such as resilience, optimism, and social support—rather than solely on economic factors, policymakers and community leaders can develop environments where individuals can flourish. Empowering community members through strengths-based interventions and participatory research is essential. These approaches ensure that community members have an active role in designing and implementing wellness initiatives, which can lead to more sustainable and impactful outcomes.

Furthermore, community psychology, a field closely related to positive psychology, emphasizes the importance of ecological perspectives. This means considering the broader social, cultural, and environmental contexts in which individuals live. By integrating positive psychological principles with an ecological approach, interventions can be more comprehensive, addressing both individual and community needs.

Individual wellness is a catalyst for community change. Positive psychology provides the tools and frameworks to harness this potential, promoting both personal flourishing and collective well-being. By focusing on empowerment, strengths-based interventions, and an ecological perspective, positive psychology can drive meaningful and lasting community transformation.

Application of Positive Psychology in Community Well-being

Positive psychology, which focuses on developing positive emotions, strengths, and virtues, has significant applications in promoting community wellness. By integrating principles of positive psychology with community-based approaches, we can create environments that support individual and collective flourishing. Here are key applications of positive psychology in community wellness:

1. **Enhancing Social Connectedness:** Positive psychology interventions can strengthen social networks within communities, developing social support, trust, and civic engagement. Activities that promote gratitude, kindness, and empathy can enhance interpersonal relationships and build a sense of belonging, which is crucial for community cohesion and resilience.
2. **Building Resilience:** Resilience training programs based on positive psychology can help community members develop coping strategies and mental toughness. These programs focus on identifying and utilizing individual and collective strengths, developing a positive outlook, and encouraging adaptive responses to adversity. This is particularly valuable in communities facing economic, social, or environmental challenges.
3. **Promoting Mental Health:** Positive psychology can complement traditional mental health interventions by focusing on strengths and well-being rather than just treating pathology. Community programs can include workshops on mindfulness, stress reduction, and positive thinking to enhance overall mental health. Such initiatives can reduce the stigma associated with mental health issues and encourage proactive engagement with mental wellness.
4. **Empowering Community Members:** By developing a sense of agency and empowerment, positive psychology encourages community members to take an active role in their well-being and that of their community.

Empowerment evaluation and participatory action research allow community members to identify their strengths, set goals, and implement changes that improve their quality of life. This participatory approach ensures that interventions are culturally relevant and community-driven.

5. **Developing Positive Institutions:** Positive psychology can help develop and sustain positive institutions within communities, such as schools, workplaces, and local organizations. These institutions can implement practices that promote well-being, such as recognizing and celebrating achievements, providing opportunities for meaningful work, and fostering inclusive and supportive environments. By creating positive institutions, communities can enhance the overall well-being of their members.
6. **Creating Supportive Environments:** Environmental factors, such as access to green spaces, recreational facilities, and safe neighborhoods, play a crucial role in community wellness. Positive psychology can guide the design of community spaces that promote physical activity, social interaction, and relaxation, contributing to the overall well-being of residents. Policymakers can use insights from positive psychology to create environments that support healthy lifestyles and reduce stress.
7. **Encouraging Civic Engagement:** Encouraging civic engagement and participation in community activities is a key application of positive psychology. When community members feel connected and invested in their community, they are more likely to contribute to its development and improvement. Programs that promote volunteerism, leadership, and community service can utilize the strengths and talents of community members, leading to a more vibrant and resilient community.

By applying the principles of positive psychology to community wellness, we can create supportive, resilient, and flourishing communities. This approach not only enhances individual well-being but also builds strong, interconnected, and empowered communities that can collectively address their challenges and opportunities.

Summary

The integration of positive psychology and community psychology presents a promising pathway to enhance community wellness. Both disciplines share a commitment to developing individual and collective well-being, yet their approaches have remained largely distinct. Community psychology emphasizes understanding individuals within their environmental contexts, addressing broader social, cultural, and political influences, and advocating for citizen participation and empowerment. It challenges traditional perspectives, avoids victim-blaming, and seeks to create interventions that promote dignity and agency. Positive psychology, on the other hand, focuses on cultivating positive emotions, strengths, and virtues, promoting individual growth and resilience through strength-based interventions.

The convergence of these fields can lead to a more holistic approach to wellness that balances the needs of individuals with the goals of the community. By incorporating the ecological perspective of community psychology, positive psychology can extend its impact beyond individual well-being to develop flourishing communities. This includes creating supportive environments, enhancing social connectedness, building resilience, and promoting mental health through community-driven initiatives.

Moreover, the collaboration between positive and community psychologists can lead to innovative research and interventions that address both subjective well-being and systemic issues. Community psychology's focus on social justice and equity can complement positive psychology's emphasis on strengths and virtues, leading to more comprehensive strategies for community development. As policymakers and practitioners recognize the interconnectedness of individual and community wellness, efforts can be directed toward creating positive institutions and supportive environments that nurture both personal and collective flourishing.

Ultimately, the integration of positive psychology and community psychology holds the potential to create empowered, resilient, and cohesive communities where individuals can flourish. This synergy can drive transformative changes at both the individual and community levels, developing a more inclusive and equitable society. By utilizing the strengths of both fields, we can develop robust frameworks and interventions that promote sustainable well-being for all members of the community.

CHAPTER 10

APPLICATION OF POSITIVE PSYCHOLOGY IN THE MULTI-CULTURAL PERSPECTIVE

The application of positive psychology within a multicultural perspective represents a significant and evolving field of study, addressing the diverse ways in which human flourishing is experienced and understood across different cultural contexts. As the world becomes increasingly interconnected, the need to appreciate and incorporate varied cultural viewpoints into positive psychology becomes important. This chapter explores the emergence of positive psychology from a multicultural perspective, exploring key research areas that highlight the rich field of human strengths and virtues as seen through different cultural lenses. By identifying the core differences between Western and Eastern philosophies, we gain a deeper understanding of how cultural values shape positive psychological constructs. Additionally, this chapter evaluates the challenges inherent in studying positive psychology across cultures, such as differing definitions of well-being and cultural biases in research methodologies. Ultimately, adopting a multicultural perspective in positive psychology not only broadens our understanding of human flourishing but also develops more inclusive and applicable practices that resonate with diverse populations. Through this exploration, we aim to uncover strategies for integrating multicultural insights into the field of positive psychology, thereby enhancing its relevance and effectiveness in promoting global well-being.

Introduction

Positive psychology, with its focus on enabling individuals and communities to lead fulfilling lives and reach their maximum potential, takes a distinctive approach by prioritizing well-being over addressing psychological dysfunctions. The field aims to cultivate contentment, positivity, good health, and overall well-being, helping individuals achieve and sustain the upper reaches of their happiness spectrum, as highlighted by Seligman (2002). However, a significant challenge within this emerging field is the need to eliminate cultural barriers to make positive psychology applicable and effective worldwide.

- **Impact of Technological Advancements:** Technological advancements have made cross-cultural communication more accessible, increasing interactions with individuals from diverse cultural backgrounds. These interactions are important in our globalized world, where understanding and appreciating diverse perspectives can significantly enhance our approach to well-being. Positive psychology emphasizes the importance of understanding other cultures empathetically, non-judgmentally, and cordially. By doing so, it promotes harmonious relationships and enriches the effectiveness of positive psychological interventions.
- **Prioritizing Cultural Competence in Positive Psychology:** A multicultural perspective is essential in the research and practice of positive psychology. Researchers and practitioners must recognize that culture profoundly influences the development of human strengths and the experience of good living. Despite the recognition of cultural diversity's importance, integrating cultural considerations into the study of mental health remains a significant challenge, as noted by Snyder et al. (2010). Addressing this challenge requires a dedicated effort to prioritize cultural competence and sensitivity across all aspects of positive psychology.
- **Integrating Cultural Diversity in Positive Psychology Interventions:** Positive psychology can play a transformative role by acknowledging and valuing the unique strengths and lifestyles of different cultural groups. This approach involves moving beyond a one-size-fits-all methodology to develop interventions that are culturally relevant and effective. By engaging with diverse cultural communities, researchers can gather insights that inform the creation of designed interventions, ensuring they resonate with and benefit the populations they aim to serve. Positive psychology promotes empathy and compassion, which are crucial for cross-cultural understanding. Empathy allows individuals to appreciate the experiences and perspectives of others, fostering a sense of connection and reducing the likelihood of conflicts arising from cultural misunderstandings. Compassion motivates individuals to act with kindness and support, further enhancing intercultural harmony.

The role of positive psychology from a multicultural perspective is complex and essential. By integrating cultural diversity, promoting empathy, and developing culturally relevant interventions, positive psychology can effectively develop well-being and resilience across diverse cultural contexts. This inclusive approach not only enriches the field but also ensures that the benefits of positive psychology are accessible to individuals from all cultural backgrounds, contributing to a more empathetic and harmonious global community.

Major Research Areas in Positive Psychology From Multicultural Perspective

Intensive research on multiculturalism and its impact on positive psychology reveals the importance of acknowledging and embracing cultural diversity. Positive psychologists are advised against adopting a color-blind approach when interacting with individuals seeking psychological well-being. In this context, color blindness refers to an empathetic yet indifferent stance that disregards cultural, religious, or national differences. This ideology, often seen as a subtle form of racism, fails to acknowledge the unique experiences and perspectives of individuals from diverse backgrounds (Williams, 2011). By understanding and respecting these differences, psychologists can better support the well-being of individuals from various cultural contexts.

1. **Positive Emotions:** While positive emotions are universally experienced, their manifestation and significance can be heavily influenced by cultural factors. Some theorists, such as Carver and Scheier (1990), argue that positive emotions result from progress toward future goals and successes. In contrast, Frederickson (1998) suggests that positive emotions play a more constructive role, facilitating learning and creativity. Regardless of their origins, positive emotions have several important functions:
   a) **Broadening Thought–Action Ranges:** Positive emotions expand our cognitive and behavioral options, allowing us to think more broadly and creatively. This openness is crucial for personal growth and problem-solving.
   b) **Undoing Persistent Negative Emotions:** Experiencing positive emotions can reduce the effects of negative emotions, helping individuals recover from stressful or traumatic experiences more effectively.
   c) **Enhancing Psychological Resilience:** Positive emotions contribute to psychological resilience, enabling individuals to cope with adversity and bounce back from challenges.
   d) **Building and Triggering Upward Spirals Toward Enhanced Emotional Well-Being:** The presence of positive emotions can initiate a cycle of increasing well-being, where positive feelings lead to further positive experiences and emotions.

These benefits emphasize the significance of positive emotions not only in enhancing our immediate mood, but also in developing a deeper sense of connection with others. Waugh and Frederickson (2006) highlight that positive emotions help us feel more connected to those around us, developing empathy and understanding. This is particularly important in a multicultural context, where recognizing and appreciating different worldviews can lead to stronger, more meaningful relationships.

- **Cross-Cultural Research on Positive Emotions:** Cross-cultural studies further emphasize the role of positive emotions in bridging cultural divides. By perceiving, experiencing, and expressing positive emotions collectively, individuals can adopt a broader perspective and develop a greater capacity for empathy towards others' worldviews. This broader perspective is essential for developing strong interpersonal relationships, regardless of cultural differences.

  One notable phenomenon in this context is the cross-race effect, also known as own-race bias. This is the tendency for individuals to more easily recognize and differentiate faces from their own race compared to those of different races. Research indicates that positive emotions can reduce or eliminate this bias, enhancing our ability to recognize and connect with individuals from different racial backgrounds (Erlbaum, 2007). Studies comparing various ethnic groups, including Hispanics with Black and White participants, Black participants with White and Japanese participants, and Arabs with Israeli Jews, consistently demonstrate the universality of the cross-race effect. Positive emotions play a critical role in mitigating this bias, fostering greater inclusivity and understanding across different racial and ethnic groups.

- **Implications for Positive Psychology:** The integration of multicultural perspectives into positive psychology emphasizes the necessity of recognizing and valuing cultural diversity. Positive emotions, influenced by cultural contexts, not only enhance individual well-being but also promote broader social cohesion and empathy. By fostering positive emotions, psychologists can help diminish biases like the cross-race effect, thereby contributing to a more inclusive and empathetic society

2. **Happiness:** The perception and expression of happiness are deeply influenced by cultural and ethnic backgrounds, leading to significant variations in how happiness is valued and pursued. In many Western cultures, happiness is often regarded as an important life goal, a state of being that individuals strive to achieve and maintain.
    - **Cultural Variations in the Perception of Happiness:** Western-centric view of happiness is not universally held. Some non-Western cultures do not place the same emphasis on happiness as a crucial life goal. For instance, in certain Eastern cultures, happiness might be viewed with suspicion or considered less important than other values such as duty, family honor, or spiritual enlightenment. Joshanloo and Weijers (2013) highlight that in some cultures, individuals might even be averse to happiness. This aversion can stem from various beliefs, such as the idea that happiness might invite misfortune or that excessive happiness could lead to complacency and moral laxity.
    - **Cultural Conceptions of Happiness:** A Comprehensive Study by Graham et al. (2012) emphasizes the cultural variability in conceptions of happiness. By analyzing dictionary definitions of happiness from 30 different nations, the researchers aimed to uncover the cultural similarities and differences in how happiness is understood. Their findings revealed that while many cultures associate happiness with good luck and favorable external conditions, others emphasize favorable internal feeling states.

      For instance, in many Western contexts, happiness is often linked to individual achievements, personal freedom, and positive emotional states. Success, wealth, and personal fulfillment are seen as pathways to happiness. In contrast, some Eastern cultures might view happiness as a state of balance and harmony, both internally and within the community. Here, happiness might be associated with fulfilling social roles, maintaining family ties, and achieving inner peace through practices like meditation and mindfulness.
    - **Averseness to Happiness:** The averseness to happiness in certain cultures can be attributed to various factors. In some cases, cultural beliefs suggest that expressing happiness openly might attract negative consequences or envy from others. For example, in some East Asian cultures, there is a notion that overt displays of happiness can bring bad luck or upset the balance of one's life. This belief is rooted

in a broader cultural context that values modesty and humility over individual exuberance.

Additionally, the concept of happiness itself might be viewed differently. In some societies, happiness is seen not as an individual pursuit but as a collective experience. The well-being of the community, family, or group takes precedence over individual happiness. Therefore, actions that contribute to collective harmony and social cohesion are often valued more than those aimed at personal joy.

- **Implications for Positive Psychology:** Understanding these cultural variations is crucial for positive psychology, which aims to enhance well-being across diverse populations. Practitioners and researchers need to recognize that interventions designed to increase happiness in one cultural context may not be effective or appropriate in another. For instance, promoting individual achievements and personal freedoms might resonate well in Western cultures but could be less relevant in collectivist societies that prioritize group harmony and interdependence.

3. **Optimism:** The psychological construct of optimism, defined as the general tendency to expect positive outcomes, contrasts with pessimism, which involves expecting negative consequences. These dispositions are not uniform across different cultures, as demonstrated by research exploring how cultural contexts influence levels of optimism and pessimism. One notable study by Chang et al. (2001) investigated these cultural variations by comparing European Americans (Westerners) and Japanese (Easterners) in their predictions of positive and negative life events.

   The study revealed distinct differences in optimistic and pessimistic biases between the two cultural groups. European Americans exhibited an optimistic bias, consistently expecting positive outcomes and underestimating the likelihood of negative events. This aligns with the broader cultural tendency in Western societies to promote self-enhancement, where individuals are encouraged to maintain high self-esteem and a positive outlook on life.

   In contrast, the Japanese participants demonstrated a pessimistic bias, specifically regarding negative events. They were more likely to anticipate adverse outcomes, reflecting a cultural inclination towards self-criticism and a cautious approach to life. This difference can be understood in the context of Eastern cultural values, which often emphasize humility, interdependence, and a realistic assessment of one's abilities and circumstances.

- **Cultural Influences on Self-Enhancement and Self-Criticism** The divergent patterns of optimism and pessimism observed in Western and Eastern cultures are rooted in deeper cultural philosophies and social norms. In Western cultures, self-enhancement is a prevalent theme. Individuals are encouraged to think positively about themselves and their futures, fostering an environment where optimism is a valued trait. This cultural framework supports the belief that one can control and shape their destiny, leading to a greater emphasis on positive expectations.

  Conversely, Eastern cultures often prioritize self-criticism and a more modest self-view. In these societies, recognizing and addressing one's shortcomings is seen as a path to improvement and social harmony. This approach cultivates a form of pessimism, particularly towards potential negative events, as it prepares individuals to cope with challenges and setbacks. Such cultural norms encourage a more cautious and less presumptive outlook for the future.

- **Implications of Cultural Differences in Optimism and Pessimism:** Understanding these cultural differences in optimism and pessimism has important implications for psychological practice and cross-cultural interactions. For instance, therapeutic approaches that emphasize positive thinking and optimism may resonate well in Western contexts but might need to be adjusted for Eastern clients. Eastern clients who may find greater value in strategies that incorporate a balanced view of potential outcomes, including negative possibilities.

  In educational settings, recognizing these cultural tendencies can help educators tailor their motivational strategies. Western students might respond better to encouragement and positive reinforcement, while Eastern students might benefit more from constructive feedback that acknowledges areas for improvement.

  Furthermore, these insights are valuable in organizational contexts, where multinational teams can benefit from understanding the different motivational drivers of their colleagues. Western employees might thrive in environments that promote innovation and risk-taking, whereas Eastern employees might excel in settings that value thorough planning and risk mitigation.

By appreciating these cultural subtleties, psychologists, educators, and organizational leaders can foster more effective and culturally sensitive approaches to enhancing well-being, motivation, and productivity across diverse populations.

4. **Self Efficacy:** Albert Bandura (1994) described self-efficacy as an individual's belief in their own ability to succeed in specific situations. This belief can be profoundly influenced by the culture to which an individual belongs, as cultural contexts shape the sources and manifestations of self-efficacy. Core social systems and institutions, such as family, school, workplace, and community, play pivotal roles in this process. Conducting cross-cultural research enhances the understanding of how culture correlates with the self and increases the relevance of theories and research explaining self-functioning (Marsh, Hau, & Kong, 2002).
    - **Individualist vs. Collectivist Cultures:** Cultural dimensions vary significantly from individualist to collectivist cultures. Individualist cultures, typical of Western societies, emphasize "I" consciousness, independence, autonomy, individual identity, personal initiative, and the right to privacy. In contrast, collectivist cultures, often found in Eastern societies, stress "we" consciousness, interdependence, collective identity, and maintaining group harmony and unity (Kim et al., 1994).
    - **Self-Efficacy Theory in Different Cultural Contexts:** Self-efficacy theory, with its focus on personal control, appears particularly suited to Western, individualistic contexts. However, Bandura (1997, 2002) asserts that self-efficacy is equally relevant in collectivistic cultures. It is essential for individuals performing collectively oriented tasks, just as it is for those engaged in individually based tasks. This perspective broadens the applicability of self-efficacy theory, recognizing its significance across diverse cultural settings.

      Sources of Self-Efficacy: Oettingen (1995) identified four potential sources of self-efficacy:

      1. **Performance Experiences:** Success enhances self-efficacy, while failures tend to diminish it. Early, consistent successes can create a strong sense of self-efficacy, making subsequent failures less impactful.
      2. **Vicarious Experiences:** Observing the successes of similar others can boost one's own self-efficacy, whereas their failures can lower it.

3. **Verbal Persuasion:** Competent individuals can influence self-efficacy beliefs through encouragement and active persuasion, especially when the communicator is trusted, expert, and attractive.
4. **Physical and Emotional Reactions:** Low arousal levels when facing challenges indicate low self-efficacy, whereas high arousal levels in response to threats reflect a strong sense of self-efficacy.

- **Cultural Variation in Self-Efficacy Sources:** Different cultural contexts may emphasize different sources of self-efficacy. In Western cultures, such as those in America or Europe, performance experiences might be the most effective in enhancing self-efficacy. The emphasis on individual achievements and personal successes aligns with individualistic cultural values, where personal accomplishments are celebrated and seen as a direct reflection of one's capabilities.

  In contrast, in Eastern cultures like India and Japan, self-efficacy might be more strongly influenced by vicarious experiences. For example, in India, parents often view their children's successes as their own, reflecting a collectivist mindset where individual achievements are closely tied to the collective success of the family or community. Observing the success of others within the group can thus significantly enhance self-efficacy, reinforcing the importance of social connections and shared experiences.

- **Implications for Practice:** Understanding these cultural nuances is crucial for applying self-efficacy theory effectively across different cultural contexts. For practitioners working in Western settings, emphasizing performance experiences and individual achievements may be more effective. Encouraging individuals to engage in activities that lead to personal success and providing opportunities for skill development can boost self-efficacy.

  In Eastern settings, leveraging vicarious experiences might be more impactful. Highlighting role models within the community, sharing success stories, and fostering environments where individuals can observe and learn from the achievements of others can enhance self-efficacy. Additionally, verbal persuasion from trusted and respected figures can play a significant role in both contexts, but may be particularly influential in cultures that value authority and expertise.

Influence of Culture on Positive Psychology.

- **The Complex Link Between Positive Psychology and Culture:** To effectively implement positive psychology globally, it is crucial to understand the intricate relationship between culture and positive psychological constructs. The Oxford Dictionary of Psychology defines culture as the "sum total of the ideas, beliefs, customs, values, knowledge, and material artifacts that are handed down from one generation to the next in a society." Positive psychology, on the other hand, focuses on "valued psychological phenomena, such as contentment and satisfaction, hope and optimism, and happiness and well-being." With technological advancements facilitating increased global communication, our interactions with diverse cultural perspectives have become more frequent. This exposure necessitates an understanding of others not only from our cultural standpoint, but also from the perspectives of the cultures in which they are embedded.
- **Sources of Influence of Culture on Positive Psychology:** Cultural influences on positive psychology stem from a variety of sources, including practices, institutions, and religious or spiritual beliefs. Contemporary researchers are increasingly exploring these cultural factors. Two broad perspectives on these cultural influences are the Eastern/Western perspective and the culture-free/culturally-embedded perspective. Psychologist Richard Schweder (1990) highlights that cultural factors guide people in determining what is morally good, virtuous, and acceptable. According to Schweder, Western individuals often seek physical rewards and emphasize autonomy and personal satisfaction, while Eastern individuals transform physical compensation into spiritual rewards, prioritizing harmony and collective satisfaction.
- **Cultural Perspectives on Well-Being:** The culture-free perspective suggests that people across different cultures have universally similar basic needs regarding happiness and well-being, such as the desire to be happy and maintain good health. Conversely, the culturally-embedded perspective argues that concepts like happiness and well-being can only be accurately understood within specific cultural contexts. This perspective suggests that happiness may not be the ultimate goal for all individuals from different cultures, challenging the universality proposed by the culture-free perspective. These divergent views emphasize the importance of considering cultural contexts when studying positive psychological constructs.

- **Eastern Philosophies and Positive Psychology:** While Western philosophies have extensively explored the interaction between culture and positive psychology, Eastern philosophies offer a vast and varied perspective. Major Eastern traditions such as Confucianism, Taoism, Buddhism, and Hinduism provide rich insights into positive psychology. Confucianism emphasizes humanistic psychology and the importance of respecting and caring for others. Taoism, centered on the concept of "The Way," views energy as a continuous flow through all individuals. Buddhism teaches virtues like love, joy, compassion, and composure, which are critical areas of study for positive psychologists. Hinduism, with its focus on karma and dedication to work, has significantly influenced Western scholars and philosophers, particularly through the Vedanta philosophy.
- **Positive Psychology in Indian Culture:** Positive psychology in India is deeply rooted in ancient texts like the Vedas and the Mahabharata. The teachings of Sri Krishna to Arjuna in the Bhagavad Gita emphasize non-attachment, hope amidst adversity, and performing one's duty without attachment to outcomes. Indian culture, with its emphasis on "unity in diversity," promotes living together in peace, harmony, and happiness, despite differences in faith and beliefs.
- **Contemporary Research in Indian Psychology:** Modern Indian psychologists are also contributing to the integration of culture and positive psychology. Psychoanalyst Sudhir Kakkar, in his book "Culture and Psyche" (2008), explores the Indian psyche through a psychoanalytical and cultural lens. Clinical psychologist Dr. Aruna Broota has developed relaxation techniques that combine yogic postures and the repetition of religious words like "shanti" (peace), making thoughts more accessible and facilitating techniques such as cognitive-behavioral therapy.
- **Need for Culturally Sensitive Research:** Most empirical findings linking culture and positive psychology are based on Western expectations, highlighting the need for culturally sensitive research that considers differences in emotions and values across cultures. Developing such research will create empirical evidence that is applicable to diverse populations, enhancing the relevance and effectiveness of positive psychology interventions globally. This approach will ensure that positive psychology respects and incorporates cultural diversity, leading to more inclusive and impactful practices that enhance well-being.

Application of Positive Psychology in Multicultural Context

Applied positive psychology aims to help individuals lead fulfilling lives and reach their full potential. Its principles are relevant across various psychological domains. Integrating a multicultural perspective within positive psychology involves understanding several key tenets, in the relevant areas.

1. **Happiness and Social Bonds:** The relationship between happiness and a multicultural perspective is deeply intertwined, as engaging with diverse cultures develops mutual understanding and enriches personal experiences. Multicultural interactions broaden individuals' horizons, enhancing their sense of belonging and community. This interconnectedness and appreciation of diversity contribute significantly to overall happiness and well-being.
    a) **Building Social Bonds and Community:** Positive psychology places a strong emphasis on the importance of social connections in developing happiness. Developing strong bonds with individuals, groups, communities, or nations from diverse cultural backgrounds can significantly enhance social activity and joy. Engaging with people from different cultures broadens perspectives, enriches lives, and cultivates a sense of belonging and community. These elements are essential for personal growth and overall well-being. Social bonds formed through multicultural interactions contribute to a richer, more fulfilling life experience.
    b) **Developing Ethnocultural Empathy:** A study by Le et al. (2009) explored the impact of multicultural attitudes on the subjective well-being and happiness of 338 ethnic minority and immigrant youths. The researchers found a positive relationship between perceived multiculturalism and subjective happiness, mediated by ethnocultural empathy among African Americans, Asians, males, and females. This indicates that understanding and sharing the feelings of others from different cultural backgrounds—ethnocultural empathy—plays a crucial role in enhancing subjective well-being and happiness.
    c) **Enhancing Subjective Well-Being:** Research indicates that multicultural attitudes, mediated by ethnocultural empathy, positively impact subjective well-being. When individuals exchange ideas and information, they become more familiar with one another, support each other's development, and build stronger social bonds. This familiarity and mutual support lead to the development of ethnocultural empathy, which in turn develops subjective well-being and

happiness. Positive psychology interventions that promote cultural empathy and understanding can therefore enhance overall happiness and life satisfaction.

d) **Promoting Mutual Support and Cooperation:** Positive psychology emphasizes the importance of mutual support and cooperation in achieving well-being. In multicultural contexts, this means encouraging individuals to support each other's cultural expressions and contributions. By recognizing and valuing the unique strengths that different cultures bring, communities can create a more cohesive and supportive social fabric. This mutual support not only enhances individual happiness but also contributes to the collective well-being of the community.

e) **Facilitating Personal Growth and Resilience:** Exposure to diverse cultural perspectives encourages personal growth and resilience. Positive psychology promotes the idea that engaging with different worldviews and practices can challenge individuals to expand their thinking and adapt to new situations. This process of learning and adaptation builds psychological resilience, an important component of happiness. Resilient individuals are better equipped to handle life's challenges and are more likely to experience lasting well-being.

2. **Understanding and Reducing Stereotypes and Prejudices:** Incorporating a multicultural perspective into positive psychology can be instrumental in reducing prejudices and developing a more inclusive and harmonious society.

a) **Emphasizing Cultural Competence:** A multicultural perspective in positive psychology emphasizes the importance of cultural competence, which involves understanding, respecting, and valuing cultural differences. Practitioners who are culturally competent can design interventions that are more relevant and respectful of diverse cultural backgrounds. By acknowledging and addressing cultural details, psychologists can create more effective strategies that resonate with individuals from various cultural contexts, thereby reducing misunderstandings and biases.

b) **Encouraging Empathy and Perspective-Taking:** Positive psychology interventions can be designed to develop empathy and perspective-taking, essential components for reducing prejudices. Activities that encourage individuals to learn about and understand different cultural experiences can help break down stereotypes. For example, storytelling and the sharing of personal narratives from diverse cultural perspectives can humanize those from different backgrounds and promote empathy. This practice helps individuals see the world from others' viewpoints, reducing fear and negative assumptions about out-groups.

c) **Promoting Positive Intergroup Contact:** Research in social psychology shows that positive intergroup contact can significantly reduce prejudices. The multicultural perspective of positive psychology can facilitate such interactions by promoting activities and environments where individuals from different cultures can come together and collaborate. Community service projects, multicultural events, and inclusive social activities can create opportunities for meaningful engagement and cooperation, developing mutual understanding and respect.

d) **Highlighting the Strengths and Contributions of All Cultures:** A strengths-based approach in positive psychology can be particularly effective in a multicultural context. By focusing on the unique strengths, contributions, and positive attributes of different cultures, this approach shifts the narrative from deficits and differences to shared human potential and accomplishments. Recognizing and celebrating the achievements of various cultural groups can enhance appreciation and reduce prejudices. For example, educational programs that highlight the contributions of different cultures to science, art, and society can foster a more positive and inclusive outlook.

e) **Implementing Mindfulness and Compassion Training:** Mindfulness and compassion training are powerful tools that can help reduce prejudices by promoting awareness and non-judgmental acceptance of others. Mindfulness practices enable individuals to observe their thoughts and biases without attachment, creating space for conscious reflection and change. Compassion training encourages a deep sense of empathy and kindness towards others, regardless of cultural differences. Incorporating these practices into positive psychology interventions can help individuals develop a more open and accepting attitude toward diverse groups.

f) **Addressing Systemic and Structural Factors:** A multicultural perspective in positive psychology also involves recognizing and addressing systemic and structural factors that contribute to prejudice and discrimination. This includes understanding how historical, social, and economic contexts shape attitudes and behaviors. By advocating for social justice and equity, positive psychology can contribute to creating environments that support diversity and inclusion. Interventions can include promoting policies and practices that reduce inequality and create opportunities for all cultural groups to thrive.

g) **Enhancing Social and Emotional Learning (SEL):** Integrating social and emotional learning (SEL) with a multicultural perspective can help individuals develop the skills needed to guide and appreciate cultural diversity. SEL programs that incorporate cultural awareness and sensitivity training can teach individuals to manage their emotions, build healthy relationships, and make responsible decisions in a diverse world. These programs can be implemented in schools, workplaces, and communities to foster an inclusive environment where diversity is valued and respected.

3. **Increase in Harmony and Peace Among Nations:** A multicultural perspective of positive psychology can significantly contribute to increasing peace and harmony among nations by developing deeper understanding, enhancing cooperation, and promoting shared values. By focusing on the strengths and virtues inherent in diverse cultures, positive psychology can create a global environment where differences are celebrated and commonalities are emphasized. Here's how this approach can be elaborated upon:

a) **Promoting Cross-Cultural Empathy and Understanding:** Positive psychology's emphasis on empathy can bridge gaps between different cultural groups. Empathy allows individuals to understand and share the feelings of others, which is crucial in a multicultural world. By encouraging practices such as mindfulness and perspective-taking, positive psychology can help people from different backgrounds see the world from each other's viewpoints. This deeper understanding reduces prejudice and fosters mutual respect, making it easier for nations to cooperate and resolve conflicts amicably.

b) **Enhancing Communication and Conflict Resolution:** Effective communication is vital for maintaining peaceful international relations. Positive psychology provides tools for improving communication skills, such as active listening and nonviolent communication, which are essential in multicultural interactions. These skills help individuals and groups to express themselves clearly and understand others better, reducing the likelihood of misunderstandings and conflicts. When conflicts do arise, positive psychology's strengths-based approach to conflict resolution encourages finding solutions that honor all parties' dignity and worth, thereby promoting lasting peace.

c) **Developing Shared Goals and Collective Well-Being:** Positive psychology encourages the identification of shared values and goals that transcend cultural differences. By focusing on universal aspirations such as peace, justice, and environmental sustainability, positive psychology helps unite diverse groups to work towards common objectives. This sense of shared purpose can strengthen international bonds as nations collaborate to achieve goals that benefit humanity as a whole. When countries work together towards common goals, the likelihood of conflict diminishes, and global harmony is enhanced.

d) **Building Resilience and Positive Cultural Identity:** In a multicultural world, resilience is crucial for overcoming challenges and stresses related to cultural integration and global interdependence. Positive psychology develops resilience through practices like gratitude, optimism, and nurturing positive relationships. Moreover, by helping individuals develop a positive cultural identity, positive psychology encourages people to take pride in their heritage while also embracing a broader, global identity. This dual sense of identity enhances self-esteem and reduces feelings of alienation, promoting social cohesion and reducing tensions between cultural groups.

e) **Facilitating Cultural Exchange and Appreciation:** Cultural exchange and appreciation are essential for building harmonious international relationships. Positive psychology supports initiatives that encourage cultural exchange, such as international education programs, cultural festivals, and collaborative projects. These initiatives allow individuals to experience and appreciate different cultures firsthand, breaking down stereotypes and building trust. As people learn about and appreciate the richness of other cultures, they become more open and accepting, leading to a more peaceful and harmonious global society.

f) **Encouraging Strength-Based Approaches:** Positive psychology's focus on strengths rather than weaknesses can shift international relations in a more constructive and collaborative direction. By identifying and utilizing the strengths of different cultures, nations can learn from each other and develop innovative solutions to global challenges. This strength-based approach develops mutual respect and admiration as countries recognize and value each other's contributions to global well-being.

g) **Creating Positive Global Narratives:** By promoting stories of successful multicultural collaborations and highlighting the benefits of cultural diversity, positive psychology can inspire nations to pursue peaceful and cooperative relationships.

4. **Less Inter-Group Conflict:** Positive psychology can play a transformative role in lessening intergroup conflict within a multicultural context. By emphasizing positive interpersonal and intrapersonal dynamics, positive psychology can help to build bridges between different cultural groups, developing an environment of mutual respect, understanding, and collaboration. There are several ways in which positive psychology can contribute to reducing intergroup conflict:

   a) **Empathy and Compassion:** Positive psychology encourages the development of empathy and compassion, which are crucial for understanding and relating to individuals from different cultural backgrounds. Empathy allows individuals to put themselves in others' shoes, appreciating their experiences and perspectives. Compassion motivates individuals to act on that understanding with kindness and support. Interventions such as mindfulness practices and loving-kindness meditation can enhance these qualities, helping people to connect on a deeper emotional level and reducing the likelihood of conflicts arising from misunderstandings or prejudices.

   b) **Enhancing Communication Skills:** Effective communication is a key to resolving and preventing conflicts. Positive psychology promotes active listening and assertive communication, which are essential skills for solving multicultural interactions. Active listening involves fully concentrating, understanding, responding, and remembering what is being said, which can help to reduce misunderstandings. Assertive communication allows individuals to express their needs and concerns clearly and respectfully. By improving these skills, positive psychology helps individuals from different cultural backgrounds engage in more constructive and respectful dialogues, thereby reducing the potential for conflict.

c) **Building Positive Intergroup Relationships:** Positive psychology emphasizes the importance of building positive relationships, which can bridge divides between different cultural groups. By developing qualities such as trust, respect, and cooperation, positive psychology can help create a sense of community and belonging among diverse groups. Activities that promote team-building, collaborative projects, and social bonding can strengthen these relationships. When people from different cultural backgrounds work together towards common goals, they are more likely to form positive impressions of each other and less likely to engage in conflict.

d) **Encouraging a Growth Mindset:** Positive psychology promotes the concept of a growth mindset, which is the belief that abilities and intelligence can be developed through dedication and hard work. This mindset can be applied to intercultural competence as well. By encouraging individuals to view intercultural interactions as opportunities for learning and growth, positive psychology helps to reduce anxiety and defensiveness that can lead to conflict. People become more open to understanding and adapting to different cultural perspectives, which enhances cooperation and harmony.

e) **Cultivating Resilience and Coping Skills:** Conflict often arises from stress and adversity. Positive psychology interventions that build resilience and effective coping skills can help individuals and groups manage stress and recover from conflicts more effectively. Practices such as gratitude, optimism, and maintaining positive relationships can enhance emotional resilience. Resilient individuals and communities are better equipped to handle cultural differences and conflicts constructively, viewing challenges as opportunities for growth rather than threats.

f) **Facilitating Forgiveness and Reconciliation:** Forgiveness is a powerful tool in resolving conflicts and healing divisions. Positive psychology research highlights the benefits of forgiveness for both individuals and groups. Encouraging forgiveness can help break cycles of resentment and retaliation that fuel intergroup conflict. Programs that facilitate dialogue and understanding, such as restorative justice initiatives, can promote forgiveness and reconciliation between cultural groups, paving the way for lasting peace and cooperation.

5. **Increase in Culturally Sensitive Researches:** Positive psychology can greatly enhance culturally sensitive research from a multicultural

perspective. By integrating principles from positive psychology, researchers and theorists can better prepare studies that are inclusive, unbiased, and reflective of diverse cultural contexts. There are several ways in which positive psychology contributes to culturally sensitive research:

a) **Promoting Cultural Competence and Awareness:** Researchers who are trained in positive psychology are more likely to recognize their own cultural biases and understand the importance of considering different cultural perspectives. This self-awareness helps them design studies that are respectful and inclusive of various cultural backgrounds. By practicing empathy, researchers can put themselves in the shoes of participants from different cultures, leading to more sensitive and relevant research questions and methodologies.

b) **Emphasizing Strengths and Well-Being Across Cultures:** A core tenet of positive psychology is the focus on strengths and well-being. When applied to multicultural research, this approach encourages researchers to look beyond deficits and problems in different cultural groups and instead highlight their strengths and contributions. This positive focus can lead to research that celebrates cultural diversity and identifies how different cultural practices contribute to well-being. By valuing the strengths of various cultures, researchers can avoid the pitfalls of ethnocentrism and develop a more balanced and appreciative understanding of cultural differences.

c) **Facilitating Inclusive and Participatory Research Methods:** Positive psychology promotes participatory and inclusive research methods, which are crucial for culturally sensitive research. By involving community members and participants from diverse cultural backgrounds in the research process, researchers can ensure that their studies are relevant and respectful. This participatory approach can include community consultations, collaborative study designs, and feedback loops where participants help shape the research outcomes. Inclusive methods help to ensure that the research is grounded in the lived experiences and perspectives of the cultural groups being studied.

d) **Encouraging Openness and Flexibility:** Positive psychology fosters a growth mindset, which encourages openness to new ideas and flexibility in thinking. Researchers with a growth mindset are more likely to be open to learning from different cultures and adapting their research approaches accordingly. This flexibility is essential for conducting culturally sensitive research, as it allows researchers to modify their methods and hypotheses in response to cultural insights and feedback. By being open and adaptable, researchers can better accommodate the nuances and complexities of different cultural contexts.

e) **Reducing In-Group Bias Through Mindfulness and Reflection:** Positive psychology incorporates mindfulness practices that can help researchers become more aware of their own biases and preconceptions. Mindfulness encourages non-judgmental awareness of one's thoughts and feelings, which can reduce in-group bias and develop a more objective and respectful approach to research. By regularly reflecting on their own cultural assumptions and the potential impact on their research, researchers can minimize bias and promote more equitable and fair studies.

f) **Building Trust and Rapport with Diverse Communities:** Trust and rapport are critical for effective and ethical research, particularly in multicultural contexts. Positive psychology emphasizes the importance of building positive relationships, which can help researchers establish trust with participants from diverse cultural backgrounds. By demonstrating respect, empathy, and genuine interest in participants' experiences, researchers can create a supportive environment where participants feel valued and heard. This trust and rapport can lead to more honest and open participation, enriching the quality and depth of the research data.

g) **Integrating Culturally Relevant Measures and Interventions:** Positive psychology encourages the use of culturally relevant measures and interventions that resonate with the specific cultural contexts being studied. Researchers can adapt existing psychological measures to better fit the cultural norms and values of different groups, or develop new tools that are culturally appropriate. This ensures that the research findings are valid and meaningful across different cultural settings. Moreover, interventions derived from positive psychology, such as strengths-based approaches or resilience training, can be tailored to align with cultural practices and beliefs, enhancing their effectiveness and acceptance.

Summary

The application of positive psychology from a multicultural perspective necessitates an understanding of the intricate relationship between culture and human strengths. Positive psychologists must incorporate the multicultural perspective into their research and practice, acknowledging culture as a crucial factor in the development of positive traits and well-being. Key research areas in positive psychology, such as positive emotions, happiness, optimism, and self-efficacy, must be examined from the perspective of cultural diversity.

Positive emotions not only enhance personal well-being but also develop a sense of connection with others. However, cultural differences significantly influence the perception and pursuit of happiness. In many Western cultures, happiness is deemed a primary life goal, whereas some non-Western cultures may not prioritize happiness in the same way. Individualist cultures, which emphasize independence and personal identity, differ markedly from collectivist cultures, which value group harmony and collective identity.

Research indicates that Western individuals often seek tangible rewards and personal satisfaction, whereas Eastern cultures tend to value spiritual fulfillment and societal harmony. This cultural variance underscores the importance of tailoring positive psychology interventions to fit the cultural context.

In India, the principles of positive psychology are deeply rooted in ancient texts like the Vedas and the Bhagavad Gita, which advocate non-attachment and the pursuit of one's duty (karma) as pathways to happiness and resilience. These cultural teachings highlight the significance of maintaining hope and equilibrium in the face of challenges.

By integrating these cultural ideas, positive psychology can more effectively promote well-being and develop a deeper understanding of human strengths across diverse cultural landscapes. This culturally sensitive approach ensures that positive psychology is inclusive and relevant to people from all cultural backgrounds.

REFERENCES

1. Aknin, L. B., Norton, M. I., & Dunn, E. W. (2009). From wealth to well-being? Money matters, but less than people think, The Journal of Positive Psychology, 4, 523–527.
2. American Psychiatric Association. (2013). Diagnostic and statistical manual of mental disorders (5th ed.).
3. Atchley, R. C. (1989). A Continuity Theory of Normal Aging. The Gerontologist, 29(2), 183–190.
4. Bandura, A. (1994). Self-efficacy. In R. J. Corsini (Ed.), Encyclopedia of psychology (2nd ed., Vol. 3, 368–369). Wiley.
5. Barraza, J. A., & Zak, P. J. (2009). Empathy towards strangers triggers oxytocin release and subsequent generosity. Annals of the New York Academy of Sciences, 1167, 182–189.
6. Basford, T. E., &Offermann, L. R. (2012). Beyond leadership: The impact of coworker relationships on employee motivation and intent to stay. Journal of Management & Organization, 8, 807–817.
7. Bass, S., Caro, F. J., & Chen, Y. P. (1993). Toward a productive aging society. Westport, CT: Auburn House.
8. Baumeister, R. F., Vohs, K. D., Aaker, J., & Garbinsky, E. N. (2012). Some key differences between a happy life and a meaningful life. Journal of Positive Psychology, 8, 505–516.
9. Baumrind, D. (1971). Current patterns of parental authority. Developmental Psychology Monographs, 4(1, Pt.2), 1–103. doi:10.1037/h0030372
10. Baumrind, D. (1991). The influence of parenting style on adolescent competence and substance use. Journal of Early Adolescence, 11(1), 56–95.
11. Boehm, J. K., Peterson, C., Kinimaki, M., & Kubzansky, L. D. (2011). Heart health when life is satisfying: evidence from the Whitehall II cohort study. *European Heart Journal, 32, 2672–2677. [PMC free article] [PubMed] [Google Scholar]
12. Boiman-Meshita, M., & Littman-Ovadia, H. (2021). The marital version of three good things: A mixed-method study. The Journal of Positive Psychology, 16(3), 367378.
13. Bowker. J. (1970). Problems of suffering in religions of the world. New York: Cambridge University Press.

14. Bowlby, J. (1979). The bowlby-ainsworth attachment theory. Behavioral and Brain Sciences, 2(4), 637–638.
15. Bowling, A., & Dieppe, P. (2005). What is successful ageing and who should define it?. Bmj, 331(7531), 1548–1551.
16. Brennan, K. A., Clark, C. L., & Shaver, P. R. (1998). Self-report measurement of adult attachment: An integrative overview.
17. Breuer, J. & Freud, S. (2004). Studies on hysteria. Penguin. Original work published 1895.
18. Bronfenbrenner, U. (1977). Toward an experimental ecology of human development. American psychologist, 32(7), 513. Applications of Positive Psychology in Everyday Life–I
19. Bronfenbrenner, U., & Morris, P. A. (2006). The Bioecological Model of Human Development. In R. M. Lerner & W. Damon (Eds.), Handbook of child psychology: Theoretical models of human development (pp. 793–828). John Wiley & Sons Inc
20. Cacioppo, J. T., Hawkley, L. C., Norman, G. J., &Berntson, G.G. (2011). Social isolation. Annals of the New York Academy of Sciences, 1231(1), 17–22.
21. Calhoun, L. G., & Tedeschi, R. G. (2001). Posttraumatic growth: The positive lessons of loss. In R. A. Neimeyer (Ed.), Meaning reconstruction & the experience of loss (pp. 157–172). Washington, DC: American Psychological Association.
22. Carstensen, L. L. (1992). Motivation for social contact across the life span: A theory of socioemotional selectivity. Nebraska Symposium on Motivation, 40, 209–254. PMID: 1340521.
23. Carstensen, L. L., Fung, H. H., & Charles, S. T. (2003). Socioemotional selectivity theory and the regulation of emotion in the second half of life. Motivation and emotion, 27(2), 103–123.
24. Center on the Developing Child at Harvard University (2021). Three Principles to Improve Outcomes for Children and Families, 2021 Update. https://46y5eh11fhgw3ve3ytpwxt9r-wpengine.netdna-ssl.com/wp uploads/2017/10/3Principles_Update2021v2.pdf content/ http://www.developingchild.harvard.edu
25. Centers for Disease Control (2014). Positive parenting tips. Retrieved from https://www.cdc.gov/ncbddd/childdevelopment/positiveparenting/
26. Chander, S. (2022). Adolescents and issues related to learning and academic achievement. In S. Patra (Ed.) Adolescence in India: Issues, challenges and possibilities. Springer.
27. CliftonCohen, S. (2004). Social relationships and health. American Psychologist, 59(8), 676–684. [PubMed] [Google Scholar]
28. Collins, J. (2001). Good to great. New York: Harper Collins.

29. Cook, J. M., & Poulsen, S. S. (2011). Utilizing photographs with the genogram: A technique for enhancing couple therapy. Journal of Systemic Therapies, 30(1), 1423.
30. Cornelissen, T. (2016). Do social interactions in the workplace lead to productivity spillover among co-workers? IZA World of Labor, 314, 1–10.
31. Csikszentmihalyi, M. (1990). The psychology of optimal experience. Harper & Row Publishers.
32. Deci, E. L., & Ryan, R. M. (1985) intrinsic motivation and self-determination in human behavior. Springer.
33. Deci, E. L., & Ryan, R. M. (2008). Self-Determination Theory: A macrotheory of human motivation, development, and health. Canadian Psychology/ Psychologie Canadienne, 49, 182–185.
34. Deci, E. L., & Ryan, R. M. (2012). Motivation, personality, and development within embedded social contexts: An overview of self-determination theory. In R. M. Ryan (Ed.), Oxford handbook of human motivation (pp. 85–107). Oxford, UK: Oxford University Press.
35. Devi & Patra, (2020a). Review of School Based Positive Psychology Interventions: Efforts to promote mental health among Adolescents. The Learning Curve, IX, p. 57–65
36. Diener, E. (2009). Assessing well-being. The collected works of Ed Diener. Springer.
37. Diener, E., & Seligman, M. E. (2002). Very happy people. Psychological Science, 13(1), 81–84.
38. Dumas, J. E. (2005). Mindfulness-based parent training: Strategies to lessen the grip of automaticity in families with disruptive children. Journal of Clinical Child and Adolescent Psychology, 34(4), 779–791. https://doi.org/10.1207/s15374424jccp3404_20
39. Dunbar, R., & Dunbar, R. I. M. (1998). Grooming, gossip, and the evolution of language. Harvard University Press.
40. Dunn D. S. (2019). Understanding the Experience of Disability: Perspectives from Social and Rehabilitation Psychology. Oxford, UK: Oxford University Press. [Google Scholar]
41. Dunn, E. W., Aknin, L. B., & Norton, M. I. (2008). Spending money on others promotes happiness. Science, 319, 1687–1688.
42. Dweck, C. S. (2007). Mindset: The new psychology of success. Ballantine Books.
43. Fowler, J. H., & Christakis, N. A. (2008). Dynamic spread of happiness in a large social network: Longitudinal analysis over 20 years in the Framingham Heart Study. The BMJ, 337.

44. Frankl, V. E. (1992). Man's search for meaning: An introduction to logotherapy (4th ed.) (I. Lasch, Trans.). Beacon Press. Original work published 1946.
45. Frankl, V.E. (1963). Man's search for meaning—An introduction to logotherapy. New York: Washington Square Press.
46. Frederickson, B. (2009). Positivity: Groundbreaking research to release your inner optimist and thrive. Oxford, England: Oneworld Publications.
47. Fredrickson, B. L. (2003). The value of positive emotions. American Scientist, 91(4), 330–335. https://doi.org/10.1511/2003.26.865
48. Fredrickson, B. L. (2004). The broaden-and-build theory of positive emotions. Philosophical Transactions of the Royal Society B: Biological Sciences, 359(1449), 1367–1378.
49. Fredrickson, B. L. (2004). The broaden–and–build theory of positive emotions. Philosophical Transactions of the Royal Society of London. Series B: Biological Sciences, 359(1449), 1367–1377.
50. Freud, S. (1997). Interpretation of dreams. Wordsworth Editions. Original work published 1900.
51. Freund, A. M., Riedger, M. Successful Aging. In Weiner, I. B. (Ed.). Handbook of Psychology. Volume 6. Developmental Psychology. New Jersey: John Wiley & Sons, Inc., 2003.
52. Froh, J. J. (2004). The history of positive psychology: Truth be told. NYS Psychologist, 16(3), 18–20.
53. Gable, S. L., & Gosnell, C. L. (2011). The positive side of close relationships. In K. M. Sheldon, T. B., Kashdan, & M. F. Steger (Eds.), Designing positive psychology: Taking stock and moving forward (pp. 265–279). Oxford University Press.
54. Gallup (n.d.) The history of CliftonStrengths. Accessed on Dec 08, 2022 from https://www.gallup.com/cliftonstrengths/en/253754/history-cliftonstrengths.aspx
55. Gallup. (2015). State of the global workforce [Report]. Retrieved from https://www.gallup.com/workplace/238079/state-global-workplace-2017.aspx
56. Gana, K., Alaphilippe, D., & Bailly, N. (2004). Positive illusions and mental and physical health in later life. Aging & mental health, 8(1), 58–64.
57. Geue, P. E., (2017). Positive practices in the workplace: Impact on team climate, work engagement, and task performance. Emerging Leadership Journeys, 10, 70–99
58. Gilman, R., Huebner, S. & Buckman, M. (2008). Positive schooling. In S.J. Lopez (Ed.), Positive psychology exploring the best in people. Westport, CT: Greenwood Publishing Co.

59. Gilpin, J. M. (2008). Teaching happiness: The role of positive psychology in the classroom (Master's thesis, Salve Regina University, Newport, Rhode Island).
60. Gottman, J. M., & Gottman, J. S. (2013). Difficulties with clients in Gottman method couples therapy.
61. Green, S., Anthony, T., & Rynsaardt, J. (2007). Evidence-based life coaching for senior high school students: Building hardiness and hope. International Coaching Psychology Review, 2, 24–32.
62. Hamilton, E. A. (2007). Firm friendship: Examining functions and outcomes of workplace friendship among law firm associates (Unpublished doctoral dissertation). Boston College, Boston, MA.
63. Harvard Health Publishing. (2008). Positive psychology in practice. Harvard Mental Health Letter. Retrieved from https://www.health.harvard.edu/mind-and-mood/positive_psychology_in_practice
64. Harvey, J. H., &Omarzu, J. (1997). Minding the close relationship. Personality and Social Psychology Review, 1(3), 224–240.
65. Havighurst, R. J. (1963). Successful aging. Processes of aging: Social and psychological perspectives, 1, 299–320.
66. Havighurst, R. J., Neugarten, B. L., & Tobin, S. (1964). Disengagement and Patterns of Aging. Journal of Gerontology, 4(1), 24.
67. Herman, J. L. (1992). Trauma and recovery: The aftermath of violence–from domestic abuse to political terror. HarperCollins.
68. Holt-Lunstad, J., Smith, T. B., Baker, M., Harris, T., & Stephenson, D. (2015). Loneliness, and social isolation as risk factors for mortality: A meta-analytic review. Perspectives on Psychological Sciences, 10(2), 227–237.
69. House, J. S., Landis, K. R., & Umberson, D. (1988). Social relationships and health. Science, 241(4865), 540–545. [PubMed] [Google Scholar]
70. Howell, R. T., & Hill, G. (2009). The mediators of experiential purchases: Determining the impact of psychological needs satisfaction and social comparison. The Journal of Positive Psychology, 4, 511–522.
71. Hudgins, K. (2019). Psychodrama revisited: Through the lens of the internal role map of the therapeutic spiral model to promote post-traumatic growth. Zeitschrift für Psychodrama und Soziometrie, 18(1), 59–74.
72. Hudgins, K., & Durost, S. W. (2022). Experiential therapy from trauma to posttraumatic growth: Therapeutic spiral model psychodrama. Springer.
73. Huebner, S. (2010). Feelings Count: Conceptualizing and Measuring Students' Happiness in Schools. Communiqué: The newspaper of the National Association of School Psychologists, 39, 1.
74. Jenkinson, C. E., Dickens, A. P., Jones, K., Thompson-Coon, J., Taylor, R. S., Rogers, M., Bambra, C. L., , & Richards, S. H. (2013). Is volunteering a public

health intervention? A systematic review and meta-analysis of the health and survival of volunteers. BMC Public Health, 13, 773–782.

75. Joseph, S. (2004). Client-centred therapy, post-traumatic stress, and post-traumatic growth: Theoretical perspectives and practical implications. Psychology and Psychotherapy: Theory, Research and Practice, 77, 101–120.
76. Joseph, S., & Linley, P.A. (2004). Positive change following trauma and trauma: A review. Journal of Traumatic Stress, 17, 11–21.
77. Joseph, S. (2013). What doesn't kill us: A guide to overcoming adversity and moving forward. Piatkus.
78. Jung, C. G. (1994). Duše moderního člověka. Brno: Atlanits.
79. Kabat-Zinn, M., & Kabat-Zinn, J. (1997). Everyday blessings. The inner work of mindful parenting. Hachette Books.
80. Kauffman, C., & Silberman, J. (2009). Finding and fostering the positive in relationships: Positive interventions in couples therapy. Journal of Clinical Psychology, 65(5), 520531.
81. Keyes, C. L. (June 2002). The mental health continuum: From languishing to flourishing in life. Journal of Health and Social Behavior, 43(2), 207–222. doi:10.2307/3090197
82. Khanna, P. (2016). Validation of Positive Psychological Interventions for Indian School Students. A Ph.d Thesis. Department of Humanities and Social Sciences. Indian Institute of Technology Delhi (IITD). New Delhi.
83. Khoshkharam, N., &Golzari, M. (2011). Efficacy of hope therapy on the rate of increasing marital satisfaction and change in insecure attachment style in married university students.
84. Kiyimba, N., Buxton, C., Shuttleworth, J., & Pathe, E. (2022). Discourses of psychological trauma. Springer.
85. Kjerulf, A. (2016, January 18). The 5 most important findings from the science of happiness that apply at work. The Chief Happiness Officer Blog. Retrieved from https://positivesharing.com/2016/01/positive-psychology-at-work/
86. Krathwohl, D.R., Bloom, B.S., & Masia, B.B. (1964). Taxonomy of educational objectives. The classification of educational goals, Handbook II: Affective domain. New York: David Mckay Company Inc.
87. Lachapelle Y., Wehmeyer M. L., Haelewyck M.-C., Courbois Y., Keith K. D., Schalock R., et al.. (2005). The relationship between quality of life and self-determination: an international study. J. Ment. Defic. Res. 49, 740–744. doi: 10.1111/j.1365-2788.2005.00743.x [PubMed] [CrossRef] [Google Scholar]
88. Layous, K., Nelson, S. K., Oberle, E., Schonert-Reichl, K. A., & Lyubomirsky, S. (2012). Kindness counts: Prompting prosocial behavior in preadolescents boosts peer acceptance and well-being. PLoS ONE, 7.

89. Lehr, U. (2007). Psychologie des Alters. Wiebelsheim: Quelle & Meyer Verlag GmbH & Co.
90. Lemon, B. W., Bengtson, V. L., & Peterson, J. A. (1972). An exploration of the activity theory of aging: Activity types and life satisfaction among in-movers to a retirement community. Journal of gerontology, 27(4), 511–523.
91. Lyubomirsky, S., King, L., & Diener, E. (2005). The benefits of frequent positive affect: Does happiness lead to success? Psychological Bulletin, 131, 803–855.
92. Martin, L. G., & Kinsella, K. (1994). Research on the Demography of Aging in Developing Countries. In L. G. Martin & S. H. Preston (Eds.), Demography of Aging Washington: National Academy Press.
93. Maslow, A.H. (1970). Motivation and Personality (2nd ed). New York: Harper & Row.
94. Mentor Coach LLC. (n.d.). What IS positive psychology? MentorCoach – Positive Psychology & Coaching. Retrieved from http://www.mentorcoach.com/positive-psychology-coaching/
95. Morgeson, F. P., & Humphrey, S. E. (2006). The Work Design Questionnaire (WDQ): Developing and validating a comprehensive measure for assessing job design and the nature of work. Journal of Applied Psychology, 91(6), 1321–1339.
96. Nigg, B., & Steidl, S. (2005). Gerontologie, Geriatrie und Gerontopsychiatrie. Wien: Facultas Universitätsverlag.
97. Noddings, N. (1995). A morally defensible mission for schools in the twenty first century. The Phi Delta Kappan, 76, 365–368.
98. Nolan, T. &Küpers, W. (2009). Organizational climate, organizational culture, and workplace relationships. In R. L. Morrison & S. L. Wright (Eds.), Friends and enemies in organizations (pp. 57–77). Palgrave Macmillan.
99. Norrish, J. M., Williams, P., O'Connor, M., & Robinson, J. (2013). An applied framework for positive education. International Journal of Well-being, 3(2), 147–161.
100. Nowlan, J. S., Wuthrich, V. M., Rapee, R. M., Kinsella, J. M., & Barker, G. (2016). A comparison of single-session positive reappraisal, cognitive restructuring and supportive counselling for older adults with type 2 diabetes. Cognitive Therapy and Research, 40(2), 216–229. https://doi-org.ezproxy.uakron.edu:2443/10.1007/s10608-015-9737-x
101. Oh, H., Chung, M.-H., &Labianca, G. (2004), Group social capital and group effectiveness: the role of informal socializing ties. Academy of Management Journal, 47, 860–875.
102. Oswald, D. L. (2017). Maintaining long-lasting friendships. The psychology of friendship, 267–282.

103. Parker, S. K., Van den Broeck, A., & Holman, D. (2017). Work design influences: A synthesis of multilevel factors that affect the design of jobs. Academy of Management Annals, 11(1), 267–308.
104. Patra, S. (2022). Is There a Right Way to Parent?: Focusing on Mindful Parenting. In S. Gupta (Eds.), Handbook of Research on Clinical Applications of Meditation and Mindfulness-Based Interventions in Mental Health (pp. 3554). IGI Global. http://doi:10.4018/978-1-7998-8682-2.ch003
105. Peppercorn, S. (2014). The benefits of positive psychology coaching. Positive Workplace Partners. Retrieved from http://positiveworkplacepartners.com/the-benefits-of-positive-psychology-coaching/
106. Peterson C. (2009). "Foreword," in Oxford Handbook of Positive Psychology. 2nd Edn. eds. Snyder C. R., Lopez S. J. (Oxford, UK: Oxford University Press;), 23–24. [Google Scholar]
107. Peterson, C. (2008). What is positive psychology, and what is it not? Psychology Today. Retrieved from https://www.psychologytoday.com/us/blog/the-good-life/200805/what-is-positive-psychology-and-what-is-it-not
108. Pulkkinen, L. (2000). Developmental Psychology. In K. Pawlik & M. R. Rosenzweig (Eds.), International Handbook of Psychology: Vol. 2. Adulthood and Aging. Thousand Oaks, CA: Sage Publications Ltd.
109. Ranzijn, R. (2002). Towards a positive psychology of ageing: Potentials and barriers. Australian Psychologist, 37(2), 79–85. https://doiorg.ezproxy.uakron.edu:2443/10.1080/00050060210001706716
110. Rowe, J. W., & Kahn, R. L. (1998). Successful aging: The MacArthur Foundation Study. New York: Pantheon.
111. Ryan R. M., Deci E. L. (2000). Self-determination theory and the facilitation of intrinsic motivation, social development, and well-being. Am. Psychol. 55, 68–78. doi: 10.1037/0003-066X.55.1.68, PMID: [PubMed] [CrossRef] [Google Scholar]
112. Ryan R. M., Deci E. L. (2017). Self-Determination Theory: Basic Psychological Needs in Motivation, Development, and Wellness. New York: Guilford Press. [Google Scholar]
113. Ryan, R. M., & Deci, E. L. (2000). Self-determination theory and the facilitation of intrinsic motivation, social development, and well-being. American Psychologist, 55(1), 68–78. doi:10.1037/0003-066X.55.1.68.
114. Ryan, R. M., & Deci, E. L. (2017). Self-determination theory: Basic psychological needs in motivation, development, and wellness. New York: Guilford Publishing.
115. Ryan, R. M., & Deci, E. L. (2018). Self-determination theory: Basic psychological needs in motivation, development, and wellness. Guilford Press.

116. Ryff, C. D. (1982). Successful aging: A developmental approach. The Gerontologist, 22(2), 209–214.
117. Ryff, C. D., Singer, B. H., & Love, G. D. (2004). Positive health: connecting well-being with biology. Philosophical Transactions of the Royal Society of London. Series B, Biological Sciences, 359, 1383–1394. [PMC free article] [PubMed] [Google Scholar]
118. Schalock R. L. (1996). Quality of Life: Vol. 1. Conceptualization and Measurement. Washington, DC: American Association on Mental Retardation. [Google Scholar]
119. Schalock R. L., Verdugo M. A. (2013). "The impact of the quality of life concept on the field of intellectual disability," in The Oxford Handbook of Positive Psychology and Disability. ed. Wehmeyer M. L. (Oxford, UK: Oxford University Press;), 37–47. [Google Scholar]
120. Schubert, C. F., Schmidt, U., & Rosner, R. (2015). Posttraumatic growth in populations with posttraumatic stress disorder: A systematic review on growth-related psychological constructs and biological variables. Clinical Psychology & Psychotherapy, 23(6), 469–486.
121. Scott, B. A., & Barnes, C. M. (2011). A multilevel field investigation of emotional labor, affect, work withdrawal, and gender. Academy of Management Journal, 54, 116–136.
122. Seay, A., Freysteinson, W. M., & McFarlane, J. (2014). Positive parenting. Nursing Forum, 49(3), 200–208.
123. Seeman, J. (1989). Toward a model of positive health. American Psychologist, 44, 1099–1109. [PubMed] [Google Scholar]
124. Seligman M. E. P., Csikszentmihalyi M. (2000). Positive psychology: an introduction. Am. Psychol. 55, 5–14. doi: 10.1037/0003-066X.55.1.5 [PubMed] [CrossRef] [Google Scholar]
125. Seligman, M. E. (2002). Positive psychology, positive prevention, and positive therapy. Handbook of positive psychology, 2(2002), 3–12.
126. Seligman, M. E. P. (2011). Flourish: A visionary new understanding of happiness and well-being. New York, NY: Free Press.
127. Seligman, M. E. P. (2011). Flourish: A visionary new understanding of happiness and well-Being. Atria Books.
128. Seligman, M. E. P. (2011). Flourish: A visionary new understanding of happiness and well-being. New York City, NY: Atria Books.
129. Seligman, M. E. P., & Csikszentmihalyi, M. (2000). Positive psychology: An introduction. American Psychologist, 55, 5–14. [PubMed] [Google Scholar]
130. Seligman, M. E. P., Steen, T. A., Park, N., & Peterson, S. (2005). Positive psychology progress: Empirical validation of interventions. American Psychologist, 60, 410–421.

131. Shaver, P. R., &Mikulincer, M. (2014). Attachment bonds in romantic relationships.
132. Shogren K. A. (2013). "Positive psychology and disability: a historical analysis," in The Oxford Handbook of Positive Psychology and Disability. ed. Wehmeyer M. L. (Oxford, UK: Oxford University Press;), 19–33. [Google Scholar]
133. Shogren K. A., Lopez S. J., Wehmeyer M. L., Little T. D., Pressgrove C. L. (2006a). The role of positive psychology constructs in predicting life satisfaction in adolescents with and without cognitive disabilities: an exploratory study. J. Posit. Psychol. 1, 37–52. doi: 10.1080/17439760500373174 [CrossRef] [Google Scholar]
134. Shogren K. A., Singh N. N., Niemiec R. M., Wehmeyer M. L. (2017). "Character strengths and mindfulness," in The Oxford Handbook of Positive Psychology and Disability. ed. Wehmeyer M. L. (Oxford, UK: Oxford University Press;). [Google Scholar]
135. Shogren K. A., Wehmeyer M. L., Buchanan C. L., Lopez S. J. (2006b). The application of positive psychology and self-determination to research in intellectual disability: a content analysis of 30 years of literature. Res. Pract. Persons Severe Disabl. 31, 338–345. doi: 10.1177/154079690603100408 [CrossRef] [Google Scholar]
136. Shogren K., Palmer S., Wehmeyer M. L., Williams-Diehm K., Little T. (2012). Effect of intervention with the self-determined learning model of instruction on access and goal attainment. Remedial Spec. Educ. 33, 320–330. doi: 10.1177/0741932511410072, PMID: [PMC free article] [PubMed] [CrossRef] [Google Scholar]
137. Sias, P. (2005). Workplace relationship quality and employee information experiences. Communication Studies, 56, 375–395.
138. Sias, P. M., Krone, K. J., &Jablin, F. M. (2002). An ecological systems perspective on workplace relationships. In M. L. Knapp & J. Daly (Eds.), Handbook of interpersonal communication (3rd ed.) (pp. 615–642). Sage.
139. Sin, N. L., & Lyubomirsky, S. (2009). Enhancing Well- Being and Alleviating Depressive Symptoms with Positive Psychology Interventions: A Practice Friendly Meta- Analysis. Journal of Clinical Psychology, 65(5), 467- 487.
140. Smith J L, Bryant F B. (2019) Enhancing positive perceptions of aging by savoringlife lessons. , Aging Ment Health 23(6), 762–770.
141. Smith, J. L., & Hollinger-Smith, L. (2015). Savoring, resilience, and psychological well-being in older adults. Aging & Mental Health, 19(3), 192–200. https://doiorg.ezproxy.uakron.edu:2443/10.1080/13607863.2014.986647

142. Snyder, C., & Lopez, S. J. (2005). Handbook of positive psychology. Oxford University Press.
143. Snyder, C.R., Lopez, S.J., & Pedrotti, J.T. (2011). Positive psychology: The scientific and practical explorations of human strengths. 2nd ed. New Delhi: Sage
144. Snyder, C.R., Lopez, S.J., & Pedrotti, J.T. (2011). Positive psychology: The scientific and practical explorations of human strengths (2nd ed.). New Delhi: Sage.
145. Sternberg, R. J. (1986). A triangular theory of love. Psychological review, 93(2), 119.
Andrews E. A., Forber-Pratt A. F. (2021). "Disability culture, identity, and language," in Understanding Disability: The Positive Psychology of Personal Factors. eds. Wehmeyer M. L., Dunn D. S. (Baltimore, MD: Lexington Press;), 31–45. [Google Scholar]
146. Tartler, R. (1961). Das Alter in der modernen Gesellschaft. Stuttgart: Ferdinand Enke Verlag.
147. Tedeschi, R. G., & Calhoun, L. G. (1996). The Posttraumatic Growth Inventory: Measuring the positive legacy of trauma. Journal of Traumatic Stress, 9(3), 455–471.
148. Thomae, H. (1951). Persönlichkeit: Eine dynamische Interpretation. Bonn: H. Bouvier u. Co.
149. Thompson J. R., Wehmeyer M. L., Shogren K. A., Seo H. (2017). "The supports paradigm in intellectual and developmental disabilities," in Handbook of Positive Psychology in Intellectual and Developmental Disabilities: Translating Research into Practice. eds. Shogren K. A., Wehmeyer M. L., Singh N. N. (New York: Springer;), 23–35. [Google Scholar]
150. Ulrich, D. (1997). Human resource champions. Boston, MA: Harvard Business School.
151. Umberson, D., & Montez, J. K. (2010). Social relationships and health: A flashpoint for health policy. Journal of Health and Social Behavior, 51, S54–S66.
152. Wang, X-H. F., Fang, Y., Qureshi, I., & Janssen, O. (2015). Understanding employee innovative behavior: Integrating the social network and leader-member exchange perspectives. Journal of Organizational Behavior, 36, 403–420.
153. Weare, K. (2015). Partnership for well-beng and mental health in schools. London: National Children's Bureau. www.ncb.org.uk
154. Weare, K. (2015). Partnership for well-beng and mental health in schools. London: National Children's Bureau. www.ncb.org.uk

155. Weathers, F. W., Bovin, M. J., Lee, D. J., Sloan, D. M., Schnurr, P. P., Kaloupek, D. G., Keane, T. M., & Marx, B. P. (2017). The Clinician-Administered PTSD Scale for DSM-5 (CAPS-5): Development and initial evaluation in military veterans. Psychological Assessment, 30(3), 383–395.
156. Wehmeyer M. L. (1992). Self-determination and the education of students with mental retardation. Educ. Train. Ment. Retard. 27, 302–314. [Google Scholar]
157. Wehmeyer M. L. (2001). "Self-determination and mental retardation," in International Review of Research in Mental Retardation. ed. Glidden L. (San Diego, CA: Academic Press;), 1–48. [Google Scholar]
158. Wehmeyer M. L. (2013a). The Story of Intellectual Disability: An Evolution of Meaning, Understanding, and Public Perception. Baltimore: Brookes Publishing Company. [Google Scholar]
159. Wehmeyer M. L. (2013b). The Oxford Handbook of Positive Psychology and Disability. Oxford, UK: Oxford University Press. [Google Scholar]
160. Wehmeyer M. L. (2020). The importance of self-determination to the quality of life of people with intellectual disability: a perspective. Int. J. Environ. Res. Public Health 17, 3–13. doi: 10.3390/ijerph17197121 [PMC free article] [PubMed] [CrossRef] [Google Scholar]
161. World Health Organization (2001). International Classification of Functioning, Disability, and Health (ICF). Geneva: Author. [Google Scholar]
162. World Health Organization. (1946). Preamble to the Constitution of the World Health Organization as adopted by the International Health Conference, New York, 19–22 June, 1946. Official Records of the World Health Organization. Geneva, Switzerland: World Health Organization.